PRAISE FOR GARY COLLINS

Cabot Island

"Collins' focus on an ordinary event taking place under extraordinary circumstances sheds a tender, respectful light on how strength of character can be forged at the anguished intersection of isolation and bereavement."
DOWNHOME

"The story is intriguing . . ."
THE CHRONICLE HERALD

The Last Farewell

"The writing here is at its best when the danger and beauty of the sea is subtly described." — ATLANTIC BOOKS TODAY

"*The Last Farewell* tells a true story, but Collins' vivid description and well-realized characters make it read like a novel." — THE CHRONICLE HERALD

"Read *The Last Farewell* not only because it is a moving historical tale of needless tragedy but also because it's a book enriched with abundant details of Newfoundland life not so widespread anymore."— THE PILOT

"[*The Last Farewell:*] *The Loss of the Collett* is informative and intriguing, and not merely for experienced sailors or Newfoundlanders." — THE NORTHERN MARINER

What Colour is the Ocean?

"Delightful rhyming story."
RESOURCE LINKS

"Scott Keating's illustrations are an asset to the book. The double page illustrations revealing the colour of the ocean are particularly successful in conveying the moods of the ocean and the land." — CM: CANADIAN REVIEW OF MATERIALS

"This tale, set by the sea in Newfoundland, is told in a simple repetitive refrain that will capture the imagination of young readers. . . . Illustrations by Scott Keating, award-winning artist and illustrator, capture the beauty of Newfoundland and the many seasons and moods of the ocean." — ATLANTIC BOOKS TODAY

Soulis Joe's Lost Mine

"There is a magic in the interior of this island that few will write about or speak of to others—an endless fascination with the land. Gary Collins is entranced in the same way that the allure of rock, tree, and bog seized the indomitable Allan Keats, and before him, his ancestor, the Mi'kmaq Soulis Joe. This book gives voice not only to these men but to the great and wonderful wilderness of Newfoundland. Read it and be prepared for the wonder and love of the wild places. It will grab and hold on to you, too." — J.A. RICKETTS, AUTHOR OF *THE BADGER RIOT*

A Day on the Ridge

"The 22 pieces in [*A Day on the Ridge*] vary considerably: a serious accident to a man canoeing with a friend down a remote and dangerous river; the life and death of a big bull moose; coming home from the woods for Christmas; the New Year's Day Orange Parade and getting caught in an otter trap—and escaping from it. Every one of these pieces is exciting and well worth reading; each is well-written, too. This may be Collins' best book, though his other six rank high, too."

THE PEI GUARDIAN

The Gale of 1929

"This book is gripping . . ."

THE PEI GUARDIAN

"Not unlike the seasoned schoonermen battling the famous gale, Collins manages to navigate his way around each story as seen through the eyes of the characters involved. It may be that I, myself, had an affinity for the characters, having been through a similar situation on a 115-foot schooner. But, it felt to me like Collins took me up and down each wave, and let me inside each heroic task of survival." — ARTS EAST

Left to Die

THE STORY OF THE SS NEWFOUNDLAND SEALING DISASTER

ILLUSTRATION BY CLINT COLLINS

Left to Die

THE STORY OF THE SS NEWFOUNDLAND SEALING DISASTER

GARY COLLINS

FLANKER PRESS LIMITED
ST. JOHN'S

Library and Archives Canada Cataloguing in Publication

Collins, Gary, 1949-, author
    Left to die : the story of the SS Newfoundland Sealing
Disaster / Gary Collins.

Includes bibliographical references and index.
Issued in print and electronic formats.
ISBN 978-1-77117-472-5 (paperback).--ISBN 978-1-77117-329-2 (epub).--
ISBN 978-1-77117-330-8 (kindle).--ISBN 978-1-77117-331-5 (pdf)

    1. Newfoundland Sealing Disaster, Newfoundland, 1914. 2. Sealing--
Newfoundland and Labrador--History--20th century. I. Title.

SH362.C64 2014   639.2'909718   C2014-900117-7
                                                                  C2014-900118-5

PRINTED IN CANADA

MIX
Paper from
responsible sources
FSC
www.fsc.org   FSC® C016245

This paper has been certified to meet the environmental and social standards of the Forest Stewardship Council® (FSC®) and comes from responsibly managed forests, and verified recycled sources.

Cover Design by Graham Blair   Illustration by Clint Collins   Maps by Albert Taylor

FLANKER PRESS LTD.
PO BOX 2522, STATION C
ST. JOHN'S, NL
CANADA

TELEPHONE: (709) 739-4477   FAX: (709) 739-4420   TOLL-FREE: 1-866-739-4420
WWW.FLANKERPRESS.COM

9 8 7 6 5 4 3 2 1

Canada Canada Council   Conseil des Arts   Newfoundland
                          for the Arts   du Canada   Labrador

We acknowledge the financial support of the Government of Canada through the Canada Book Fund (CBF) and the Government of Newfoundland and Labrador, Department of Business, Tourism, Culture and Rural Development for our publishing activities. We acknowledge the support of the Canada Council for the Arts, which last year invested $153 million to bring the arts to Canadians throughout the country. Nous remercions le Conseil des arts du Canada de son soutien. L'an dernier, le Conseil a investi 153 millions de dollars pour mettre de l'art dans la vie des Canadiennes et des Canadiens de tout le pays.

For my wife, Rose, who has all of the human attributes so prevalent throughout this book: Loyal. True. Noble. Faithful. Friend. Mate.

Ever-loved.

Now go, write it before them on a tablet, and inscribe it in a book, that it may be for the time to come for ever and ever.

Isaiah 30:8

Preface

"*T*HEY DIDN'T DIE LIKE FLIES, you know, like I've heard some reporters say over the years. Oh no, it wasn't like that a'tall. The men who died didn't just drop like flies. There was nothing quick or easy about it. They had frozen feet, and fingers too numb and cramped with the cold to wipe the tears from their eyes. Tears from tough, fearless, grown men. And a good many of them young, too! Most of them just lay down on the ice, frozen solid, almost, weak from hunger and too tired to get back up. They gave up the ghost. Died of despair, most of 'em did. And with tears frozen to their cheeks, too. 'Twas cruel to look upon, you know. We figured no one was lookin' fer us. Oh, my boy, that was the saddest part of all! We figured we were left to die. Turns out we were right, too."

Sitting next to me in the cab of our five-ton Ford truck was my wife, Rose, and beside her, staring out the passenger-side window, was Cecil Mouland, one of the last living survivors of the *Newfoundland* sealing disaster. The old gentleman's white head was bent in sorrow, his memories overwhelming him. No one spoke for a while as the truck's engine whined. The transmission clicked as I geared down halfway up a steep grade somewhere west of Clarenville on the Trans-Canada Highway. Behind the cab, the stake-bodied deck of my truck was loaded with the last of Cecil's worldly possessions. It was the fall of 1971. The day was warm and the country we were driving through was resplendent with autumn colours. But the story we were listening to was a dark and cold one.

Up until that very day, Cecil Mouland had been a resident of my hometown, Hare Bay, and his wife was the former Jessie Collins from the same community. The two had lived in other places, including an extended stay in the US, but in their senior years they had returned to Newfoundland, where they lived in a modest bungalow in the east end of our community. The couple lived a frugal, independent, modest, and unassuming life.

They were devout Christians and were loved and respected by everyone. Jessie had died two years before, on July 15, 1969, at seventy-four years of age. They had no children, so, rather than allow himself to become a burden to anyone in his advanced age, Cecil decided he would move to a seniors' home in St. John's.

We had loaded all of Uncle Cecil's furniture, bed and baggage, and secured it to the truck the evening before. We were lucky it hadn't rained because the load was not covered. Uncle Cecil wasn't really my blood relative, but in the Newfoundland way he was called uncle by everyone. The man had a jovial manner. Laughter came easy and he was seldom seen without a smile. He was content with his lot and had that true zest for life which comes from someone who had nearly lost it. Everyone knew Uncle Cecil was a survivor of the great *Newfoundland* sealing disaster, and as the years went by he became the last. Like many others in our community, I had heard snippets of his courageous ordeal on the ice floes in the spring of 1914, but I had never heard the full story.

As the old truck laboured along the TCH, we would not only hear the amazing tale of the tragedy; we would hear it from a man who had lived through it. I had never seen a person become so animated when telling a story. He spoke with great emotion and moved his hands and arms for emphasis. He laughed aloud and cried real tears as his storytelling warranted.

At one point he said, "I have to show you how it was!" Dropping to his knees on the dirty floor of the truck, he clasped his hands together forcefully as if in prayer, his knuckles white with the exertion. He did this so fervently it was as if he were supplicating to Almighty God, even now after all those years, to spare his fellow hunters. The old man wept so hard he had to remove his glasses to wipe away the tears.

He got back up on the seat, replaced his glasses, and said, "It must be told again and again, you know. So people will know how it was, you see. What we went through, and so, pray God, it will never happen again."

We stopped for gas and a snack, and after settling onto the road again, I asked Uncle Cecil about his life after the disaster. He tried his very best to make a living in Newfoundland, he told me. He fished for a while and worked at whatever was available. There wasn't much work in the Doting Cove area during the early years of his marriage.

"We didn't need much, though, my Jessie and me. Never ones for material things, we weren't. There was only the two of us, you know. No children came our way. Would have liked children of my own. My Jessie, too, loved children, she did."

The 1930s were the hardest. Fish prices dropped and everything else slid downhill with it. The economy was really bad and there was no work to be had anywhere, he said. Many Newfoundlanders left to find work in Canada and others went to the United States. Cecil and Jessie joined the latter.

I listened without interrupting, though I wanted to hear more about the seal hunt. It was as though he wanted a break after talking about so much death and sadness. With a ready smile on his face again, he burst out laughing, as hard as he had cried moments before, while he recounted this little story.

Cecil scraped together enough money for passage from St. John's to Brooklyn, New York. In 1940, he and Jessie lived on 642 10th Street, Kings, New York. The first job he managed to get—jobs were not easy to come by in the states, either—was in a carpenter shop, though he said he couldn't drive a nail straight or follow a line with a handsaw. The first day on the job, the foreman asked him if he could build a door. Cecil, with his confident Newfoundland outport attitude, assured him he could. After all, how hard could it be to construct something as simple as a door? It was all easy work, nothing to it.

The foreman showed him the tools and the lumber he would need, gave him the door measurements, and left the shop. Cecil worked on the door all morning. The wood was pine, it smelled good, and it was easy to work with. He had the door finished by midday, but after sizing up the job, he wasn't very pleased with his creation. It wasn't square—or even rectangular—as a door should be. He could see every nailhead and the joints gaped open. It looked more like a splitting table than a door. Fearing the foreman's return, he decided to hide it. He pushed the door under the workbench, buried it in the sawdust and shavings that were all over the floor—most of them of his own making—and started to build a second one.

He worked frantically now, not knowing when the foreman would return. Just before quitting time at six that evening, Cecil had made another door and decided it wasn't much better than the first one, when the foreman entered the shop. The man stood beside Cecil at the bench, looked at the door, and for the longest time said nothing.

Then: "Well, Mouland, there is one thing I know. You can only get better, because there is no way in hell you will ever find a door as bad as that one."

And though it might mean his job, Cecil could not resist saying, "Oh yes there is, sir!"

And with that he pulled the first door out of its hiding place. The foreman stared in disbelief from one door to the other before he burst out laughing. The two men became good friends and, under his guidance, Cecil Mouland learned the art of carpentry—even how to build a good door.

Uncle Cecil removed his glasses, and this time the tears he

wiped away were from genuine laughter. He greatly enjoyed spinning yarns, and like the true storyteller he was, he had included the carpentry story as a bridge between bad episodes of his life. When I gently inquired about the shipboard conditions aboard the old SS *Newfoundland*, his demeanour changed and the man returned to the year 1914. So vivid and passionate was his description, he took me back with him.

"Oh, Lord save us," he said. "What a filthy ship she was. And the smell of her bilge! It remains in my head still. Funny thing about that, eh? How a man can hold such a thing as a bad smell in his head for so long?"

"Did you ever go back to the seal hunt, Uncle Cec?" Rose asked.

"No, my darling maid, I did not," he replied. "Been asked that same question many times since. Everyone figured I couldn't go back to the hunt because of what I had witnessed out there on the ice, you see. So much pain and death I had seen up close like a man should never see. 'Twasn't that a'tall. I was young then and would get over that part of it, like many others did. Went back to the seal hunt, they did, them as had endured the same thing as me.

"But to be honest 'twas two things which kept me from returning. The first was the grime and filth of the ship that I could not abide. I saw the first rat in my life aboard that ship. Imagine that! A great bilge rat. Big as a cat, it was. And we jammed in solid out on that white sea of ice! I found lice in me blankets, too, and that, too, was a first fer me. Mind ye, I wasn't raised with a silver spoon nor satin sheets for my bed, either, but my mother's table, sparse though it was at times, was always a spotless one and my bed was ever a clean one."

Uncle Cecil stopped and I was afraid he wouldn't continue. He drew his hand through his thinning hair.

"I've never had one louse since. Course, if I did they would be easy to spot now, eh?" Then he laughed his hearty laugh again, which I knew was his way of easing himself back into the sad part of his tale. "The second reason was the all-consuming fear that if I ever got stranded on the ice no one would come lookin' fer me. The utter despair I saw in the eyes of men. The despair of it all. That was the thing of it. I will take that cruel memory of being abandoned and left to die to my grave."

Uncle Cecil was silent for a while after that.

"I should have died out there, you know," he said quietly, his voice soft and very serious. "I would have, too, but for two people, and both of them with the same name . . . and both Collinses, too," he said with a grin, looking directly at me. "The first was the man Jesse Collins from Newport, the hardest, toughest man I've ever known. He kept me and a good many others alive. The other was my sweetheart, Jessie Collins, from your town, Hare Bay.

"My, my, what a beautiful girl she was then, and oh how I loved her. I loves her still, of course. A man never stops lovin' his first—and for me, my only—true love. I promised her I would return and marry her, you see. And she said she would wait for me. It was a love pledge between the two of us. Still, if it weren't for the other Jesse Collins"—here he raised his two arms as if to ask, *Who knows?*—"I might not have kept my pledge."

Cecil grew silent again, remembering. His eyes filled with tears once more, thinking, I was sure, of the woman who was no longer a part of his aging years. I sensed his story was done and didn't ask him any more questions.

Cecil and I off-loaded his belongings at his modest apartment in St. John's. He gave Rose a hug as well as a wall ornament he had made. Turning to me, he shook my hand, and when I told him I wanted only gas money for the trip, he grasped my hand warmly in both of his and said simply, "Thank you, my boy, and may God bless you."

"Thanks for the tale," I said.

"Oh, I will forever tell it, my boy. I would to God there was no tale to tell!"

We left him then, and he stood waving with one hand and drying his eyes with the other until I turned out onto the busy street and lost him in the truck mirrors.

It would be more than forty years before I would come to realize the true value of what I had heard. Luckily, when I sat down to try and retell, in my own way, the story of that horrific sealing disaster, the voice of the old gentleman huddled with emotion in the cab of my truck came back to me with astounding clarity.

When I was a boy, there was another man who lived in our town who had also survived that same disaster. His name was Jesse Collins, the man considered by many—especially Cecil Mouland—as one of the heroes of the *Newfoundland* sealing disaster. He moved to Hare Bay from Newport, one of the de-settled fishing communities eighteen miles or so north by the coast. I use *de-settled* because I know of few that were forced to leave their birthplaces who were ever truly resettled.

Jesse died on February 7, 1959, at seventy-four, when I was ten years old. He lived just two houses up the gravel road from mine. I remember him as an old man who often walked down the road pulling on a curved pipe with a stream of tobacco smoke trailing over his left shoulder. He was always well-groomed and wore a tie, even on weekdays. I don't remember speaking to him, but I remember the day he was carried along the gravel road of our town to his grave. It was cold and snowing and the road was snow-packed and slippery. His coffin was sticking out of the back of a truck. There were chains strapped to the back tires, clicking and rattling as the truck slowly drove by. Dark-clad mourners walked behind in silence. The blinds and curtains at every window were drawn as the funeral procession passed. Horses drawing sleds laden with logs were *whoa*ed, their reins sawed tight until the cortège passed.

When I asked my mother, who was peering out the window, she whispered, "Hush! They are burying the ol' ice hunter Uncle Jesse Collins today." Jesse and his wife, Alice, had five children.

Today many of his descendants still live in Hare Bay, and his name lives on in the same garden where he spent his last days.

The night I received the call from Garry Cranford, the president of Flanker Press, asking me to consider telling the story of the *Newfoundland* sealing disaster of the spring of 1914, is a memorable one. I was stunned. That night has been recorded in my private journals along with my first reaction to his request. My editor, Jerry Cranford, part of the executive of Flanker Press, felt that after 100 years, the story should be told again. The only real, authoritative story on that event, *Death on the Ice*, had been written by Cassie Brown. Margo Cranford, also on the executive board of Flanker Press, is the niece of the late Cassie. Margo agreed that it was time for those events to be retold. I was humbled to be asked to take on such a story. I was also flattered, but mostly I was frightened. How could I dare disturb the unique work of the late Cassie Brown?

But the truth of it was that I had for some time secretly wanted to retell the story in my own way. After considerable thought I agreed to write it. During the initial course of my research for this book, I refused to read *Death on the Ice*. I didn't want to be influenced by Cassie's work. I am fiercely independent—well, as independent as a writer can be when he bears in mind that with a historical, fact-based work he has to rely on information from others.

But no matter the avenue I pursued, all roads seemed to lead back to *Death on the Ice*. It was the only thorough account written about the event. There was no alternative. I read it again and I gleaned from the pages of Cassie Brown's stellar book many facts and accounts of real events that were to be found nowhere else, but as far as it was in my power to do so, I have left her work undisturbed. With the first draft of my manuscript written, its framework describing many scenes of ice and seals and men, I started to feel my way toward the climactic conclusion of the book. I was actually afraid of it! Again, I felt as if I were intruding in some way upon Cassie's great masterpiece. After all, *Death on the Ice* is iconic in Newfoundland and Labrador and can be found in nearly as many homes as the Bible.

I was bolstered and reassured by my family in this endeavour. With every page my wife read, and after searching my own memory of that long-ago day in the cab of my truck with Uncle Cecil Mouland, I finally came to realize that the story I would tell was to be mine alone and no one else's. I continued with a free mind, then, and completed the story in great earnest.

Though the story you are about to read is a dramatic retelling of the events surrounding the Great Newfoundland Sealing Disaster of 1914, with new information and new sources interviewed, I respectfully acknowledge the writings of Cassie Brown, Newfoundland and Labrador's First Lady of Literature, and her book *Death on the Ice*.

1

*T*HERE IS A PLACE BEYOND the edge of winter daylight where for weeks at a time the sun does not appear. It leaves for a dismal time on the barren northlands an inactive, lethargic existence for the dark-skinned humans who live there; but away from the rim of this sunless land and on the frosty, thickening sea where no human dares, there is an even bleaker, more forbidding place. The warmth of the greatest light in the heavens barely creases the line between Arctic day and night.

The night is infinite, immeasurable, absolute, and sterile. No living thing is here. No living thing can survive here. Surface-dwelling and pelagic fishes have gone into the nether depths to escape the death sentence of freezing gills. Air-breathing mammals, with warm, four-chambered hearts, have left for open water or have long since hidden elsewhere on the distant land. The might of the rolling ocean is at last humbled, quelled, and arrested. Conquered and defeated, the ocean is claimed and frozen by the most formidable of Earth's winter spells—the long polar night.

A polar rigor mortis has stolen silently through the Arctic night. Waves are frozen in motion, their undulations captured and painted on the ocean's surface. Ice crystals form and burst open before thickening. The Arctic night has transformed the water into a crystalline solid, which only a warming sun will release hundreds of miles to the south. The dark time is as silent and still as it is black; there is no sky, there is no earth, just an unfeeling, depthless, interminable night. With no definition between dark and light, it is as if the daytime has never been. The mindless polar night defies even the Christian god, who on His first day of creation commanded light to *be* upon the dark wastes of all the earth. Now even His omnipresence does not come up over the northern slope of the sea.

Then, beaded lights appear in the dense, black heavens. It is as if they are being lit by a swift, invisible lamplighter, and subtly they are placed in the inky sky. The stars glitter and gleam. They look like silver streams twisting and shimmering down the length of the night sky. The firmament is in its starry glory. There is no moon. The sky is eternal, as if the passage of time has been halted. Now the sky is flecked with countless silvery eyes that wink and tremble, until the whole is like a mantle of glittering, haloed diamonds.

But there is no one below to admire the scene. The Big Dipper of the north sky is upright, holding all of its wondrous mysteries inside its seven stars. Directly below that downward-curving handle of the Great Bear constellation, a shimmer of light suddenly appears on the horizon.

A lip of moon appears slowly, as if wondering whether or not it should shed its light on the barren plain. The giant, steel-silver orb rises steadily, a creeping, searching light where before there had been only darkness. Its glow gives shape and creates shadows where none has been. A frozen, snow-humped plain appears. Clearing its earthly bonds, the moon, which now has assumed a whitish glow, hangs silently and unmoving just over the rim of the northern world. Now the scene is complete, and still there is no one to admire the artistry. Nothing moves in that show of light. There is no sound. The movement of night air is a rustle as it bears over the sea of frozen runnels and dusty snow. This coming together of ice and an all-enveloping sky could have taken a millennium to create—or just one polar night.

* * * * *

HE WAS CHRISTENED PHILLIP HOLLOWAY, which in Newfoundland meant everyone shortened his name to Phil. Everyone, that is, but his mother, who always called him by his full name—especially when she was mad at him. His mother was a churchgoer and had heard the name Phillip from the Church of England minister who came periodically to their outport fishing village of Newport on the north side of Bonavista Bay. She liked the name Phillip and, according to the minister, who spoke in monotone from the pulpit, Phillip of the Bible was brother to King Herod. He was a preacher and healer and had much wisdom, and for that reason she gave her son his name. She knew it was also the name of one of Christ's lesser-known apostles. He wouldn't tell his mother, but Phillip preferred to be called Phil.

Months after his birth, which she told him had been an easy one, with him eager to enter the world, the circuit-sailing preacher came flushing in through the narrow harbour entrance. The schooner's stained-brown sails clattered down the masts as the sheets were let go. Phillip had screamed like a bugger when he was anointed with holy water. In his defence, she added the water was so cold the minister had to break the ice in the stone font before dipping his fingers in and fairly dousing the water over her sleeping son. Now at forty-five, Phil smiled as he remembered the story while hammering the last few nails into a new spire for that church near the landwash high above the sea. It was dangerous work, but he wasn't afraid of heights.

Phil heard his name. It was twenty-nine-year-old Jesse Collins. The two men were good friends despite their ages.

"The 'arbour froze over last night, Phil b'y. Won't be long

now before we'll be scunnin' across from side to side on the ice. I loves it!"

"Me too," Phil said as he climbed down the ladder.

"You'll be headin' in the woods again this fine marnin', I s'pose?"

"Well, you knows now, Jess b'y, tomorrow is Sunday an' I won't be tendin' to me trapline. It's been two days since I've been in, so I'll be a bit late this day, I'm thinkin'."

"Well, 'ave a care on the trail, Phil. I'll be seein' you this evenin' in the twine loft, I s'pose? We'll talk more about gettin' that berth to the ice fer you this spring."

"Well, you knows now we will! Though I'll be bringin' dark on me shoulder, I 'lows. 'Specially if I stands here all day jawin' with you!"

Jesse grinned as he always did and turned away down the footpath to his wharf at the sea edge, smoke from his pipe curling behind his neck, his feet crunching in the new snow.

Leaving the path where the harbour bent around itself, Phil made his way up through the drung to the hills overlooking the settlement. Here he paused and looked back. He never tired of the view from the hills above the hamlet of Newport. Jesse was right about the ice. Though without wind, last night's deep cold had frozen their harbour all the way out to its narrow entrance. Woodsmoke curled out of every black funnel below him and hung motionless like a grey pallor over the village. A few dogs barked, the ones on the opposite side of the harbour answering the yelps of those on the near side. The morning was so calm Phil could hear the rattle of a chain that held one of the dogs.

The sun was up out of the sea and the west side of the harbour was brightening while the east side still lay in shadows. The north end of the harbour ended in a rocky canyon called "the rattle." The ebb and flow of the daily tides surged in and out of Salt Water Pond, which turned perpendicular to the rattle in an east-west direction. It was little more than a mile long and less than a mile wide. Fat sea trout came up through the rattle in season, and even codfish swam from the sea into the brackish pond. Leaving the edge of the community, its forested rim long since denuded by the community's need for wood, Phil headed for the pond. On the other side of it, green stands of spruce and fir stretched toward the northwest. Twisted brooks and streams ran from every hill and marshland, and in each valley lay secluded ponds and steadies. All of them had their complement of soft-skinned otter, beaver, and muskrat, which were Phil's only source of ready cash. Snowshoe hares abounded—the locals called them rabbits—and where there were hares there were fox. This was Phillip Holloway's area for trapping and he was good at it. At forty-six years old he was known all over the area for his ability at "furrin.'"

When he had set his traps and snares just two days ago, Phillip had crossed the pond in a dory. He had rowed the dory up through the rattle at high tide and left it on the community side of the pond. This morning, however, after two nights and days of freezing, he expected he would be able to cross the pond on the ice.

Stepping gingerly out onto the new ice, Phil tested its thickness with his axe. Just over an inch, he figured. It took his weight well enough, though a water ripple went ahead of him as he walked out. Phil was a true woodsman, stepping lightly and keeping his lungs filled with air as he walked on the thin ice.

Nearing the centre of the pond, where he knew the current was strongest and the ice at its thinnest, it started to buckle. It was the way of young saltwater ice. It bent in warning before it broke, unlike freshwater ice, which would break away under a man's weight without any warning at all. Not standing in place long enough to break through, Phil chopped holes and rapidly splashed water ahead of and behind him as he walked. The temperature was well below freezing, so the water would quickly freeze and strengthen the ice for his return trip, which would be in the dark. Passing the centre without incident, he continued on and reached the north side of Salt Water Pond.

Looking back, he took a mark on the pond's far side to guide his return trip. Then he headed up through the forest on an ancient path, his footsteps silent on the virgin snow.

* * * * *

BACK IN NEWPORT, JESSE COLLINS shaved splinters from a plug of tobacco, crushed and worried the plug between his calloused hands, and pressed it into a short-stemmed clay pipe. He snicked a match head against a jagged thumbnail, and when the stick flared he cupped the flame against the pipe's bowl. He sucked until his cheeks collapsed and the tobacco glowed and he was finally rewarded with a plume of greyish blue smoke which escaped through the thin crease on the right side of his mouth.

Jesse had spent most of his day mending torn salmon nets. He wished he had enough twine to make new ones, but the last fishing season had not been kind and he couldn't afford to buy the materials he needed. Fishing for the silvery salmon was his passion. He loved nothing better than leaving the sheltered harbour in the pre-dawn summer mornings, seated alone in his punt, and with drawing sail heading for the salmon berths to haul his nets.

Atlantic salmon, pressed in salt for three days and then slow-cured by the smoke of the native blackberry bush, was considered a delicacy. Only a few fishermen around the area would take the time and had patience to smoke the salmon. Most of them salted the fish away in barrels and shipped it along with their summer's catch of cod in the fall. Jesse knew one man who was firm in his curing method. They had to be in salt three days, and three days in smoke, no more and no less.

Jesse had a different way, though. He cut his salmon down the back and splayed them open, held under salt with weights, or in press, until they were firm. Then he placed them in his smoker until they passed his taste test. He even had a method for that. After a few days—usually more than three—he would open the smoker door, allow most of the smoke to baffle out through the door, and then, bending down, he would enter. With his knife he would slice into the thickest part of one of the salmon. Squeezing the fish, he would watch the juices running out the cut he had made. Too much juice and the fish were not done to his liking; too little juice and they were overcooked. When their natural juices oozed just right and their flesh was golden brown outside and had a pinkish hue inside, then they were ready.

Now the sun was down among the hills and the evening shadows were in the harbour, and Jesse's thoughts turned toward cod fishing. He fished for cod each year after the salmon run was done; he handlined for them as did many others. It was a common practice. Even with his catch of salmon and cod, Jesse rarely saw any money for his work. Like all the others, he slaved under a truck system. The merchants merely exchanged his entire catch for provisions. No matter how plentiful the year's catch, it was never enough for him to make a profit. The fishermen were always in debt to the merchants and chandlers. The only hard cash money Jesse Collins ever received came from the spring seal hunt, something he excelled at.

Several trap crews worked from Newport, and this past summer one of the crews had suffered a great loss during the capelin scull. The trap fishing was at its peak. With the capelin came hundreds of humpback whales. They had feasted on the schools of capelin for weeks. Often the leviathans would follow their prey right up to the shoreline. One such daring whale had become tangled in one of the cod traps fastened to the shore. For three days the fishermen watched helplessly as the huge mammal tried to free itself from miles of twine. Early the fourth morning the anxious fishermen returned to find the whale had finally freed itself, but of their precious trap there remained a mass of useless netting. They hauled it aboard their trap skiff and pulled it up on the land. When Jesse inquired about the trap, he was told that if he had guts enough to repair it, he could have it. Knowing it was too much work for one man to take on, he approached his friend Phil and Phil's brother Joshua.

After much consideration, the three men decided to take on repairing the discarded cod trap and buddy up fishing with it the following spring. It would not be easy and would take all winter for the three men to complete. Fortunately, Phillip Holloway's hands were as adept at netting traps as they were at skinning fur. The speed of the twine needle in his hands as it clicked and twirled mending (also called "making") the net was the talk around every twine loft in the community. There was one other thing they would need in order to fish with a large cod trap: a bigger boat.

They knew where to purchase one in Greenspond, another isolated outport island community just a few miles north of Newport. The price for the thirty-one-foot boat—complete with a five-horsepower Atlantic one-lunger engine—was $75. Neither of the three men had a cent to their name. Phil agreed to put more time in on his trapline and to put what extra dollars he could earn into their new enterprise. He also asked Jesse to use his influence with the sealing skippers to get him and Joshua a berth at the ice on the same ship. Joshua had spent six years to the ice and was an experienced hand.

Jesse agreed. The income from that hunt, no matter how little it would be, was still cash. The three men figured that this money would be enough to set themselves up as trapmen.

* * * * *

ON THE OTHER SIDE OF Salt Water Pond, with the day just about gone and close to an hour's walk from home, Phil had his mind on another kind of trap. It was a big leg-hold trap for an otter which he had set in the animal's lead by the side of a brook. Despite his occupation, Phil hated to see animals suffer, and this evening was no different. He had trapped an otter by its left hind foot and the animal was crazed with pain and fear as he approached it. It was a young male, full of fight and anger. It snarled and spat at the hunter as he crouched among the trees, axe in hand. Each time the otter sprang to free itself, the small mesh chain leash attached to the steel trap jangled tight and yanked the otter back onto its haunches, trembling. It took several minutes before the otter tired and Phil got the chance to dispatch it with a blow to its head with the pole of his axe. Phil was sweating. He had been hurrying on the trail all day, wanting to cross the pond before full dark.

Bending down to remove the trap, he shivered as the cold leaked into his open collar. Phil saw the wound to the otter's leg. He removed the trap, cleaned the blood from it, and covered the mechanism with fir boughs before resetting it in the same lead. Crouched low, he inspected his kill, running both hands first against and then with the grain of the luxurious fur. The otter's fur was thick, and though the animal was sleek, it was well-muscled and would make good eating.

He was about to stand when he felt hot liquid running down over his top lip. He knew immediately what it was—blood. Phillip Holloway was prone to bad nosebleeds. He had always had them, even when he was a young man, but they had been less frequent then. Sometimes he would go years without one. But as he got older they occurred more often, sometimes two or even four times a year. Not only were they occurring more frequently, they were also becoming more severe. He noticed over the years that the bleeding came on more often when he was sweating, or sometimes soon after engaging in strenuous work. Blood dripped rapidly from both his nostrils in huge, hot drops that kept on coming. At intervals it spurted from his nose. In just a few seconds the snow around his feet was covered with bright red blood.

Phil wasn't worried too much about it, for though a bad episode might leave him feeling weak, the bleeding always stopped. Someone had told him to sit up straight, lean his head forward, and pinch his nostrils tight for several minutes until the bleeding stopped.

He sat against a tree and tilted his head forward. By now his blood had stained the snow all around him. It dripped onto the dark skin of the otter. He tasted the sweet metallic stickiness of it on his lips and felt it run down over his chin. Before he had stemmed the initial flow between his thumb and forefinger, both his hands were bright red and his clothing was smeared with it. Phil sat motionlessly for several minutes, feeling tired and weak. He didn't know if he should release the pressure on his nose or not. The warmth of his blood tickled his throat and he spat it out. Sweating and shivering, he steeled himself against the urge to straighten up and remove his fingers. Gradually, he began releasing the pressure from his nostrils. When he took his fingers away, his left nostril was glued shut with his blood and the other had stopped bleeding. He stood shakily to his feet, lifting the dead otter with him. Leaning against the tree, he waited longer than usual for his strength to return. This had been his worst nosebleed yet. Taking his time, he staggered a bit as he headed down the trail toward the pond and home.

Later that evening, Phil entered the stage with the otter in his hand just as Jesse was climbing the steps up to the twine loft. Phil could hear Joshua working on the twine loft floor above the stage ceiling.

"Died hard, did he?" Jesse commented, looking at the bloodstained otter.

"Yeah, well you knows how hard it is to get a good smack at 'em sometimes." Phil fastened the otter to a hook in the beam overhead, where the animal spun slowly in the lantern light, a rictus grin on its face. Jesse stepped back from the ladder.

"Some of the b'ys were out on the 'ead this evenin' and said they saw a few turrs flyin' in the bay. I was thinkin' maybe we could haul my punt out over the ice tomorrow marnin' and row down to Greenspond. I'll get a message wired off fer our berths to the ice and we'll shoot a meal of turrs there and back."

"I only got a dozen or so shells," said Phil. "Been meanin' to fill a few more."

"I've about the same. Josh got about the same, he told me. We'll make sure to fire at doubles at least. We'll do all right." Jesse was always confident. "Be wonderful good if we could talk to one of the sealin' skipper's face to face, Phil b'y. Them bloody merchants in S'n John's don't know if they're punched er bored er tore wit' a jigger! 'Tis the skippers who'll get the berth fer us!" He headed for the steps again. "We'll get in a couple o' hours of nettin' twine before we heads home, eh Phil?"

"Just as soon as I skins the otter, Jess b'y. Can't let 'em stiffen up too much. 'Ard to skin when they're froze." As Jesse disappeared through the hatch above, Phil pulled out his skinning knife and stepped to the turning otter. He moved it into the lantern's glow as night deepened outside the stage. Frost descended on the sleeping village, smoke drifted out of every funnel, and the harbour ice thickened.

Jesse, Phil, and Joshua had lots of help hauling their rowboat out over the harbour ice very early the next morning. Others were also going turr hunting, so everyone was only too willing to help. It was the outport way. They slipped their four-oared punt into the slob ice at the edge and had to rock the boat back and forth to get it through and into open water. Phil sat on the front thwart and pulled with the two oars while Joshua worked the oars on the middle seat. Jesse stood near the after seat with the sculling oar tucked in his arms, sculling and guiding the craft along. The sea was calm and had an oily, silvery smooth look after last night's heavy frost.

They hadn't gone far before they saw their first turr. Jesse put down the sculling oar and picked up his shotgun. Phil and Joshua looked over their shoulders and rowed hard toward the plump black-and-white seabird.

"Steady now!" said Jesse.

The two men stopped rowing and allowed the punt to drift closer to the bird. The boat rose and fell on the swell as Jesse aimed and fired. The bird tried to rise but fell over on its back, showing its white belly and its feet twitching in death.

"T'ought we was goin' to shoot doubles!" exclaimed Phil.

"Oh! Well, that was just a practice shot, Phil b'y."

Jesse dropped an iron bolt down the barrel of his old twelve-gauge gun, forcing the spent shell out. He placed the shell in a leather bag to be packed with shot and powder and used again later. He rammed another shell into the gun with the heel of his hand, placed the gun down with its muzzle leaning up over the low gunnel, and picked up the oar. After fishing the turr out of the water with a dip net, they continued on in a northerly direction.

2

*I*T TOOK THE THREE MEN a couple of hours of rowing and hunting before they reached the community of Greenspond. By that time they had fifteen fat turrs in the bottom of their punt, their white feathers spattered with blood. The birds flew in from the open sea and they figured on killing a few more on the way back. The tickle in Greenspond was slobbed over and the men had to rally the punt from side to side to get close enough to tie up to one of the wharves.

Two ships were moored in the narrow tickle. Jesse recognized them as sealing vessels. He would learn later that several more sealing ships were moored in Pond Tickle, the thin waterway separating Greenspond Island from the mainland. It was a common practice for some of the merchants from the mainland to secure their vessels in or near Greenspond, fearing that a hard winter freeze-up in their own inland harbours would keep them from getting to the spring ice floes with the other vessels in time for the seal hunt.

With a population of more than 1,600 to Newport's 200 souls, Greenspond was considered a metropolis. This "capital of the north" was the oldest continuously inhabited outport in Newfoundland. Greenspond had a resident doctor, a court, a customs house, and three churches. A few of the houses were rumoured to be brothels. There was a cobbler and cooper, a blacksmith, and even a tinsmith on the little island. Greenspond also boasted the most sealing captains from anywhere else in Newfoundland—fifty-one of them! More than three-quarters of all vessels involved in the annual Newfoundland seal hunt set sail from the port of Greenspond.

Even before the St. John's merchants took sealers to the icefields to kill seals with clubs, the industrious fishermen from Greenspond had realized the financial potential of these migratory mammals. They killed them with rifle and heavy shot while in the open sea, but mostly they "fished" for them using fishing nets. One year, the fishermen from Greenspond caught more than 18,000 seals with their nets. Now they used nets that were designed for use in this seal fishery. The seal nets were stronger and had a bigger mesh than the others. Netting for seals became an annual spring event that offered the only considerable source of money to most of the struggling fishermen. When the seal hunt finally evolved into a serious money-making venture involving dozens of great ships and thousands of men, the name "seal fishery," a name the fishermen of Greenspond had given to the seal harvest, had stuck.

It was nearly midday when Jesse, Joshua, and Phil climbed up onto the wharf, tied up their boat, and walked ashore. Children were piling out of the big schoolhouse and running home for dinner, exciting several barking dogs as they went. Some of the rowdy children chased a lone two-wheeled dray piled with fishing gear as it was pulled along by a plodding dark brown pony. The teamster cursed and shouted at them.

Clothes hung from drooping clotheslines while smoke rose into the air from cheap black funnels and expensive brick chimneys alike. Behind picket fences men sawed firewood into short stove lengths with rasping bucksaws. Men split stove junks into smaller pieces, their axes ringing and thudding clearly. Others strolled and hurried along the narrow roads, stood in groups on wharves, and chatted at stage doors.

One of the Greenspond men recognized Collins and the Holloways as they approached.

"Well now, Jesse Collins from New Harbour! Furrin' Phil and his little brother wit' ya, too." Many people in the area, including some of Greenspond's own residents, referred to Newport as New Harbour. It was the community's original name. "Yer the ones who's been makin' all them little poppin' sounds up in the reach this fine marnin'! Shootin' them scrawny bull birds fer a pot o' soup, I s'pose ya was!"

"I didn't see any blood in your boat, Job Easton. Eatin' canned bully beef these days, are ye?" the young Collins shot back with his quick tongue, smiling as he did.

"Ha ha! Bully beef fer all of us again this spring at the swile hunt, I 'lows," said Easton. "'Orse meat I says they puts in them cans! Ya knows the merchants are takin' names already fer berths to the ice, I s'pose?"

Jesse assured Easton and the others that they did know. Not only that, he told them, he and the two Holloway boys were hoping to ship out together. They were planning on trap fishing as a crew for cod next year, and they figured they would all try and get to the ice on the same ship. Jesse, who had acquired an excellent reputation with the sealing skippers as a seal hunter, had agreed to use his influence to get them on a ship with him.

They talked more for a while about seals, or swiles as some of them called the animals, about skippers they wished to sail with and some they wished they hadn't sailed with, about ice conditions, pelt prices, and the pay they might receive.

"That bloody Abe Kean. Got 'e's name as top jowler offa our backs, he did," said one of the men with Job Easton. Jowler was the name given to the most successful of sealing captains. "Not fit to sail with, that man idden, the way he treats his swilers."

"Knows where to find the seals, though," another chimed in. "Can't stick him fer that. He kin smell 'em, they says."

"Oh, aye, he kin find the bloody swiles, all right. But 'tis the likes o' we as does the killing."

"'Twill be a bad year fer ice, I'm 'lowin'," another interjected, changing the subject.

They talked on, about sealing skippers and their hunting methods, about ships and the fierce conditions aboard these hunting vessels, about the many near-death experiences they had encountered while at the seal hunt, about food "I wouldn't give me dog," about the filthy shipboard conditions of the seal hunt, about sleeping on the bloody sculps, about the paltry dollars they had been paid last year. But to a man they agreed they would sell their souls to go to the hunt again.

Soon the three Newport men took their leave, with many encouraging shouts ringing in their ears.

"Good luck to ye!"

"'Ope ye gets a top berth!"

"Mark yer X fer Killer Kean!"

"Don't shoot no mooty birds on the way back!"

"Can't beat rabbit's piss fer fox bait!"

This last was directed at the man everyone in these parts knew as "Furrin' Phil."

Although the fishing season was over, Greenspond was still bustling with business. Chandlers and merchants, blacksmiths, coopers, and tinsmiths still plied their trade. Goods from all over the northeast side of Newfoundland came to this port for shipment to Europe and beyond. Barrels of partridgeberries picked from the hills in the bays, casks of pickled Atlantic salmon and herring, dried capelin seined and cured months ago, and thousands of quintals of sun-dried codfish all readied to leave before the winter winds came to stay, had to be exported. Bales of cordage and twine, rusted iron grapnels, barrels of tar, tons of coal, and mountains of salt were imported into this busy, poorly sheltered harbour. Lumber and billets of birch firewood from the bay communities were stacked beside bulging warehouses. And then there were the preparations needed for the massive seal hunt just over two months away. Many companies from St. John's had established themselves here in this seaport. One of them was Harvey and Company, one of the major seal hunting firms in Newfoundland. It was the Harvey's premises that the men from Newport were headed for.

A figure clad in a fur coat walked ahead of them. The fur came down to the tops of the man's expensive-looking boots, making him look bigger than he actually was. He appeared to be headed toward the Harvey's building, too. His shoulders were rounded but not stooped and he walked with a decisive step. On his head was a hat made of sealskin.

"By God, Captain Kean!" Phil whispered hoarsely to his companions. "Jest the man we wants to see! You speak to 'im, Jess."

"Skipper Kean, sir! A word, if ya don't mind, sir!" Jesse called to the black figure ahead of them.

The man stopped and turned slowly, as if the speaker behind him were a hindrance to be admonished. The clean-shaven man was Abram Kean's youngest son, Westbury. For three years Wes Kean had been sealing skipper of the SS *Newfoundland* with Harvey and Company out of St. John's, and everyone knew he was trying to step out of his famous father's shadow with a big seal kill of his own. It hadn't happened yet. Wes recognized Jesse Collins.

"Rowed across in punt, did ya, Collins? Fine marnin' fer a few turrs!"

"'Tis so, sir. We got a few. Yer welcome to a meal of 'em if you'd like, sir." Collins hoped to please the young sealing skipper. "If I took all the turrs offered to me since last evenin' and this marning here in Pond—all picked an' ready fer the pot, too, mind ye—I'd need a four-thwart trap skiff to put 'em in."

Kean waved a big hand in dismissal of Jesse's offer. "Now if 'twas saltwater ducks you was offerin'! Ah, my man, dem's the good eatin'! None about yet, they tells me. What word did ye want with me, Collins?" Kean had wasted enough of his time discussing seabirds.

Jesse stepped forward. He was one of the few men who

wasn't intimidated by the Keans, father or son. In his strong, determined voice, brazen with youth, he said, "I heard you was to be skipper on the *Newfoundland* again this year, sir. I sailed with ye before, sir, and this year the t'ree of us would like to go to the ice with you."

Phil shifted uneasily on his feet. He was a quiet man who didn't like confrontations, especially in public. He was sure one was coming now.

"There's no need fer a man who can hunt swiles like you to be bribin' me with a few turrs, Collins. What about yer buddies? Good as yerself, I s'pose they are."

"Better, sir," was Jesse's brash answer. "Phil is a trapper an' skins otters and such better than me."

Wes Kean showed one of his rare grins. He loved a man with confidence. "Haulin' the pelts offa dem freshwater animals is one thing, and sculpin' saltwater swiles is another thing altogether. Come with me!"

And with that the man turned and clumped up the few steps to the office door. He entered without knocking and stepped inside as if he owned the place. He didn't kick the snow from his boots. The three men from Newport followed him.

They entered a bare room with a wooden floor and two tiny, frost-covered windows on either side. A small bogie near the back wall showed a flicker of flame from the cracks around its cast-iron door. Beside the stove, which the men noted gave off little heat, was a bucket half filled with lumps of coal. Sticking up over the bucket's broad lip was a short-handled steel shovel.

At the front of the chilly room was a large desk cluttered with ledgers and papers scrawled with ink. Behind the desk was a small man with a drooping black moustache. He wore a winter coat and a salt and pepper hat. A large glass ashtray was nestled among the many papers on one corner of the messy desk and it was filled to the brim with the grey dottle from a long-stemmed pipe resting on top of the ashes.

The clerk squinted as though he needed spectacles. His shirt collar was buttoned tightly to his thin neck, around which was knotted a red tie stained with food. When he looked up and saw Captain Kean, he was visibly shaken. His mouth gaped open, showing tobacco-stained teeth, and his eyes opened wide.

"G-good marnin', Skipper Wes, I'm sure, sir!"

To add to the man's discomfort, Wes pulled the big ledger the clerk had been working on out of his hands. Kean didn't acknowledge the man's greeting. Instead, he scanned the list of names printed with care on several pages.

"No shortage of names, I see."

"Oh, no, Skipper, sir. More than ye'll be needin', sir. The first of 'em come by wire from the main office in S'n John's, sir."

"Well, here's t'ree more men fer ye to enter in yer ledger."

"Indeed I will, sir! I'll put 'em down on the last page right away, sir!"

Kean grabbed the pen from the clerk's fingers, dragged its nib over the first three names on the first page, and gave the book back to the startled clerk.

"Put the names o' the New Harbour men beside the ones I jest scratched out and put the S'n John's names on the last page!" He turned toward the Newport men, who stood in silence. "Sign yer names or mark yer X accordin' to yer means, my b'ys!"

Without another word, he exited the office and closed the door behind him.

3

ON THE NORTHEAST COAST OF the North American continent is a serrated edge of innumerable bays and inlets. Ancient mountain ranges, worn smooth with age or still rugged with youth, hide their formidable bases beneath the seas. It is a wild, formidable area of the earth sparsely inhabited by the planet's most prolific of mammals—humans. For the dark-skinned ones who had finally found their way here, the journey had not been an easy one. Before history was recorded on paper or vellum, their amazing trek had begun when the northern part of the Americas was still joined to Asia by a thin bridge of land. Well north of the warm plains and beyond the tree-lined taiga, these winter clans dwelled and roamed the vast tundra of the Arctic regions. Only the immeasurable ocean could halt one of mankind's greatest migrations and thus end their journey.

But upon the heaving breast of that same frigid sea, where two-legged mammals dared not go, another odyssey continued. Warm-blooded seals, their numbers dwarfing the men who hunted them, were beginning their annual migration. Fierce hood seals were on the move, warring among themselves during the time of mating, the males sprouting pinkish, bulbous hoods on their broad heads. Smaller ring seals—this breed had no visible ears—which seldom roamed from the Arctic seas, were abroad in lesser numbers. But outnumbering them all, and carrying upon their backs what some have called the harp of David—the Christian king—were the gentle harp seals, whose other distinguishing marks were their black eyes.

The harp seals spend so much time in the water they are more like fish than mammals. Maybe it is the animal's love of open water that motivates them to wander south. More likely it is an inbred urge, a primordial sense that is beyond their control, which moves them. Whatever the reason, it is always the same. The harp seals leave the Arctic and head south when the freeze-up begins. For an animal that appears to revel in the coldest of waters and live on the ice floes, it remains a mystery, but when ice forms in the northern bays of Canada's eastern Arctic, the seals leave.

They come from as far north as there is open water, leaving the places that have European names; from the upper reaches of Kane Basin, which separates the icy shores of western Greenland from Ellesmere, Canada's northernmost island. Away from the freezing bights of Baffin Bay they swim south and to the east, from the slobbed-over crevices of Lancaster Sound they come cavorting over the freezing sea. They leave the upper islands of Hudson's Bay and Foxe Basin and are hurried along by the current of Hudson Strait to join the gathering herd. In herds of dozens, and then by the hundreds and finally thousands, they gather on the open sea and swim south, past wonderful, terrible headlands and heaving bodies of water bearing the exotic native names of the first peoples of the Americas: Ungava Bay and Akpatok Island; Cape Kakkiviak; Nachvak Fjord; and Saglek Bay. They are hunted and killed on the open sea, shot with long-barrelled rifles and shotguns, speared by harpoons, and drowned in fishing nets. The scattered sniping and swiping has as little effect on their vast numbers as a small waterway that leaves a mighty river. Without stopping they pass Kikkertavak and Tunungayualok islands on the western edge of the Labrador Sea, their numbers growing steadily, until several million have reached the suck of the Strait of Belle Isle, and here, surprisingly, they are divided.

The Labrador Current is the name given to the movement of water that begins in the polar seas. A powerful current beginning on the east coast of Greenland, the world's largest island, rounds its most southerly point at Cape Farewell, then heads north. The impenetrable plains of ice turn the current west and then south to become the Baffin Current, until it mixes with the North Atlantic in the Labrador Sea. Here the Labrador Current moves steadily southward outside the northeast coast of Newfoundland. Huge eddies can be seen in places, miles in length and traced by the white froth of turbulent undertows. It merges with the greatest of all ocean currents flowing northward from the world's largest maw of ocean, the Gulf of Mexico, on the Grand Banks of Newfoundland. Here the mingling of cold northern water with the warm southern currents creates the planet's richest fishing grounds. Still farther south and west, the tide from the Labrador Sea continues, until it nears Cape Hatteras of North Carolina and its mighty flow is slowed and finally defeated.

Large numbers of the harps break ranks with the rest of the herd and plunge into the Strait of Belle Isle. Barking, crying, and mumbling, they dip and thrash in and out of the water, most of them bearing east toward the open sea, others swimming west into the opening of the strait, but all of them headed unerringly south.

By day they mill around the same area of ocean, resting and diving beneath calm rolling seas or wind-tossed waves. They feast on millions of fish by day. The tender, white flesh of the ground-dwelling cod is their favourite. But when night casts its shadow over the sea, they continue their quest, and the new dawn finds them miles farther south.

The seals on the back side—or the Gulf of St. Lawrence side—of Newfoundland journey as far south as the Îles de la Madeleine and St. Paul Island, northeast of Cape North, off the coast of Cape Breton. The herd that favours the front—or east side—of the island of Newfoundland journeys farther. They have been seen as far south as Sable Island, off the southeast coast of Nova Scotia. It is here in these warming waters that the harp seals' southward migration ends, but their amazing odyssey, far from over, is really just beginning, for now the herds return northward to rendezvous with fate.

∗ ∗ ∗ ∗ ∗

THE BONAVISTA PENINSULA IS MADE up of the island-strewn Bonavista Bay on its north side and the windy maw of Trinity Bay on its south. The island of Newfoundland defines its northernmost end at Cape Bauld and the most southerly point at Cape Pine, the latter of which is largely treeless despite its name. The island is inundated with peninsulas. Some of them appear to be straining to break free of the immense island to which they are tethered.

On the northeast tip of the Bonavista Peninsula, just five miles south of the jutting Bonavista Cape itself and on the Trinity Bay side of that cape, there is a long indentation leading into the granite headland where families of fishermen live. It is a place that holds little shelter from the sea. Standing to the east from this cove are two small, rocky, barren islands where nesting birds land during the short summer season. It is from the island bird colonies that the cove, in its lee, got its simple name: Bird Island Cove. By 1914, the name of the cove had been changed again. The first Methodist minster of the Bird Island Cove settlement, who bravely tried to pluck his wayward flock from the waters of sin, was William Ellis. Despite the preacher's fruitless efforts to convert the hard-nosed fishermen to his way of thinking, out of respect the settlement was renamed Elliston.

This windswept area with the poor anchorage had been well-known to fish merchants from Europe for hundreds of years. Other, more daring men knew about the place, too. Masterless men from Ireland, seeking freedom from an oppressed land, escaped to drungs and wooded valleys inland from the community's shoreline.

Here, codfish teemed in the shallow waters just off the landwash. The men who fished—as well as their families, who shared in the work of reaping and curing this market-driven bounty—were the toughest of breeds. Born on the edge of a merciless ocean and with a dubious future for them beyond it, they shouldered their load and for the most part leaned willingly into the tangled traces of outport life.

With sharpened stakes and gnarled spikes pounded into jagged crevices—all fastened with nail-driven lungers—they constructed works of wooden genius. Laddered slipways built in the few places where boats could be hauled up on the land were swept away by autumn gales. Denied even the comfort of wharves for docking and for off-loading fish, still the intrepid fishermen demanded another favour from the ocean: a place to moor their vessels when not in use. Summer anchorages were also known as holding grounds or collars.

Small punts and rodneys with rounded stems, and bigger boats with lone masts—called sloops—swung from their lines. Similar boats held unique outport names, like bullies and scows, knockabouts and trap skiffs. Sleek schooners with black hulls sported sails that were barked brown and tied vertically to the masts. These vessels bowed to the winds and swung with the tides "on collar" in the roads off Elliston. But when the autumn liners signalled the end of the fishing season, and the dark seas rolling up from the deep Atlantic portended gales of wind, vessels large and small were released from their collars. The smaller boats were hauled up to every available crevice on land.

With great fanfare and much shouting, well-organized men and boys used ropes and tackles to pull the vessels out of the storms' path. They sailed the schooners to safer ports and took them into deep bays and sheltered coves. It was a major event in coastal communities. For men who had worked hard since early spring, this time of relative inactivity was largely a time of idle hands. Few of them liked it.

Some of them spent the late fall and winter months trapping animals on the peninsula and beyond. Many of them went looking for work in the lumber camps, some as far away as central Newfoundland. Employment opportunities such as these were few and far between yet offered ready cash to the industrious workers. But whether the fishermen were standing on stagehead or in twine loft, meeting by chance on a lonely trapline, or gathering for nightly chats in a dimly lit logging camp, their talk was the same: the coming seal hunt.

Those who had been to the hunt before tantalized the others with tales of incredible adventure. Young men not yet sixteen years old—but with years of work behind them—listened intently. Many had lied about their ages and succeeded in getting out to the hunt, but this was a risky venture. Those who tried sometimes found themselves, after walking for days to get there, standing with their hands in empty pockets on a St. John's waterfront and watching their would-be passage sail away without them.

*　*　*　*　*

THOUGH HE HAD WANTED TO go last year, Albert Crewe had no intention of risking his chance for adventure by being found as a stowaway. Now he was sixteen years old, strong with youth, and like a cat on his feet, one of the best abilities a sealer can possess. He begged his forty-nine-year-old father, a veteran sealer named Reuben Crewe, to use his influence to get him a berth to the ice, but his request fell on deaf ears. Reuben had had a frightening experience on the Arctic ice floes three years before. The near-death ordeal had turned him from the seal hunt and he had sworn to his wife, Mary, that he would never go again. Nor would he speak to the ship captains, most of whom he knew, for his young son to go. Reuben tried his best to discourage his son from going to the ice.

But Albert would not be swayed by his doting father. All of the dangers associated with hunting seals on the open Atlantic simply added to the boy's enthusiasm. He would go a-swilin'. Nothing would stop him. Not his father's warnings, nor his mother's tearful overtures. He was accoutred with the might of youth. He was invincible. In desperation, Albert approached his uncle Ben.

Ben knew all about Reuben's fears. He knew also about Reuben's terrifying experience on a sealing ship in the Gulf of St. Lawrence. It was fresh in his memory and a tale that Reuben had recounted many times. However, Benjamin reasoned, Reuben had survived the ordeal. Not only that, Reuben had been a much older man and probably past his prime. Young Albert was flush with the boundless energy of youth. He was fleet of foot and as tough as nails. Ben listened to his nephew's questions for weeks before finally giving in and, using his own influence, obtained a berth to the ice that coming spring for the boy. Ben never told Reuben what he had done, and for the longest time neither did Albert. The weeks went by, and Reuben suspected something had happened when his usually persistent son had not mentioned the seal hunt. He decided to confront Albert.

"'Tis good fer me to see you've given up on that bert' to the ice, my son. 'Tis not fit fer a man to be at, anyway."

"Well—I—'tis like—I mean . . ." Albert stammered, fearing his father's wrath. "I've—I've got me bert', Pop. I'm going to the ice this spring," Albert finished, his voice resolute.

"What do 'e mean, you've got a bert'? 'Tis not possible! 'Ow could a boy of sixteen get a . . . by God, 'twas that bloody Ben who spoke fer 'e, wudnit? I knowed it! Well, 'twon't happen, I tell 'e. Yer mother will never allow it. Her 'eart will pine away when you go, I tell 'e! I'll be havin' a few choice words with Ben before this day dies, too!"

"'Tis no use fer you to rage, Pop! Nor Mom, either, fer me

mind's made up! I'm a man and can make me own bed. And 'tis not Uncle Ben's fault! I pestered him somethin' fierce fer months before he gave in. Besides, he has wired into S'n John's these many days ago and arranged fer me to go. I've only to make me mark alongside me name when I goes in there this spring. I'll be sailin' on the SS *Newfoundland*." Albert finished in a flourish, proud yet fearing that his father's influence with the sealing skippers could still upset his chances at getting a berth.

It was late evening in the deep wintertime. The land was frozen and snow covered everything except the black, tarred roofs of Elliston. Lamplight shone from every house, including Mary Crewe's, as father and son walked up the hard-packed snow trail toward her kitchen.

"Inside!" roared Reuben Crewe. And despite Albert's recent statement of being a man, he stepped ahead of his stern father into his mother's bright, warm kitchen like a boy.

In the kitchen, with a pot filled with a steaming hot supper burbling on the wood stove, the argument continued. Albert's mother wasn't angry like his father. Mary Crewe was deeply hurt and begged her boy to reason it out and to understand her view. Mary remembered all too well her husband's bare escape from the icefields in the Gulf three years ago. The event had shaken her man so badly he had not gone seal hunting again. And she was glad of it.

She had being tired of the waiting when he was away, the nights of staring out over an empty black sea, the agony of not knowing. And now it would begin all over again. She stood at the short counter below the windowpanes and for a time stared out into the still winter night. Behind her, seated at the table, her husband and son shouted at each other with the snow from their boots melting on her clean floor. It was the first real argument she had ever seen at her kitchen table and Mary didn't like it at all. It saddened her all the more.

She measured flour and a touch of cherished baking powder into a brown earthen bowl, added water, rolled and fashioned the flour in her hands into several balls, and laid them in a large white plate hard by the bowl. The rolled white flour looked like snowballs. At the table opposite her husband, her son was defying Reuben for the first time. Mary picked up the plate of duff, walked to the stove, and removed the lid from the bubbling pot filled with vegetables. A cloud of sweet-smelling steam lifted into the air. The smell reached the two men at the table and they turned toward it for an instant before continuing with their argument. Mary dropped the dumplings one by one down among the yellowed turnips, pale potatoes, and softened green cabbage leaves.

"Duff's in!" Mary announced loudly.

She dropped the boiler lid onto the stove where it clattered noisily on the hot cast-iron surface. Father and son turned toward the noise without speaking. Mary's back was to them, but they could see her deft fingers touching the floating dumplings and settling them among the hot vegetables according to her liking.

The argument was over. Reuben knew it was rare for his nimble-fingered woman to drop anything, and even if she did she certainly wouldn't let the pot lid lie there. As if reading his thoughts, Mary picked up the cover by its wooden knob and placed it back on the pot. Reuben knew, too, that her cry of "Duff's in!" wasn't so much to let them know that supper was almost done as it was to tell them to stop arguing in her kitchen.

Albert placed his hands on the table edge, pushed himself to his feet, and walked toward the door. He stepped quietly out into the winter night. Just past the kerosene light from his mother's kitchen window, he stopped and looked back at the house. He felt bad about the fierce disagreement he had just had with his father, but at the same time he was glad. The discussion was done. His mother had ended it. Albert knew it would not be brought up again. Framed in the lamplit window, his mother's head was bent as if examining her cooking, but inside the quiet kitchen, Mary's eyes had misted over in worry for her son who would go a-sealin'.

The winter night crept down over the village of Elliston by the sea. A frothy white spindrift licked at the layers of sedimentary shoreline, the only semblance of light on an otherwise black ocean.

*   *   *   *   *

THE SEALS SCATTER AS THEY range farther south from the Gulf of St. Lawrence and out from the southwest coast of Newfoundland, breaking their ranks into smaller herds and strings. When it reaches the shallow waters off Sable Island, the depleted vanguard suddenly stops its southward migration They reach waist high out of the seas, treading the water with their scutters, appearing to be studying, with black, shifting eyes, this tiny lace of land mass adrift in the open sea.

Sable Island is an atoll, in the shape of a new moon, that dares above the Atlantic waters more than 100 miles southeast of the coast of Nova Scotia. The island is settled down low in the sea. It is little more than twenty-six miles long and at its broadest point is barely three-quarters of a mile wide. It looks as though it should have vanished beneath the sea long ago, and the waters continue to try to erode its very foundation. Yet it remains defiant of wind and wave. For hundreds of years mariners have called it the graveyard of the Atlantic, and with good reason. Its treacherous coastline has taken many ships and men who had sailed too close. It is good for sailors to be wary.

The harp seals do not travel farther south. The sound of wave upon land is a hissing, crashing cacophony. The pounding surf snarls angrily as it tries to erase what little piece of land is left, and it has startled the seals from their southward campaign. Turning as one, they bend northward.

Now begins a frenetic pace unique to the animal world. The seals forge north from Sable and from the shores of the Magdeline Islands and away from Cape North. They stop infrequently for food now. They dive deep into the water, bursting forth again as sleek as dolphins, their flippers bunched in mid-air for the next onward thrust. They give off an eager coughing, barking sound as they forge ahead. And sometimes there is no sound at all save for the rush of water on their bodies. They swim north by instinct. North to the oncoming fields of ice and to the pains of birth. North to home. North to death.

4

*H*E WAS NINETEEN YEARS OLD and had never killed
a seal. In fact, Cecil Mouland had never killed much of
anything outside of a few seabirds and didn't consider himself
to be a hunter. He was a crack shot with the shotgun, though,
and considered himself good with a rifle, which he used at target
shooting on the rare occasion he could get his hands on a few
bullets. He was living where he had been born, in the fishing
hamlet of Doting Cove. It was a wild cove sparsely populated
by hardy fishermen and their families on the southern part of
Notre Dame Bay. Many of the locals considered Muddy Point,
just to the windward of Doting Cove, to be the real southern
beginning to Notre Dame Bay, and not Cape Freels, which lies
at the end of a straight shore of white, sandy beaches more
than twenty miles south of Doting Cove. Wherever its defined
points, "Our Lady Bay" is the pride of Newfoundland bays. Not
only is it the largest of all the many bays around the island's
coastline, it holds the greatest number of smaller islands in
any of Newfoundland's bays, and into its salt water flows the
mightiest of Newfoundland's rivers, the Exploits.

Cecil was bursting with the joy of life, filled with energy,
eager to please, and something more. Young Cecil was in love
with the pretty Salvation Army schoolteacher who had just

been stationed at Doting Cove. Her name was Jessie Collins. She was an eager young cadet in the Salvation Army movement and would be the very first teacher in a brand new schoolhouse under construction. Nineteen-year-old Jessie was from the logging and lumbering community of Hare Bay, which lay in the sprawling forested hills on the north side of Bonavista Bay. This was her first teaching position and she was very nervous. And now she had the handsomest young man in the cove asking to walk out with her, which only added to her unease.

She hadn't told him yet, but Jessie loved Cecil. She had never met anyone quite like him. He was good-looking and always kept himself meticulously groomed, especially his thick head of hair— even when she caught glimpses of him working around the busy shoreline. He always had a ready smile, and it was this that made the attractive schoolteacher flash her dark eyes his way the first time they passed each other on the gravel road of Doting Cove. Word around the community was that Cecil was the real devilskin, always drivin' works and doing anything for a laugh. He reminded her of Tom Sawyer, another devilskin Jessie had read about.

For Cecil's part, he was quite willing to give up all of his youthful antics if such devilish antics were cause for Jessie to stop looking his way. The first time he had seen the young woman walking by the fences lining the road near his home, he had been enamoured with her. She had been wearing store-bought gloves and a new coat. But it was her dark, secretive eyes that had enthralled him. They became sweethearts in that wonderful autumn of 1913. Their love flourished, with the warmth of simply holding hands, and the bliss of sweet kisses stolen in the hidden places that lovers knew. The name of the little village was not lost on the couple. Cecil believed the warmth of Jessie's touch, her lingering scent, and the very taste of her mouth would sustain and strengthen him enough to get through any ordeal.

*   *   *   *   *

WINTER BEGAN BEFORE ITS DUE date in 1913. Long before Christmas, the fresh waters froze solid and deep snows covered the land. George Tuff was from Templeman, a shallow, rocky, islet-bound cove in the lee of the point of land on which loomed the scattered houses of Newtown. Tuff had seen many early winters in his time, and now, walking along the road in Templeman, last night's snowfall barely slowed his stride. At this early hour there were no other tracks but his own on the path he was following. George was an early riser. Neither warm summer dawns nor cold winter mornings would find him in bed. The land around him was relatively flat, with humps of land to the west over which a low drift of snow was carried by a cold, moderate west wind. Amid the light snow, tall yellow grasses bent and rustled over the bawns.

To the east, the open blue sea lay broken and dented near the shoreline by hundreds of rocks and tiny islands, all of them worn smooth by eons of pounding seas. In the offing, many hidden reefs betrayed their danger when they breached among the waves. This morning, the ocean was displaying its calmer side. The wind from the west and northwest had blown away from the land for days, easing some of the otherwise unruly winter seas. Lanes of deep navy and some softer blues on the water scunned away from the land, the colours changing whenever the clouds overhead allowed the morning sun through.

Templeman was a fishing community of rugged beauty, but George Tuff barely gave the scene a glance as he trudged by. He was a lean, work-hardened man of thirty-two years. His face was stern, sculpted, clean-shaven, weathered, and tough. His eyes were pellucid, steel grey, and intense. His rough appearance throughout could be attributed more to a harsh way of life than to any genetic profile in his lineage. Tuff had a voice that was as clipped and curt as was his appearance. Seeing two men step onto the path ahead of him, he said:

"Ready to go to the telegraph office in Newtown, are ye, b'ys?" He added, "Checkin' yer names off fer a bert' to the ice!"

He knew the answer. Last evening they had talked about going across to Newtown.

"Oh, we're ready, a'right. Seen ya comin' down the road, Jarge b'y," said James Howell in his slow, pleasant voice.

"Fine civil marnin' 'tis, too, Jarge," Henry Dowding joined in. "Can't wait to get me name down fer swilin', I can't! More's the better to be shippin' with you, Jarge b'y. Are we walkin' down or shovin' across the arm in punt?" Henry was an eager, talkative man. All three men were good friends.

"Punt!" George said, the lone word hanging in the air as if he had been insulted.

Tuff came from a breed of men who would walk over the roughest ice floes without complaint for hours, but given the chance, no matter how short the crossing, like all outport men, he would go in boat rather than walk. The three men shoved a punt down a rickety slip greased with snow. The boat rocked with their weight as they stepped aboard. They swept the seats free of snow with mittened hands and Tuff sat facing the bow on the middle thwart. James shipped the after oars and, with Henry pulling from the bow oars, the punt shot away from the land. Small waves appeared at her bow, and frothy bubbles rose up from her heart-shaped counter to disappear again in her wake. The two rowers kept up a lively conversation despite their vigorous rowing. Their voices rose and fell, but the figure seated in the middle didn't say much as his body moved instinctively with the rhythm of the boat.

With seventeen years of hard experience at the icefields, George Tuff was one of the most seasoned and respected sealers to be found anywhere around the coast of Newfoundland. For ten of those years he had been given the job of master watch, a position of leadership up the greasy rungs of the sealing ladder. For the last three springs Tuff had been hunting seals with Captain Westbury Kean, the youngest son of Abram Kean, on the old wooden ship SS *Newfoundland*.

Wes Kean, as pleased with Tuff's easygoing, take-it-as-it-comes manner as he was with his ability to handle men, had recently told Tuff he wanted him to ship with him again in the spring of 1914 as first mate, or, as it was better known, his second hand. George should have been very pleased with himself. It was an amazing accolade for an uneducated, unassuming man to have the captain's ear, and in fact to have control of the ship and her crew. But, in reality, George Tuff hadn't been asked; he had been told he was to take the position as second hand. It irked him, but he accepted the job without comment. His old reluctance to resist authority figures, which had plagued him in his youth, was alive and well throughout his manhood. Secretly, Tuff preferred to follow, to work without responsibility, than to carry the burden of leadership.

Tuff had sailed and hunted with Westbury's father and had earned Abe Kean's grudging respect. Abe wanted his son, who was eagerly striving to make a name for himself in the sealing industry, to have the best of men around him. There was no one better to teach, and more importantly to serve, his ambitious son than George Tuff.

George was born in another century, in the year 1882. He was little different from other lads of his age and era, save for one trait. Tuff took orders from authority without question. Shortly after ten years of age he was doing the work of men. He learned the way of ropes and boats, sails and oars, wild seas and calm waters, and the catching and curing of all fish. Under the tutelage of parents and elders, George excelled without complaint. He loved being on the open sea. While his muscles were yet soft, he endured the kick of the muzzleloader against his shoulder, proudly bearing the bruises as a rite of passage toward being a gunner.

Tuff loved it all but yearned for more. He wanted to go seal hunting, and not searching for the scattered heads poking out of calm seas while he waited with gun in hand. He wanted to go to the Arctic ice floes and hunt the seals where they lived and gave birth by the millions. When he was fifteen, he was tempted to try and stow away aboard one of the sealing vessels, but tales of unpaid menial tasks heaped upon stowaways deterred him. When he went to the hunt, as he was determined to do, he would go not only as a man but as a paid hunter.

And so it was. In the spring of 1897, when George Tuff was sixteen years old, he went to the ice. From the first day when he was ordered over the side with the rest of the sealers, Tuff relished the hunt and quickly mastered the killing of seals and the ability to think on his feet. With his bloodied skinning knife he ran swiftly over settling ice pans as deftly as the best of them. And the very next spring, aboard the SS *Greenland* in 1898, George Tuff would give witness to a living nightmare that has been recorded as one of Newfoundland's worst disasters at sea.

The punt approached a wharf in Barbour's Tickle, Newtown. With a quick flip of their forearms, both rowers shipped the oars from the thole-pins and flicked them inside the boat. The long wooden oars rattled as they came down against the thwarts. Henry sprang out of the boat with painter in hand, climbed up the wharf lungers, and secured the bow to the wooden grump. James pulled the stern of the boat parallel to the high wharf, tied it off, and scrambled up. By the time he stood on the worn wharf planking, the fleet-footed Tuff was striding away.

They hurried down the road to the post office and were met by other men who had seen the punt coming down the bight. One of them was Mark Howell, also from Templeman, and the others were seal hunters from Newtown who had secured tickets to the ice. They stopped and talked for a while until the impatient Tuff, eager as always to get the job done, walked away.

*　*　*　*　*

ALONG THE ENTIRE NORTHEAST COAST, the Christmas month of 1913 was an unusually cold one, even for Newfoundland. Woodland valleys were choked with snow which fell almost daily, and save for the occasional black outcropping that stared out of the headlands, the landscape was white.

In all the "places," as everyone called the communities of coastal habitation, there was little activity on the sea. A few small boats were seen rowing outside the frozen harbours to hunt seabirds. The one true sign of spring on the northeast coast—the Arctic ice floes—was still three months away, but wherever fishermen gathered, the seal hunt was the main point of discussion. News was trickling back from the north of an exceptionally cold winter. Ice conditions were expected to be heavy for the coming spring and were predicted to come early. The snow and heavy frost on the island kept on coming, making the talk of a bad spring all the more believable.

The frozen harbour of Newport was now a well-travelled bridge used by young and old to visit both sides of the community. Dogs ran barking behind yelling children, who raced down hillsides and out onto the icy harbour on homemade sleds. Below the cliffs at the harbour entrance, where the ice ended and the open sea began, the ice edge was several inches thick. A beaten snow path led from the inner harbour out to the very edge. Three punts had been hauled out of the water and now rested on their sides several boat lengths away from the edge. The boats were used to hunt turrs, puffins, eider ducks, and even the little bull birds, which the locals enjoyed in bird soup. The same boats would be used to hunt seals when the first of them appeared. For many in these isolated outports, the migrating mammals would provide the first welcome source of meat for the entire year.

But for now the sturdy little boats that played such a role in outport life lay in wait. It was Christmas Eve.

The harbour was quiet now, save for the barking of a single dog, chained and sounding hungry. A brisk west wind that had come with the dawn now faded as west winds sometimes do when the sun goes down behind the long hills. It lessened to a gentle but much colder night wind. A bright moon halved by a single dark cloud appeared over the hills of the outer harbour. Heat rising from each blackened funnel turned to grey smoke when it hit the night air. The soft wind seemed to play with the smoke for a time and furled it above each rooftop before carrying it away.

A sparsely decorated fir Christmas tree tied with twine was in a corner opposite the stove in Phillip Holloway's warm kitchen. The heat from the kitchen stove sent the tree's rich smell to every corner of the room. Phillip's wife, Maryann, had placed every trinket on the tree as delicately as if they were all store-bought breakables. She had precious few such items, so for the most part the tree was adorned with her own creative ideas. Twisted lengths of colourful worsted wool and spirals of rare orange peels—saved for this very day—hung from the tips of limbs. Pieces of coloured yarn were lovingly wound through the branches. Several rabbit bladders, long since pricked and drained, blown tight with air and painted with gay colours, hung like vellum pouches, along with pairs of hand-knitted baby's booties long out of use, pieces of blue mussel shells, their pearly insides glistening in the lamplight as they slowly spun with the heat from the stove, pine cones yawing open to the heat to reveal the silvery gossamer seed inside and pieces of paper and scraps of materials that dangled and twirled. A few rare Christmas cards from past years were draped like tents over the twine that held the tree upright. On top of the lovingly decorated tree was a silver star Phillip had made from a piece of pine board and painted with Silver Dazzle, a shiny paint used to bedeck kitchen stoves.

Their children tucked in bed, Maryann and Phil talked over a cup of tea and a slice of bread smeared with partridgeberry jam. Phil assured Maryann they were going to have a bright future. When the cod fishery started up this summer they would have a cod trap, a bigger boat, and for once a better chance at making a go of it. But their immediate future hinged on the spring seal hunt and the cash money Phillip would bring home. Reports of this spring's bad ice meant nothing to him. After all, he was to ship out with Jesse Collins, a seasoned seal hunter, and best of all he had secured a berth aboard the SS *Newfoundland* with Captain Wes Kean, the son of the most famous seal killer of all.

Maryann cleared the table, poured the dregs of the teapot onto the smouldering ashes in the stove, and with lamp in hand turned to mount the stairs before she noticed something different. Phil was standing at the foot of the stairs, waiting to walk up to bed with her. It was a rare thing. She liked it.

"Merry Christmas, Maryann," he said in a soft voice.

"Oh! Merry Christmas to you, too, my love." She added quietly, "Just a minute, Phil."

Remembering she had not put the loaf of bread away, she stepped to the counter beside the kitchen window. She placed the half-eaten loaf inside a small wooden box with a door in its side. Stopping at the bottom of the stairs once again and holding the lamp higher, she looked around for her man, but the only shadow reaching long up the stairs was hers.

*   *   *   *   *

IT WAS THE EVENING OF January 6, 1914, in Elliston, the last day of Christmas, or, as it was better known to everyone in Newfoundland, Old Christmas Day. It was the day of Epiphany on the church calendar. It was also the last night for the mummers—that ridiculously disguised group of citizens young and old who went door to door throughout the season. They were always welcomed inside to engage in revelry, music, and antics—but only if their faces were hidden—to entertain the households until their hosts correctly identified them, after which they would dance their way out the door. The snow melt from their heavy footwear, which could be anything from woollen mitts to snowshoes worn backwards, was hastily mopped up in readiness for the next troupe of mummers, who were already coming down the lane, rattling the pickets on the fence as they came. It was during this time of celebration and good cheer, with the dancing mummers buckling his kitchen floor, that Reuben Crewe hoped his wife, Mary, could enjoy herself on this last night of Christmas.

He had been withholding something from her for weeks and he didn't like it at all. All through the days of Christmas and sleepless nights of Christmas, lying awake next to his woman, Reuben was torn with the decision he had made. Now, with the last mummers for the night gone from their kitchen, the strains of their accordion music fading away outside, and with the warmth of the season still upon them, it was time.

Mary returned from the porch where she had taken the mop after wiping the floor. Reuben had never once seen his wife go to bed leaving a dirty floor.

"'Twas a good Christmastime, Mary, my love," Reuben began.

"Oh, 'twas all that, Reub b'y. It's my favourite time of year, as you well know."

"Mine too. Especially the mummers. Dirty buggers, though!"

"No need fer cursin' now, Reub. 'Sides, a few flicks with the mop is a pittance to pay fer a night of enjoyment!"

"I'm going to the ice this spring, Mary maid." Reuben blurted it out without softening the announcement.

"I know, Reuben," came the soft reply.

Reuben turned with surprise, as much with Mary's use of his full name as with her knowledge of his returning to the seal hunt. She only called him Reuben when he had done something she didn't like—or when she had learned of sad news.

"'Ow could 'e know, Mary? I've kept it bottled up inside me like a festerin' sore these many weeks an' 'ave told no man!"

"Oh, Reuben, after all these years together, do you think you can keep sech a thing from me? Why, our Albert is a man now, as ye well know. Yet he can't go out in punt or head in to cut a slide load of firewood wit'out you chargin' him to mind the wind or the sharp axe. Still 'n all, I've never heard you speak a word to the boy about havin' a care at the sealin'. So then I knew you was goin' along wit' Albert, jest to 'ave an eye on 'im. To be honest, Reub b'y, 'tis a great load off my mind knowing you'll be alongside of 'im."

And as simple as that, Reuben's secret was out. Not only that, Mary was calling him Reub again. He felt a great weight lift off his own shoulders. Reuben hated keeping things from Mary. Feeling better than he had for a long time, he went upstairs to bed.

But Mary stayed for a time and puttered around her kitchen as housewives do. The stove pinged and creaked as the heat died. The kettle stopped its burbling when she removed it from the stovetop, and hissed gently when she placed it on the cooler hob. She walked on slippered feet across her neat kitchen and stood at the window facing the bay. The woman was mentally preparing herself for the time when she would stand at this same window night after night and stare into the nothingness of the black sea.

She turned with the oil lamp in her hand and walked away from the window. Reaching for the banister, her wedding ring clicked as her hand came in contact with the polished wood. Her gaze fell first upon the gold ring which shone with a soft lustre under the pale glow of the yellow lamplight, and then back to the featureless window. Sighing, she turned and stepped quickly up the thirteen steps to her room.

*   *   *   *   *

NORTH BY THE WINTRY COAST, the same silvery moonlight was witness to the plans of another, much younger couple. The night had deepened as it aged, but standing in the lun under the eaves of a scaly, red-painted stage in Doting Cove, in the warmth of each other's arms, Cecil Mouland and Jessie Collins didn't feel the cold. Earlier they had walked hand in hand, watching the moon rise up out of the sea as if pushed from below by an unseen force. There were no high hills for the winter light to wash over and no canyon walls where dark shadows could hide. There was just the wide-open sea, out of which the pale moon climbed to shed its mystic light on the black water, and the broad, flat landwash strewn with tuckamore just out of the light's reach. The rote of the nearby sea, though persistent, was largely ignored by the two lovers.

They tore their mouths free from a hundred passionate kisses. Cecil clutched Jessie fiercely to his chest, his face buried against her neck. Her secret woman smell emanated, warm and intoxicating, from beneath her brown tresses. He sought her moist, red, sensuous mouth again, seeking, searching, exploring. Jessie tore her mouth away from the kisses that were clouding her senses and gasped for air.

"Oh my! Oh my! I—I—we, I cannot—we mustn't—'tis not right."

"Oh, Jessie! My darling! My love!" cried Cecil. "You are mine! You must be mine forever! Will you be my wife?"

And the young Jessie went back into his embrace and murmured, "Yes, I will! I will! Oh, I will, my love!" It was the best Christmas gift he would ever receive.

"I'll be buildin' you a home, Jessie, my love," Cecil said after they had made their pledge. "I've been meanin' to tell you, I'm going to the ice this spring! 'Tis been arranged fer me. 'Twill be guaranteed money!"

"Oh, you're to be an ice hunter!" Jessie cried excitedly. Communities deep in Bonavista Bay always referred to seal hunters as ice hunters. "They stay at my father's house in Hare Bay every year," she continued.

"Well, I don't know about ice hunters, Jessie, my love. Sealers, or swilers, we are called around 'ere. Though I know you crowd in the bay have a different name for everyt'ing," Cecil said, laughing in his good-natured way. Secretly, though, he was pleased. Ice hunter was a proud title for a young man to wear.

The two lovers soon left and walked down the snowy road together in the light of the moon. Stealing a few more kisses at the open gate of Jessie's home, the couple finally said good night. Jessie Collins went inside and closed the door behind her without a sound, and Cecil Mouland, the proud young ice hunter, bent his way home.

5

*I*N ST. JOHN'S, THE OLDEST European city in the Americas, the light of the last day of Christmas was also fading. Night was quickly filling the harbour, hiding the castle-like tower high above the north side of The Notch. It crept around old buildings in need of paint. Lights came on, some of them yellow and faint.

In dingy harbour taverns, beer was spilling over onto polished bar tops. Imported black rums were poured, blended harsh to burn a man's throat. In the drinking establishments of the old city on the sea edge, this last night of Christmas was just another excuse to drink. But over the bustling harbour, from atop one of the darkened hills, a church bell pealed out its belief and beckoned the faithful to witness the true celebration of the season.

The snow that had fallen on the city was no longer white. Coal soot from a thousand chimneys and the tread of a thousand more feet had left the cobblestoned streets a grimy muck. Spattered among the dirty snow were greenish splotches of manure dropped by horses pulling drays. Above the outer edge of the city, where The Notch met the Atlantic Ocean, the hills on both sides were splayed winter white.

Dozens of vessels were moored inside this narrow entrance

and around the circumference of this best of harbours, and in several places where the slope of the rugged land allowed, small boats were hauled up for the season just out of reach of the sea. On one fence rail rested a discarded net with gaping, rotten holes, its cork floats tapping against the rail with the evening wind. Below the fence, the wooden claws of killicks—that ingenious Newfoundland invention that used rocks in lieu of steel grapnels—protruded out of the snow.

Ships were tied to the harbour wall and schooners with downed sails were hanked onto wharves and piers that poked like fingers into the greasy harbour waters. Hemp and bass and manila hawsers bigger than a man's forearm were secured to worn bollards, creaking with the strain of holding the ships to the shore. From a few of the vessels came the smells of an evening meal cooking, the smells as foreign as the tongues of sailors who smoked while staring down over the bulwarks.

There were schooners, some of them tied to the docks and some of them hooked to collars off the land. All of them had furled sails and appeared to have been at rest for some time. Their decks were covered with trackless snow and their plimsoll lines had the same icy tidewater mark as did the cliffs.

Some of the steel ships in the harbour looked worn and rusty. Layers of ice coated their decks and rigging. One of them, with a deep-grey hull and a bright white superstructure, had built up a head of steam in preparation for leaving and was being pulled away from a northside dock by a stout little tug. Somewhere inside the vessel, a valve was released. The steam's release sent a screeching sound around the harbour that no one noticed. The tug huffed a plume of smoke out of its lone stack as it wedged itself between the ship's bow and the dock. Then, looking small and vulnerable beneath the huge liner, it pushed its charge into midstream. With the ship's bow pointed seaward, the harbour tug burst away from the liner. Its whistle sounded and it plunged toward The Narrows. The liner made way and followed.

The seabound liner's portholes were bright with light as

she slipped out of the harbour, but only a glimmer of light showed from the black windows high up on her bridge. No captain would allow light on his bridge to hamper his visibility, especially not while making way through The Notch of St. John's harbour. Smoke from the huge ship's furnaces shot out of her stacks, only to fall lazily to her afterdeck and trail along in the vessel's slipstream like a sooty curtain.

A deep, rumbling sound came from her vitals as well as a hiss of disturbed water as the ship went by the land. Still following the fussy little tug and taking the first of the Atlantic combers at the harbour mouth, the liner tipped her broad stern to the old city.

Secured to the many wooden docks and harbour aprons were several ships used extensively in the sealing industry. Only two of them were lit, showing a little activity. The others were silent save for the frequent wrenching and chafing at their tethers and the suck of the tide along their hulls. Coils of cordage and tangled lines smeared with snow lay on their decks as if huddling against the cold. Derricks, covered with snow, rested horizontally in their chocks. Huge windlasses in the bows were moulded in casts of snow. The big spring-lines and main bowsers that held the vessels to the docks were also covered with a layer of snow, except where they bagged down and dipped into the water between ship and wharf.

A sealing vessel moored some distance apart from the others looked ragged and dishevelled. She was in total darkness, with only the new snow on her deck to give her any semblance of cleanliness or light. She had a lone stack which rose above her bridge and reached halfway up her two masts. The forward mast was taller than the after mast, and from its top dangled a long piece of rigging that hung limply and stirred with the vessel's movements. She had a small list to port as if she were leaking or carried an uneven weight somewhere inside her battered hull.

Two men appeared on the dock abaft of the black ship. They walked quickly toward a gangway that leaned down from the vessel's listing port bulwark. The gangway, which was little more than two planks nailed together, was fastened to the bulwark, rising and falling and moving side to side with each motion of the ship. The men's boots crunched on the snow as they approached the rickety walkway. One of them lugged a wooden tool box that swung by a handle from his left hand. Suddenly, he stumbled and fell backwards, the tool box spilling some of its contents onto the dock. The man bent to pick them up and cursed on the snow while the other man swore at him for falling. The tools clinked as he threw them back into the box.

They hesitated when they reached the gangway. It was covered with trackless snow. There were no rails or steps, and a single misstep would likely spill them into the icy harbour. After some discussion and more cursing, one of them scurried awkwardly up the makeshift gangway and stepped onto the deck of the ship. After a moment he found a rope and threw it down to the other. The man on the dock fastened the line to the tool box and waited as his companion pulled it up the walkway. After some coaxing from the man on board, the other finally made his way up. They walked like thieves toward a door and fumbled with its frozen lock. The door finally opened with a groan against its rusty hinges and the frost. Stepping inside, they lit a match, illuminating the windows.

After a while, the light went out again and the door creaked open as before. The two men appeared above the gangway and one of them went slipping, half running onto the dock. Inside the tool box was another large box, which the man aboard the ship lowered down. Finally, he stepped onto the gang-board, his arms spread out for balance. He tried creeping down. It didn't work. He stumbled forward like a battered pugilist, stumbling and narrowly missing the empty air between plank and harbour, until he finally landed face down on the snowy dock. His partner roared with laughter. The two men grabbed the handle of the tool box, much heavier now, and walked quickly away with the chest between them. And the black box of modern wireless technology they had come for went with them.

The distant shriek of the steamer's whistle and the answering farewell from the tug came through The Notch. And soon a throaty rumble came from the harbour entrance. A bright masthead light appeared and soon a green starboard and red port light. A white flush of water burst from her bows as the busy little tugboat came into view. The tug came roaring along the length of the sealing vessel the two men had just vacated. The tug's engines were cut and she was heeled hard to starboard, her momentum swinging her under the broad stern of the quiet sealing ship. The tug slammed quickly and without ceremony against the dock, her rubbers chafing at the blow. Like a young athlete, a crewman jumped onto the dock from the shivering tugboat and dropped the sturdy bights of rope over the steel grumps fore and aft. A spring line was thrown and tied and the engine was shut down. The lights of the tug went out. The skipper jumped ashore and the two-man crew walked away to home.

The old sealing vessel pulled at her lines when the wash of the powerful tug rudely disturbed her sleep. The gang-board was plucked upwards with the indignity of the tug's after waves, and when it came down it banged against the dock. While the ship twisted in the tug's wake, for a moment her black windows picked up glimmers of light from the city. Then the dirty windows of the old SS *Newfoundland* fell dark with night again.

* * * * *

THE OCEAN'S SURFACE HAS UNDERGONE a dramatic transformation under the curtain of Arctic night. With the terrible night winds, layers of snow have accumulated into countless humped, white shapes. At times during that long, lightless polar time, lifelike sounds where there was no life reverberated for miles along the expansive seascape: the rending and tearing of ice under pressure groaned and protested; it whined and screeched. There came rustling, crushing, pulverizing sounds, and sometimes a hissing and flushing, as if a troubled river flowed nearby.

The light returns gradually, reluctantly, revealing spectral scenes of white and grey. Now the deep, bitter night is penetrated by light. The blackest of skies grows dusky. Then comes the longest, most spectacular of gloamings. Deep smears of purple blend with pinks and shaded blues to dazzle the horizon.

This time of murky light, with all of its beautiful hues, soon passes. The sun scales out of the dark places and hangs in triumph, boldly ablaze, over a morphed landscape. And now, in the full light of day, where there had been a huge, grey, muted ocean, emerges a white plain without end.

It is incredible to look upon. It stretches so far as to shrink with the curvature of the ocean. Black points of land jut into its fringed borders. Huge, formidable-looking headlands with blunted and scarred waists stand like ramparts on the perimeters of this wasteland. There is no sign of life. Nor does it appear to be a place where life can exist. It is barren and beautiful.

Rising out of this white plain are several mountainous ice formations. Like the unbroken field of ice, the majestic icebergs were not here when the polar night had begun. Under the sun's new light the ice floes gleam and glitter, basking in revelation after its time in the Arctic womb. Still, the ice is not finished with its amazing spectacle. Something even more incredible is happening. The immensity is moving. It is as if the entire northern world is in motion, propelled by a power beyond imagination. It is moving!

The two greatest natural forces on the earth came together to create this phenomenon. First, the relentless north wind blew upon each hummock and rise of ice. Every piece of snow and ice above sea level became a sail against which the wind pressed with all its might. And then, below the surface of ice, the greatest force of all was exerted: the power of moving water. Once in motion, nothing can stop it. Along its ordained route to the south, the ice will rise up over countless reefs and atolls. It will be pulverized by wind and wave and heaved against merciless headlands. Millions of gallons of water will melt off it and flow back into the sea.

But for now it is still ice. The pounding it takes, while decreasing its height and weight, merely increases its area. Eventually it will be destroyed by the same forces that bring it south for man to see. The frigid winds and demanding tides that had created and befriended the plain and forced it from static to kinetic energy will gradually turn from cold to warm. And that is little more than a seasonal relief, for even as the fields of ice finally succumb to warmer climes, already the land of its birth will prepare to freeze the northern ocean all over again.

Ice in motion is a spectacular feature of the polar seas that is unsurpassed by any other natural movement on earth. The constant pull and press of wind and tide is finally rewarded by the release of ice from the land. It begins at the edges of frozen bays and offshore islands encased in ice, until the hundreds of miles of ice becomes, as a whole, the Great White Plain. Down from the northern bays and inlets, the ice is gathered and moved as if by some hidden director. It is torn from shingled beaches and muddy coves where it tears kelp beds away in its haste to be a part of the icy roundup. The ice is driven away from the Arctic coasts and out into the ice roads of the North Atlantic. It slides beyond Hatton Headland and Button Island, past Ryan's Bay and the Hebron shore, until it pushes to the very edge of Labrador at Battle Harbour, where the maw of the Strait of Belle Isle and the currents of the Labrador Sea and the colliding tides from the St. Lawrence Gulf will debate and ultimately decide its fate.

From windy headlands and kitchen windows, in Cook's Harbour and Wild Bight, in the shadow of Cape Norman and across the mouth of the shallow Pistolet Bay, to Savage Cove in the western lee of the oddly named Cape Onion, and farther east to Quirpon, sheltered behind the naked Cape Bauld, that northernmost point on the mainland of Newfoundland, the hunters of seals are watching and waiting. For those in the know, the clouded cast of white that appears on the horizon above a strangely untroubled sea is the portent of a welcome spring visitor. The ice is coming! Days earlier, great sludgy masses of slob ice had come out of the north. It is a grey mass of pounded ice crystals on the sea, too thick for a man to row a punt through. It always comes ahead of the main ice pack. Eider ducks by the thousands had come at the first light of dawn in swirling flocks, looking for open water. The marauding fields of ice behind them had crowded the birds away from the shoals and bays where they had been feeding.

For days small clumps of pure white ice appear, scattered and derelict from the main patch of ice. The salty tang of the open sea is replaced by a knifing wind that burns a man's face and waters his eyes. With all the signs of its approach, and with a tangible feel of it in the sea air, the greatest migration on earth has begun. And with it will come the harp seal herd, the largest population of migratory mammals.

The people who have lived long and who have watched for the Arctic ice's annual arrival say there is a place where the Great White Plain stops. It is that huge stretch of the Labrador Sea at the north end of the Belle Isle Strait, usually between Battle Harbour, on the Labrador side, and Belle Isle itself on the Atlantic side. It is said that here it is decision time for the ice floes. It is not a matter of if, but how much of its weight will be pushed down into the Strait if Belle Isle and the ever-widening St. Lawrence Gulf, and how much of it will flow down the open, Atlantic side of the island of Newfoundland. The wedge-shaped Belle Isle is the equalizer. It will turn huge tracts of ice east and west. Little more than nine miles long and barely three miles wide, the island itself lords out over the ocean just a dozen miles or so north from where the island of Newfoundland ends. From its beginning thousands of miles away in the United States, Belle Isle's north head is the northernmost end of the Appalachian chain of mountains.

Hidden beneath and swirling around its snarl of coastline, two great ocean currents are at work. Here the cold Labrador

Current, pouring steadily out of the northwest, collides with the smaller and much warmer tributary pushing up through the Belle Isle Strait from the St. Lawrence Gulf. The two mighty ocean rivers collide and torment the waters around Belle Isle.

Then, without warning, the Great White Plain advances toward the island of Newfoundland. It stills the seas and calms the waters with a surface that is spattered with the black heads of seals. Now the Strait of Belle Isle is clogged with ice from shore to shore, and for a while Newfoundland is not an island. It is connected to the rest of North America by a bridge that surrounds the north of the island like a white caul.

It pushes into Red Bay, beneath the vermilion granite cliffs where, 500 years before, the Basque adventurers of France and Spain had dwelled. And in that quiet bay, resting below the threatening, scouring ice, the remains of the Basque whalers' ancient chalupas with blubber-soaked ribs await discovery.

Into Jellyfish Cove the vanguard of the ice is forced onto shore-lined rocks and against solid landwash. Rising over the irregular, unpredictable ice surface and looking like embattled parapets are larger pieces of ice. Away from the edge of the invasive ice and across the salted flats of dead grasses and tangled gorse, standing mutely over the wintry scene are several large oval mounds with sod tops drifted bare of snow. Hidden and preserved beneath the grassy mounds are hundreds of artifacts that predate the Basque hunters on the other side of the strait by hundreds of years. The knolls are the long-deserted sod houses of seafaring Norsemen who ventured over the North Atlantic Ocean to this point of land 2,000 years before. In Jellyfish Cove and L'Anse aux Meadows, these markings of European exploration, which no one yet believes in and which will change the history of the Americas, also remain to be discovered.

The north headlands of the island of Newfoundland shudder with the impact of hundreds of square miles of moving ice pressing on them. The island shoulders the ice aside, dividing the immense ice floe which will keep coming for weeks, sending it east and west. Seals approach the moving plain, their numbers increasing by the millions. They appear with heads bobbing and flippers clawing, clumsily hauling themselves out of the sea. They crowd the miniature dark-water bays and sea-ponds held within the icefield. They peer up through ice rents and bobbing-holes and squeeze their sleek, supple bodies around the edges of countless ice pans. Their numbers increase until, on the Great White Plain, the largest colony of mammals adrift on any ocean has gathered. With the exception of juvenile seals of last year's birth among the herd, they are all adults. Hollow grunts, a few deep, throaty rumbles, and sometimes vibrating clicking sounds come from the scattered herds. Adult males sometimes snarl and spit with clacking teeth at smaller females with swollen bellies as much as they do at rival males, but for the most part the huge rookery is strangely quiet.

In the harsh mid-winter of 1914, this incredible spectacle of one of nature's wonders is lost on the hunters who wait on land. For hard-bitten men who watch their women try to make table from bare cupboards, who have to reach into near-empty flour barrels to feed hungry bellies, the ice and its visitors mean only one thing: meat! Rich, tasty, fatty, sustaining meat in abundance.

Tough men with steely nerves venture off the land and out onto the ice with heavy wooden gaffs in hand. They spring and leap across dangerous swatches of open water between shifting pans of ice. It is extremely dangerous work. It is so demanding that sometimes a man must make decisions in mid-jump. The slob between the pans, though frozen and beckoning, is not to be trusted. Every move is a challenge. It is work that would tire a mountaineer. The ice is uneven and slippery. It moves and swells underfoot. The pans are deceiving. It takes a quick, knowing eye to decide which of them will take the weight of a burly man. To land on one that will not could mean death. And all the while a man must keep a careful eye for the safety of the land behind him and a hunter's eye on the wary seals ahead. The sealer sweats as much from the surge of hunter's adrenaline as from the exertion of the stalk.

For all but a few scarred adult seals that had survived previous ocean migrations, it is their first glimpse of a creature standing on two limbs. The old seals rise up on their bellies, for a better look at what is coming for them, before slumping back on the ice. With the weight of their bodies, their fat is splayed flat and level beneath them on the ice surface. Their black eyes roll. Their nostrils flare, seeking the smell of the intruders. And when the stench of the beasts with two legs sprinting toward them invades their senses, they flee. They make great, lumbering lunges, their fat bodies wallowing as they dive head first into nearby blowholes. They sink tail first into open swatches and crevices, rising back up out of the water for one last look, before disappearing beneath the ice. They flee by the thousands, but not all of them make it. Black-clad hunters with raised clubs suddenly appear around the high edges of ice and they bludgeon the skulls of seals with one sure blow. The successful hunters trudge homewards with bent backs, towing the bloody carcasses of meat behind them.

And when the winds die and the tide slackens, the ice pressure loosens from the land and miles of black lakes of open water appear for men to row out in small boats for the harvest. They fire volleys of shot from long heavy guns at the bobbing heads of seals in the water. They kill unwary seals basking on the pans. They haul the bodies of seals in over the gunnels of their punts, where the slain animals' dark blood runs along the timbers toward the stern of the boat. Back on shore the seals are quickly butchered. Now it is cut-and-come-again until the entire village, starving for fresh meat, is satisfied. This method of seal hunting will continue for the landsmen until the ice floe has passed, taking the seal herds with it.

Now the Great White Plain has been stained with its first blood and the death of mammals. But it pales when compared to the deadly hunt to come.

6

"*T*HE ICE HUNTERS ARE COMIN'!" Young children, who were always the first to see the sealers, shouted excitedly around the frozen harbours of Trinity, Dover, and Hare Bay on the north side of Bonavista Bay. The annual swilers' walk had begun! Every late winter they watched for the ice hunters, a dark line of men coming up over the bay ice from Butchers Cove at Hare Bay harbour's east end, always in the late evening. They were considered fearless hunters, adventurers as strong and invincible as Vikings. It would continue for days—they would walk for miles out of the northern coastal outports and make their way to the railhead at Gambo and from there to the sealing ships in St. John's harbour.

Some of the sealers were luckier than others. Word had come that the sealing ship *Newfoundland* would make a stop in the small seaport of Wesleyville this year. For seal hunters who had secured berths on the *Newfoundland* from as far away as Notre Dame Bay, this was good news. But if you lived elsewhere along the coast, getting to St. John's on her sail date was your problem. They walked over logging roads, through deep forests, and across frozen ponds. They struggled through deep, unbroken snow, over trackless bogs and windy barrens, over bays and inner coves, to get the train to St. John's.

Some walked the whole distance to St. John's over the railbed. Others took their chances and snuck aboard unheated freight cars. One would-be sealer, after travelling a full day in a freight car, arrived at the St. John's station, jumped out of the car, and landed on frostbitten feet. By rail or horse-drawn sleigh, by dog team or on their own two feet, 1,500 men, seasoned sealers and neophytes alike, made it to St. John's harbour in the winter of 1914.

Most of the swilers who walked into Hare Bay towed small sleds carrying their duffle bags. Other sleds had wooden boxes tied to them. Some of the ice hunter boxes were painted and some were not. They were rectangular, small but sturdy, and for the most part looked battered and worn with use. Their covers were fastened with thick leather straps and a loop of rope for carrying them hung from either end. Many of the seasoned sealers used the boxes year after year, not trusting their few valuables to canvas bags. The boxes were mysterious things that contained all manner of secrets for boys with adventurous minds: seal daggers by the dozen; fancy tow ropes braided like lariats; playing cards with the queen of every suit clad in fancy underwear—or wearing no clothes at all!—tiny bottles filled with secret ingredients, known only to sealers, that kept them immune from frost. Every boy knew that ice hunters never got cold. The boxes, like the bags, also contained bare essentials: a shift of clothes, needle and thread, a razor, a Bible.

Tow ropes extended from the front of the sleds and were draped over the sealers' shoulders. Those who didn't haul sleds carried their duffle, or nunny bags, on their backs. When curious boys approached them, laughing and shouting with glee, and crackies ran yapping around their feet, the men straightened their backs, kicked at the snapping dogs, and shouted rough yet friendly greetings to their young followers. Inspired by the boisterous welcome, the men lengthened their stride until the youngest of the children found themselves running to keep up. They manoeuvred around the tidewaters that flushed up through the baddy catters where the harbour ice met the landwash. Once on the land, the swilers dispersed down long lanes hemmed in on both sides by fences and went inside welcoming houses for the night.

The boys who followed the ice hunters hoped to get their hands on one of the swilers' sleds. As a rule, they weren't much to look at. For the most part they were hastily built sleds used to get the sealers' gear to the train at Gambo and then to be discarded. But some of them were crafted by hand, and to a boy who was used to dragging heavy handcarts up steep "slidin' hills," they were a prize. All of them were lightweight, no more than three or four feet long. And no matter if it wasn't the fastest sled on Uncle Robert's Hill, just to be the proud owner of a genuine ice hunter's sled was enough. Sadly, though, despite the pleadings of brazen young boys and the rashings of food followed by Mom's partridgeberry tarts, it was rare for the sealers to part with their sleds; the ice hunters still had fifteen or more miles to walk to the railhead. There the swilers' walk ended and, much to the envy of the Hare Bay boys, the men might just as soon give their sleds to the Gambo boys.

*　*　*　*　*

THE CITY OF ST. JOHN'S, Newfoundland, had heard the soft footfalls and later the booted tramp from the countless feet of men for hundreds of years. In the beginning, a stalwart, handsome people with red-stained skin had come here, when the hills above St. John's harbour were unscarred and the pure waters issuing inside its sheltered canyon washed upon virgin shores. They chose calm days to paddle their fragile barks past the grey mountains guarding the entrance to the harbour. They bound their feet with the skins of animals and lived off the land. After a time, they left, and their footprints were not found on this shore or any other shore again.

Other explorers and adventurers came here over the years, their massive, wind-driven vessels dwarfing the canoes of the native inhabitants. They took riches from the land and pulled far more than they needed out of the boundless sea. And they would never go away. Wars were fought over this city harbour by countries far beyond its walls. Soldiers and sailors prepared for battle here for hundreds of years, but none of them came with the same fortitude and fighting spirit as the ice hunters.

They were a fierce group of men who entered the city with springing step. They came for days until more than 1,500 of their kind had claimed the waterfronts of the city. The roadstead outside the city's natural walls was its surest avenue, but few came from that direction; the North Atlantic Ocean in mid-winter was a daunting place and not well-travelled. Instead, chunky railway engines, laboriously belching coal, pulled them into the west end of the old city aboard rocking railcars. Or they walked into the city on foot, with packs on their backs or towed behind them on slides. Some came on horse-drawn sleds from the nearer outlying settlements, while others arrived by teams of one or two dogs— rarely more. A few of the lucky ones had walked for no more than a day to get here, but most of the hunters had come from great distances. Some had travelled to railway connections from all along the northeast coast of the island, out of Notre Dame Bay and up from the trackless north side of Bonavista Bay to the railhead at Gambo. Others came from the south side of that bay, around its barren headland into Trinity Bay, from Elliston and Catalina, riding on a spur line barely three years old to connect with the main trunk at Clarenville, and on east into St. John's. And those who had empty pockets walked through snow-choked forests and followed logging trails and travelled across the frozen bights of the inner bays. Many of the hunters were from within the city's limits, but the greater number came from the isolated outports of rural Newfoundland, most of them from the northeast coast. It was an annul exodus out of the bays to the city.

Most of the sealing captains hailed from Bonavista Bay. The captains from the small island community of Greenspond preferred to crew their ships with men from their own area.

They had arrived in St. John's and the city was waiting for

them. The ship owners were expecting them. These were the men who would crew their ships, and without them there would be no hunt. Without exception, all of them crowded and milled around the docks in the lower part of the harbour. They sought out their vessels and the offices of the merchants who owned them. Even those sealers who had their berths confirmed by telegraph or mail or by word of mouth were always anxious. Until he marked his X or wrote his name in a company's ledger, a sealer's berth was not secure.

Others among them hoped to get aboard the ships by fraudulent means. They used the names of others who had obtained berths but for various reasons were not now going. This practice was so common, the merchants required the sealers to sign this statement:

> If any man should sign a false name and shall proceed in the said vessel personating or representing himself to be another, it shall be the option of the Master or suppliers to withhold from him any share of the voyage.

In reality, the merchants were not all that concerned with the accuracy of the names in their ledgers but would take full advantage of the situation to get work done or obtain seal pelts without paying for them.

There were others, hopefuls, who made their way into the city on pure speculation. If men failed to show up in time to sail on a vessel, these others would stand by and gladly take their places. So coveted were these seal hunting berths that every spring there were stowaways found aboard ships long after they had cleared the harbour. Those men, underage and seasoned sealers alike, were considered either good luck or jinxes, depending on the success of the vessels the stowaways had been discovered on that spring. No matter the success of the ship, the stowaway could be made to work aboard ship or hunt on the ice with no expectation of payment. A lot depended on the master's whim. Yet it was so rare to find no stowaways that it was considered by many of the sealers to be a bad omen if one was *not* found.

Having secured their berths, the sealers next had to obtain their crop. This was the term used for the hunter's necessary gear used in the hunt. It consisted of a wooden gaff, used or new, to aid in jumping the pans but primarily to club seals. The gaff had a wooden handle several feet in length and was equipped on the business end with a steel point as well as a steel hook. Other essentials were tow ropes for hauling seals by hand, a skinning knife with a curved blade in a leather sheath, and a steel to keep the knife sharp. Some of the more seasoned sealers brought their own gaffs all the way from home and would use no other, especially the "S'n John's–made" ones. They had made the gaffs to suit themselves with the right balance and heft. The crop could be purchased with ready cash but was almost always kept in strict account to be applied against the sealer's share, to be counted after the vessel returned to harbour.

The shipowners and chandlers who provided these necessities also had other items to tempt the hunters. There were fancy knives encased in tooled leather cases, sealskin boots hand-crafted by Labrador women, woollen hats, stockings, and mittens with fancy designs on them knitted by women of Newfoundland for pennies and sold for dollars. Long greatcoats were available for purchase, as well as eyeglasses and goggles to protect the hunter's eyes from the burning pain of snow blindness; thick, rich bars of chocolate and boxes of candies guaranteed to give instant energy to a tired sealer; tins or bags of tobacco to be smoked or chewed; and pipes short-stemmed or long. One merchant sold used pipes with an advertisement scrawled above them in longhand: "Hardly fire-hardened and no teeth marks." But aside from the cheapest tobacco available, few of the sealers could afford to buy any of it.

In their haste to make their ship's sail date, most of the ice hunters had arrived in the city a day or two before. So accommodations had to be found. Some of them had friends or relatives in St. John's and made arrangement to board with them. Others knew no one in town and had to rely on other places of lodging. They could stay on their respective ships if it was convenient to do so, but they were required to work at preparing for the hunt while aboard—without pay. Or, if they wanted to, they could sleep on the floor of the shipowner's warehouses. But even then, if they ate a few meals from the ship's galley without working aboard, the cost was not considered to be part of the voyage and would be added to their crop.

By day they walked around the city in groups, usually with men from their own towns or areas. They peered into shopfront windows and sometimes walked inside to look longingly over the counters at articles for sale. The smartly dressed shopkeepers, who looked at them with much anticipation when they came in, then with disdain when they walked out empty-handed, would never know the pain of men who could not afford to buy even one small toy for a waiting child.

At night these would-be sealers slept peacefully, covered in warm blankets on feathered mattresses in the homes of friends, on the floors of cold warehouses, on relatively warmer brin-wrapped bales of cordage, or below the decks of stinking, well-worn ships. But for some of them, their first time seeing the city lights was too much to resist. For the most part the swilers were a hardened breed of men who kept to themselves. When not in groups they were usually called baymen. They bore the taunts from the townies in good fun, but they were not to be tampered with, as many of the city boys had learned.

One cold night, a group of sealers who were waiting for their ship to leave for the ice found themselves seated at the bar in a dingy grog shop just up from the docks. Between them they found enough money for a few belts of rum. The bartender, who was also the owner of the establishment, was a big man with a beer belly and was known for his dislike of baymen.

The sealers placed the glass to their lips and tipped back

the rum, feeling it sting their throats on the way down. But after a grimace and a quick spinal shiver accompanied with a smacking of lips, they ordered another round. This one came from a different bottle the barkeep poured from beneath the bar, but the sealers appeared not to notice. The night continued and the sealers talked louder. One of the sealers was a big man who had a speech problem. He was amiable enough, a hard-working fisherman who was known around the Greenspond area for his great strength. He talked slowly and, with his outport tongue combined with an Irish and Welsh brogue, was a bit difficult for the bartender to understand.

The big sealer walked to the bar and asked for one more round, this time from the real bottle. The bartender's face turned red.

"What did you say?" he roared, both of his hands under his bulging belly, which leaned half out over the bar.

"I s'id to you, sir, to pour me an' the b'ys 'ere a tum'ler of good black rum and no more of dat townie lassy water what's under the bar!" the sealer said.

"By God," yelled the indignant bartender. "I didn't understand half of what you said. You bloody baymen all sound dumb to me. No man accuses me of selling watered-down rum, calls me a townie, and gets away with it. I've a good mind to punch you in the mouth."

"Well, now, seein' 's 'ow both of we is of the same mind, in a manner of speakin', tell you what I'll do fer 'e. I'll stan' 'ere an' allow 'e to make the first smack."

"Why, you're even dumber than you look!" cried the barman.

With that, he threw a long-handed punch over the bar at the big sealer's head. The blow connected with the man's left cheek, and, true to his word, he didn't move. It drove some spittle out of the right side of his mouth and shook his head a bit, but little else. The bartender stared in disbelief that the man was still on his feet.

"Can't 'it no 'arder'n dat, can 'e?" asked the sealer. "Well, dat be as it may, now 'tis my turn!"

The bartender turned to run, but he was too slow. He had mistakenly thought the big sealer's slowness of speech was also an indicator of his wits as well as his hands. The sealer reached across the bar and grabbed the man by the throat with his right hand, twisting and pulling him halfway across the bar with a single fluid motion.

"Dis is fer callin' me dumb!" the sealer said, his right hand twisting tighter. His left hand, balled into a huge fist, came up and the bartender's eyes rolled in fear of what was to come.

"An' dis is fer sellin' we fellers pissy rum!"

And with that, the big swiler's knuckles collided with the bartender's mouth, tearing out one of the man's bottom teeth that was rotten and two on the top that were not. The sealer released his hold on the unconscious man, who slid behind the bar, knocking over bottles as he fell. The man from Greenspond picked up one of the upended bottles and poured its contents over the bartender's ashen face. He was right. It did indeed look like pissy molasses water.

* * * * *

ALL THROUGH THE LENGTHENING DAYS, preparations to ready the ships for the seal hunt continued. The sound of men and equipment resounded around the old seaport. Windlasses gave off rusted flakes of misuse as valves were opened. Winches squealed and groaned as they wound steel cables in their grip. Derricks creaked as they swung their loads in over the steel and wooden gunnels of ships. Sometimes, daring young men took a ride aboard with them. Whistles blew and valves hissed. Items were hoisted aboard the ships while others were hoisted out of them. Everything that wasn't necessary for the running of the ships was removed to create space for what the skippers hoped would be a bumper year at the hunt.

The *Newfoundland* was stripped above and below decks of all but her bare essentials before Wes Kean ordered provisions aboard for 203 men: forty-five barrels of Royal Household and thirty barrels of Golden Glow flour, along with 2,040 pounds of butter for the bread; 344 pounds of crew tea as well as eighty pounds of cabin tea; 363 gallons of sugar molasses; two barrels of sugar; 1,568 pounds of Rangoon Beans; 150 pounds of onions; and thirty pounds of sago. Men lugged other items on their backs up over the gangway and directly into the officer's quarters: four dozen pickles; one dozen marmalade; one case of salmon; one pail of jam; one pound of custard; eight dozen skinned rabbits; one dozen large pineapples; and fifteen pounds of coffee. And for one of the officers who liked spices, which likely included Captain Kean: one pound of assorted spices; one dozen bottles of Worcestershire sauce; three pounds of white pepper; and six bottles of curry powder.

With the aid of the winches, twenty-five quintals of codfish made their way into the *Newfoundland*'s larders, along with thirty-two barrels of salt pork, ten barrels of heavily salted beef, thirty-two barrels of potatoes, and fifteen barrels of turnip. Bales of cordage and kegs of gunpowder made their way aboard as well, to be used to free the ship should it become jammed in the ice. Men hoisted aboard lumber to build partitions to hold seal pelts, and kegs of nails to fasten them. Black coal disappeared into the ship's bunkers by the tons. Fresh water for the boilers and for drinking was carried aboard. Men yelled and laughed and cursed. Dogs ran around, barking at all the excitement. Sometimes in the evening, smartly dressed ladies walked by and smiled up at the seafarers, who were only too glad to return their admiration.

And outside the bustling harbour filled with seal killers, the Great White Plain was bearing steadily southward.

* * * * *

BY THE LATE EVENING OF March 9, 1914, the SS *Newfoundland* was just about ready for the hunt. The old ship would make to sea at midnight. She was one of the oldest ships of the fleet and one of the last wooden vessels to take part in the hunt. Other ships of wooden construction were also preparing for the annual seal hunt, but the old *Newfoundland* outstripped them all. Because she was made of wood and couldn't batter her way through the ice, she, along with the other wooden walls, were allowed to leave port a day ahead of the steel ships. It was her only advantage. The ship had been outfitted for her forty-second year at sea and looked her age.

It was said that every grey roller of the North Atlantic had met the hull of the old *Newfoundland*. Her high prow, once rising proudly above her decks, stood 212.5 feet forward of her stern and gave the vessel a settled look. The weight of years at sea had burdened her after part so that her stern dragged low in the water.

She was a screw-driven ship, built by naval engineer Peter Baldwin for the Newfoundland Sealing Company Ltd., constructed out of Canadian hardwoods and pitch pine in the city of Quebec, Canada. Designed for a life at the seal hunt, her keel first slid into the fresh water of the St. Lawrence River in 1872. She had both an upper and a lower deck with a beam of 29.5 feet. With both a main as well as a foremast, she was classed as a brigantine: while under sail, she could carry canvas both square-rigged and schooner, or fore and aft rigged, at the same time. The new ship was also equipped with a modern, 130-horsepower, coal-fired steam engine. A single smokestack rose out of her boiler room amidships. She was registered to carry a legal weight of 567.83 net tons and at the time of her launching was owned by John Anderson. By 1893 the *Newfoundland* had a new owner, Captain Farquhar, with a Nova Scotia registry and continued to sail to the seal hunt. Farquhar became involved in the Spanish-American war in 1898 and he used the *Newfoundland* as a blockade runner to smuggle goods to Cuba. The ship was captured with her full crew, and with war contraband aboard, she was held by the Americans at Charleston, North Carolina, for six long months.

By 1914 she had long been owned by Harvey and Company of St. John's. A lifetime at sea, forty-two springs of punching her way through fields of ice, had taken its toll. She had been repaired many times above and below deck. Her forward hull had been strengthened from her forefoot to just above her plimsoll line. Greenheart timbers and even straps of iron had been bolted to her timbers, all designed to keep her viable for the annual seal hunt.

Over the past four decades, in the off-seasons, the ship had brought in and carried out of St. John's her share of cargoes, but those who sailed in her always said the smell from forty years of freighting greasy seal pelts would stay with her until she died. It had seeped into the grain of her wood so that no amount of cleaning could remove it. Deep in the crevices of her lowest bilge, where films of seal fat had disappeared into every crack, even years of sea water could not rinse away the smell of seal blubber.

Maybe the sealers who had walked her decks were right about her smell, for on August 3, 1916, when the old sealing vessel struck a reef and sank off St. Mary's Bay, the calm streak that came up from her watery grave for days looked like blubber stains that had finally been released from her timbers.

7

*H*ARP SEALS ARE GREGARIOUS ANIMALS that live in vast herds of millions all over the North Atlantic Ocean. They range as far north as the White Sea, that huge fjord of the Barents Sea. They also breed along the coast of Greenland. But it is the coast of Newfoundland and Labrador where their numbers are the greatest.

They can grow to a length of six feet or more and weigh as much as 400 pounds. Their courting begins on land, their mating takes place in water, and they give birth to their young on the ice. They are semi-aquatic and are capable of diving to ocean depths of 1,000 feet and staying under water up to twenty minutes without breathing.

The Groenlandica name for them is *phoca*. The Inuit call the baby harp seals *kotik*. The Europeans called them harp seals due to the pattern on their backs that sometimes resembles a harp. The Newfoundlanders call them many names, depending on their state or age. One of the sealers' names for the adult harp seal is saddleback. Their dense fur is very attractive to humans. When cured properly it makes the finest clothing, as well as boots and tooled wallets and personalized pocketbooks.

The animals are protected from their harsh environment by three inches or more of fat. The boiling process of the fat gives off a stench so bad it sticks to a man's throat, but the rendered oil burns clear and is odourless. It provides the finest lubricating oil for delicate machinery and was used extensively in the textile industry in England. British women washed their skin with fine soaps made from the oil of seals and they splashed on their faces scented perfumes rendered from seal fat. So soft and pure was the oil of the harp seal, it was even used to soothe the pain of diaper rash on the bottoms of European babies.

But the prize of the hunt was the white skins of baby seals. Born a whitish yellow in the early days of March, in as little as three days their hides turn a soft white, hence the name whitecoat. From their mothers' teats they suck milk that increases their weight by as much as five pounds a day, and by mid-March they have all moulted to the same wonderful colour. But in just two weeks they begin to moult again to a colour that holds less value to humans. Newfoundlanders call the seals at this time of their life "ragged jackets." Now their fat is the only thing of any value; their fur is worthless.

The timing of the hunt was everything. To maximize the merchants' yield, the sealers had to be on the ice when the hides of the young seals were white. The white fur of the seals at birth, their most vulnerable stage of life, had adapted over time to protect them from natural predators. Polar bears followed them to the fields of ice and killed them regularly; sharks swam in the open leads looking for the unwary ones; farther north, wolves, wolverines, and lynx were seen hunting them when the ice came to shore. Sometimes the ice-coloured pelts would spare the young seals, but in 1914 their snowy hides would do nothing to hide them from the greatest predator of all: man.

* * * * *

TWO OF THE SEALERS WERE having second thoughts about boarding the *Newfoundland* on the evening of March 9. One of them was Peter Lamb. Peter was from the isolated outport of

Red Island, a small island of fisher people situated on the outer edge of the eastern channel of Placentia Bay. He had crossed Placentia Bay in rowboat with his friend John Lundrigan on March 2. The inner reaches of the bay were frozen over, so the two men walked across the arm and then ashore, on to the town of Whitbourne, where they stayed the night with friends. By the early morning of March 5, they were traipsing down the streets of St. John's. Here John said goodbye to his friend and boarded the sealing vessel *Southern Cross*, which had been making ready to take part in the hunt in the Gulf of St. Lawrence. Vessels taking part in "the Gulf hunt" to the west were allowed to leave port five days earlier than those hunting at "the Front," or east side of the island of Newfoundland.

When Peter shook his friend's hand, he took from him more than a warm farewell. He was also taking his friend's name! John Lundrigan had sold his berth on the *Newfoundland* for fifty cents. Instead of sailing in the *Newfoundland*, John had arranged a berth aboard the ship *Southern Cross*. Peter Lamb signed his friend's name both on the *Newfoundland*'s registry as well as on the required statement of pledge before boarding. Peter didn't feel good about the deceit, but, eager to join the hunt, he told himself he hadn't broken any real law. Truthfully, it was illegal to sign aboard a ship using someone else's name, but he comforted himself in the knowledge that it was a common practice. Once aboard the vessel he figured he would be just one of the crew, as far as the ship's officers were concerned. They rarely spoke to ordinary sealers, anyway. If the other sealers found out, they would never tell. They always looked after their own.

One other such hopeful was John Antle. John was from St. John's, barely fifteen years old, and had never been to the seal hunt before. He had tried and tried to secure a berth, going to the waterfront every day. He had even managed to talk to one of the owners of the sealing ships and had told him he was sixteen, but the man saw through his lie and refused him a berth. Aside from working aboard a small inshore fishing boat, slightly more than twenty feet long, young John had never been to sea, either. Antle loved the ocean and was fearless no matter the weather. Making for sea out through The Notch was all he had wanted. But now, the lure of the seal fishery, which was a rite of manhood among the outport youth of Newfoundland in 1914, was irresistible.

Besides, he knew of another man who had stowed away the year before. After being discovered, he had been allowed to hunt seals just like the other sealers, and he had returned with money in his pocket. Antle had tried his best, but he couldn't secure passage. Still, he was determined to board the SS *Newfoundland* no matter what. He just didn't know how he was going to get up the gangway without being seen. John Antle had no ticket and the ship showed all evidence of preparing to leave.

*   *   *   *   *

THERE WAS ANOTHER MAN WHO was reluctant to walk aboard the SS *Newfoundland*, but he wasn't a sealer. Navigator Charles W. Green wasn't wanted aboard and he knew it. Times were changing, and the effects of some of these changes were evident on the bridge of the SS *Newfoundland*. The island of Newfoundland was part of the dominion of the British Empire of King George V and had to abide by her rules, especially in matters naval. Everyone on the island considered it to be a nation unto itself, with its own government under elected Prime Minister Edward Morris, but Britannia still ruled these shores. According to the British Admiralty, all ships venturing upon the high seas were required to have on their bridge an officer who had been schooled in navigation and who had a master mariner's ticket. The captain of the *Newfoundland*, Westbury Kean, had neither.

Even the pull of old Abram Kean and his many associates, influential though they were, meant nothing to the British laws of the sea. And so Captain Charles Green was ordered by Harvey and Company, the owners of the *Newfoundland*, to report as navigator on board on March 9, in time to prepare himself in such matters as he might deem necessary for the voyage. He was also told in no uncertain terms that he was not to interfere in any way with the young captain in the usual operations of the ship. His role was strictly one of formality and nothing more. His interference would only be accepted in the unlikely event of an emergency.

Green walked aboard the *Newfoundland* well after dark on the evening of her sailing. A few men scurried about her deck, some of them making room for him as he strode toward the bridge with as much confidence as he could muster. A winch cluttered, its steel dogs clinking into the teeth of its gears as it hoisted aboard the last of the ship's gear. A faint, low rumble arose from the deck as he crossed, and when he stopped for a minute to observe the ship's surroundings and get the smell of her, he felt a slight vibration beneath his feet. The boilers below decks were already fired to build up steam as he climbed the bridge ladder. The *Newfoundland*'s idling engine sent black smoke out of the funnel just abaft the bridge. Her one smokestack was huge and black, reaching to half the height of her mast. Several cables strained to support it and keep it upright. It looked ponderous and ugly, as if it had been pushed above her decks as an afterthought.

Wes Kean didn't turn around as his navigator entered. He stayed at the forward window, looking at the activity on deck. There was no welcome aboard, no friendly gesture at all from the skipper. Nor did Green offer any of his own, though he realized not acknowledging him would come as a blow to the younger man's pride. Before long, the two men exchanged greetings and then fell silent. This token civility taken care of, Green resolved to keep to himself.

Wes Kean had every right to feel slighted. He was a very capable skipper. Incredibly, at just twenty-nine years of age, he had already spent fourteen years at sea. Though this spring would be his fourth as captain aboard the SS *Newfoundland*, secretly he hated the ship. She was old, cumbersome to manoeuvre among the ice, underpowered, and she shuddered as if she would break apart every time her bows shouldered the ice pans aside.

He had received his tutelage in seafaring and the seal hunt from one of the greatest seamen and sealing captains of them all, a man every sealer loved and hated: his father, Abram Kean. Wes knew the law regarding master tickets, but having Green aboard didn't make him feel any better. He could box the compass by the time he was seventeen years old, and he could find his way around the ragged, treacherous island of Newfoundland in stormy gale or foggy night as much by natural instinct as by dead reckoning. He couldn't shoot the stars with the graduated disc and pointer of the astrolabe—to make astronomical calculations of the celestial bodies, day or night, to find exactly where his ship was on the ocean—but Westbury Kean was still a good skipper. He treated his men fairly and had earned the respect of all who sailed with him.

It wasn't that he didn't want the extra help in navigation. In fact, he longed for a master's ticket. It was the embarrassment of knowing that, without returning to school, he didn't possess the education to achieve such a degree. It galled him to go back to book learning, even for a master's ticket. He had hated school just as much on the day he left it as he had the day he had first went in, though that period had not been a long one. His father had returned to school and had earned his master's certificate more than twenty years ago, when he was in his thirties, but Wes had rebelled against it. He felt he was qualified enough and didn't need the stuffy learning like the book-smart man who had just stepped onto the deck of his ship.

There was nothing stuffy about Charles W. Green. He had earned his smarts from a far different world than that of any nautical school. Green was a proven master mariner. He had been one for five years, and though he had spent just one spring at the ice as navigator aboard the *Beothic*, the Arctic floes were no stranger to him. He had three years of experience with the Canadian Government Service and had shipped aboard the SS *Arctic* as third and second officer from 1906 to 1909. He had endured the rigours and privations that come with wintering on Baffin Island's Pond Inlet during the terrible winter of 1906-07.

The very next year, 1908-09, Green was aboard the SS *Arctic*, which lay frozen in Winter Harbour on Melville Island, Northwest Territories. It was the fiercest of winters and Charles Green had proven his worth.

On April 7, 1909, he led a party of seven men from Melville Island across McClure Sound to Banks Island, on the eastern edge of the Beaufort Sea. By the time the group had returned from Bay of God's Mercy, Banks Island, they had spent an incredible forty-one days on the frozen Arctic wastes. They pulled komatiks loaded with their provisions and slept in canvas tents. They had sleeping bags made from sheepskin. The nights were so cold they had to cover their heads with the bags to keep from freezing. They discovered after a few nights out that breathing while inside the fleece bags caused moisture to collect, which froze solid and made the bags heavy and unusable. They discarded them and carried on, sleeping under ship's blankets. They survived primarily by drinking Bovril, a concentrated essence of beef, diluted with water and brought to a boil on a spirit stove. All of the men under Charles Green's leadership returned to Melville Island unharmed.

He shipped aboard the SS *Kite* to Greenland as her master for three years. In 1912 he was master of yet another vessel bound into the Arctic seas. This time it was the *Neptune*, sailing for Baffin Island with the Lucky Scott Expedition aboard.

Scott was a wealthy American mining promoter and had so much success with the discovery of rare minerals he was considered lucky. Robert Janes of Newfoundland, who prided himself as being one of only a few prospectors in Newfoundland, had been on a recent voyage to Baffin Island.

While fishing for salmon in Eclipse Sound, Janes told everyone, he dislodged with his boots a nugget of solid gold. Not only that, he boasted, but there were nuggets in many other places in the cold running water. News of Janes's discovery reached Lucky Scott and an expedition to Baffin Island was arranged with a few others. When they reached Baffin Island, Robert Janes was their leader. Under his guidance they found not one trace of gold, but coal, and even that was of poor quality. Not feeling so lucky, Janes escaped the fury of Scott and the others by fleeing over the tundra of Baffin. With bullets whizzing all around him, Janes escaped.

Charles Green was the captain who took the men off Baffin Island and returned them south. Inside the hold of the *Neptune* was a fortune, not of gold but of ivory and furs. Unknown to Green, all of it had been stolen. It was an expedition plagued with scandal—with treachery, thievery, and even murder—a blight on Arctic justice.

Such was the man who was to share the bridge of the *Newfoundland* with her captain. Despite his credentials, he could not interfere with the normal running of the ship. Both men were easygoing and even-tempered, which was a good thing, for the SS *Newfoundland* was making final preparations for sea. She was about to get under way, navigated by a man who had a certificate to be her captain, but who took orders from one who did not.

* * * * *

PETER LAMB WATCHED FOR HIS chance, and when a group of sealers went lively and laughing up the gangway to board the *Newfoundland*, he walked behind and laughed right along with them. No one noticed. Many young men were coming aboard for the first time, and it was the same every spring. No one even asked him his name. He jumped over her gunnel as quick as you please, stepped across her deck with the same confidence as the other sealers, and disappeared below. And as simple as that, Peter Lamb had boarded the *Newfoundland* under the guise of John Lundrigan.

John Antle had been walking the waterfront of St. John's since early that morning. He had spent a sleepless night, half in dread, half in anticipation of the seal hunt. He had had many chances to board the ship the day before—there was no security of any kind—but Antle reasoned that being caught aboard before she sailed would result in his immediate discharge from the vessel back onto the wharf. He decided to wait until the last minute and not risk being discovered until he was at sea. The first light of day found him walking, hands in pockets and head down like a thief, along by the ships being fitted for the voyage.

Earlier, he had seen a man around his age go aboard the ship behind a bunch of noisy sealers. Maybe it was another stowaway, he thought. He noted the man had walked slowly to the gangway and then quite suddenly had jumped behind the sealers as if it were a split decision. The others had given no indication that they knew him. For a moment he considered doing the same thing, but he decided he would stick with his plan. He had thought it out for days and decided he would sneak aboard after dark.

He had watched another man walk aboard the vessel earlier with a suitcase in his hand and climb the steps to the bridge. None of the sealers carried suitcases. This man was dressed in a greatcoat that came to his ankles, like most of the skippers wore, but it wasn't Wes Kean. Someone had pointed out Kean to Antle before. The lights of the city came on, but they did nothing to illuminate the docks. John was glad of that. The *Newfoundland* was in near-total darkness for a while before a few dull lights appeared in her portholes. The lamps looked as though they needed cleaning. The ones aloft in her rigging could have passed for candles. Dozens of shadows stirred on deck, faintly outlined by the ship's lamps and the men's glowing pipe bowls and cigarette ends. The voices of the sealers who strolled on her deck came in low tones except when they laughed or coughed.

John Antle, still dockside, caught the smell of food coming from the ship as some of the men went below. He waited, his duffle bag by his side. Presently the shapes of a couple of men were on her deck but no one was near the gangway. John figured that, after their supper was over, the sealers would be back on deck smoking and yarning again. Antle lived in the city and he knew that sealers would line the gunnels of the ship as they left port, day or night. He sped like a startled crackie across the narrow apron, the strap of his bag slung over his left shoulder sliding partway down his arm as he ran. He shouldered it again, tighter this time, and raced on. He slowed when he reached the bottom of the gangway and forced himself to run up soft and easy, to make as little noise as possible. Leaping over the gunnels of the *Newfoundland*, he landed like a bobcat, on the balls of his feet, and headed for his hiding place. He knew where he was going.

Antle had heard that one of the first places the ship's officers looked for stowaways was aboard the lifeboats, which were usually covered in heavy tarps. He would not risk hiding in such an obvious place. He would put up with the consequences after being discovered at sea, anything to go to the ice, but he would not take the chance of being discovered while still in port. The forward hatches of the *Newfoundland* were covered and battened down. The forward derricks were raised parallel to the foremast, indicating loading for that part of the vessel was complete. That part of the ship was also in plain view of anyone who might be looking out of the bridge windows.

One of the after derricks was still pointing away from the mainmast and stretching horizontally over the wharf, as if waiting for one last load to swing aboard. One of the after hatches was open and there was no one around it. Antle walked aft toward it, forcing himself to walk at a casual pace, fearing he would attract attention. His heart was pounding against his chest as he reached the hatch coaming and peered down into the ship's hold. At first he could see nothing, but he waited for a few moments to pass for his eyes to adjust. Barrels stood on their ends and boxes were stowed between them. Antle figured it would be no more than a three- or four-foot drop after lowering his body down. He sat on the edge of the coaming, swung his legs in over the edge, hung on by his arms for a second or two, and then let go. He landed on the edge of a barrel and twisted his ankle, but he didn't let out a sound.

Looking upwards through the open hatch, it seemed as though the light would give away his hiding place, but he knew it wouldn't. Still, he scrambled over the stowed gear as fast as he could on his tender ankle. He had barely made it across the tops of piles of provisions, settling himself between the hull of the ship and a bag of what smelled like oakum, when the after winch started up again. It was followed by the clatter of gears and shouts coming from a couple of the crew. While he watched, he saw the head of the jib come into his view, its top stay whining through its tackle, and then it stopped. The light of the hatch was suddenly blocked by a load of goods swinging in a loading net. Antle watched as the whip line was pulled tight across the hatch opening, where it steadied and guided the load in place. The top stay tackle whined again and the load was gently lowered down into the hold. From above, the mainstay of the derrick was released and the end of it fell down with a thump. Its standing part was rapidly pulled back through the bights of the netting, leaving Antle alone with the load, which gave him only a dim view of topside.

He could hear the derrick swing again and he thought another load was coming aboard. For a moment he was afraid of being crushed, but the hatch cover dropped with a thud and he heard someone hammering it in place. Now he was in complete darkness. He didn't like it much, but he knew there had to be a door to the after bulkhead somewhere. The main thing was that he was safe aboard the ship. He was a stowaway. He had done it! It hadn't been difficult at all. But what John Antle didn't know was that this was not the SS *Newfoundland*'s final port of call. She had to make another stop at Wesleyville, and if he were discovered, Wes Kean would put him ashore there in that isolated seaport without a second thought, leaving him a penniless stranger 300 miles from home.

8

*F*OR DAYS BEFORE IT APPEARS, the people on the northeast coast of Newfoundland can see the glow on the horizon above the ice floes. Sealers call it the "ice blink." The wind is raw and the bays are filled with northern slob, easily differentiated from local bay slob by men who know the ways of the ice. The Great White Plain is bearing south at a steady gait, but now the plain is different. The quiet of the ice has changed, for now it is spattered with stains of blood, and it cradles the countless young of the harp females. Continuing without stop day and night over a two-day period, they have given birth to their pups by the hundreds of thousands.

From the dilated genitals of the female her pup emerges as she lies on the ice bearing the pangs of birth in silence, her body extended with contraction. Following it is the clear, yellowish placenta, flecked with the blood of birth. Immediately the new mother twists and squirms around, tearing the umbilical cord out of her body, physically separating herself from her young forever. She sniffs loudly at her newborn's nose, pushing aside its filmy caul, identifying its scent and then noses the crying pup to her swollen teats. The pup cries all the more, confused, afraid, hungry, and nearly blind. So human-like are the cries of the pups, seal hunters refer to them as cradle wails.

The patient female, stretched fully on her side, nudges the infant with her head and pushes it with her flippers until it preoccupies itself with feeding. The Great White Plain is now a massive nursery. It is a spectacular sight. The whelping of the harp seals has begun. The cry and mewl of the young multiplies by the minute, the influx of newborns on the ice like waves on a beach, gentle and soft, unending, yet fierce and unstoppable with the bringing of new life.

The birthing bed is never still, but always in motion beneath the pregnant seals. It is unpredictable, not to be trusted. March winds tear across the shelterless icefields without mercy. Blizzards of snow come out of the north just in time to accompany the birthing of the seals. The Newfoundland sealers call the snowstorms the whelping batch, or lapping batch, and by some unexplained wile of nature, they almost always happen when the pups are being born. The storm can last for a day or more. For its duration it hides the vulnerable mothers and newborns from predators and gives the seals a temporary shelter.

It also kills.

The storms are so severe they sometimes separate the infant seals from their mothers in blinding snowdrifts, and the pitiful bleating of the young goes unheard. By the hundreds they die from exposure to one of the harshest calving grounds on earth. After the storms they are found entombed beneath the snow by anxious mothers. They fall into water-filled crevices and, unable to swim, drown within minutes. They are crushed between the edges of ice pans or fall into shark-infested waters.

Many are stillborn—tiny, shrunken creatures preserved within their own fluids—and slip, already dead, into an uncaring world. And for some reason known only to nature, there are others that are born mute. Ironically, perhaps cruelly, the sealers call them screechers; they starve to death without making a sound. Others die crying for mothers who have slipped down a nearby breathing hole never to return.

In such a forbidding winter realm, a great multitude of young seals are unceremoniously delivered but survive the birthing. And before the month of their birth has ended, they are deserted by their mothers. The female leaves abruptly to follow the age-old craving and will mate promiscuously for days. The pups are now forsaken, alone, defenceless, and the time of the hunter is near.

*   *   *   *   *

REUBEN CREWE WALKED THE DECK of the SS *Newfoundland* again. He had done so several times since he and his son Albert had boarded the vessel in the early afternoon of March 8. A new railway line from the main trunk at Clarenville was started in 1909, and on November 8, 1911, the rail line to Bonavista was completed. It was an easy walk from Elliston to Bonavista. There were twelve sealers in St. John's from Elliston and many others from the Bonavista area, but not all of them had the means to come by train. Most of them had walked.

Reuben Crewe and his son had travelled by train. It was Albert's first time. It was also his first time in a city, and now his first time stepping onto the deck of a steamer. The boy was ecstatic. Reuben wisely gave his son lots of slack to explore and enjoy his first visit to the city and to mingle and meet the old sealers. He had no intention of crowding Albert. Remembering his first time on such a voyage, he saw through his son's eyes the wonder of it all again. It made him feel much better about the coming seal hunt. Albert's enthusiasm for the hunt and the experience of the voyage had changed his father. Sealers Reuben had not seen for years greeted him warmly. He had to admit it felt good being aboard a sealer for another hunt. He would teach Albert everything he knew about hunting seals and about the dangers afoot on the Arctic ice floes. It would be all right. After all, he had survived one life-threatening experience at the seal hunt years ago aboard the *Harlaw*. The event had given him the foresight of what could happen. He told himself the chances of such a thing happening again were unlikely.

Albert Crewe couldn't believe he was actually going to the seal hunt. Even when his father had announced in January that he was going, too, he was still doubtful. He had heard him say many times he would never ever go back to the ice. He knew his father was only going to the hunt to "have an eye on him," but he didn't mind that. So far on this trip his dad had not interfered with his activities. Albert had roamed the streets of St. John's and marvelled at the items for sale in the shops. With his full head of flaxen hair and broad shoulders and still a couple of years of growth due him, he got his first glance of young city women who met him on the streets. With his long blond hair, Albert Crewe strode forth young and proud, looking for all the world like a Viking venturing forth on a voyage of discovery. Though Albert was a shy young man, he secretly loved the looks he received. He was having the best time of his life.

He and a couple of other young hunters had already had an amazing experience in the city. They explored the many shops, sometimes peering in the windows, sometimes growing bold and actually walking into the stores. Into one such store they had entered quietly, not bothering to kick the dirty street-snow from their heavy boots. The door closed on its own behind them. It took a minute for the boys to realize they had entered an establishment that sold woman's apparel. They were embarrassed and were about to leave when they witnessed an incredible scene in the back of the store. Standing there was a naked woman with pale white skin and long eyelashes over dark, half-closed eyes. Standing behind her and out of the view, a man's hands were caressing her fully-pointed breasts. The boys stared with gaping mouths and bulging eyes.

"Be with you in a minute," said a thin, high-pitched voice.

But when the store owner stepped around the mannequin he had been dressing, his store was empty but for the snow tracks on the floor.

Albert walked the top deck of the *Newfoundland* and watched her final preparations for sea. He was too excited to go below for supper. He didn't want to miss anything that was happening above decks. Such is the way of all young sailors who go to sea for the first time. Just after dusk, he watched in fascination as the city lights appeared, seemingly one by one, when he saw a man walk briskly astern to the after hold and promptly disappear over its coaming. *He looked young,* Albert thought, *maybe even younger than me.* One of the dockworkers, he figured. As he continued to watch, the final sling of provisions was hoisted aboard. The after hold cover was fitted tight, the winches stopped, and the dockworkers walked ashore. The young man Albert had seen jump into the hold was not among them.

A fierce rumble came from the ship's belly that made her decks tremble. It was accompanied by a burst of black smoke from her high stack and from somewhere else the hissing whine of released steam. The shoring lines were slipped from the wharf bollards and pulled up over the side of the ship. Albert Crewe felt the wooden deck vibrate from stem to stern as her bows swung slowly from the dock.

*   *   *   *   *

THE SHIP'S DOORWAYS FILLED WITH men rushing on deck to see her leave. A whistle blew from somewhere on her superstructure. It sounded hoarse and worn. Astern of the ship came the farewell whistle of the *Florizel,* captained by Wes's older brother, Joseph Kean, who was also preparing for sea. The high-pitched horn from Abram Kean aboard the *Stephano* also sounded around the harbour. The *Stephano* was the world's newest sealing vessel and her captain was acknowledging his son's departure aboard one of the oldest. Old man Kean's ship was owned by Bowring's. She was also the world's best icebreaker, and though Abram Kean had to follow the rules of steel ships leaving for the seal hunt, he hated watching and not being the first one to leave, even though its captain was his youngest son, Wes.

Despite the late hour, people had gathered on Harvey's Wharf to wave and yell goodbyes to the sealers lining the rails. Some of them had either family or friends aboard and others just came to see the first of the sealers off. It was the thing to do in St. John's each spring. The night was black without starshine or moonlight. A cold, raw wind was blowing, but deep in the bowl of St. John's harbour it was difficult to tell from which direction. Women clad in long coats with high collars buttoned, their heads covered with woollen scarves, waved their gloved hands. Men shouted encouragement from the dock. Sealers lining the *Newfoundland*'s port side yelled and whistled as the ship moved away from the wharf and the crushed harbour ice rustled along her hull. Steam whistles sounded again. The people ashore shouted. Whiskered, hard-looking men standing at her rail spat over the side and flicked cigarette butts into the water. Her hoarse whistle sounded again. Barking dogs added to the din. And at the stroke of midnight the battered and worn *Newfoundland* was under way for her historic encounter with the Great White Plain.

She looked small and appeared to be skulking by the huge old cliffs that formed the harbour entrance. Her lights looked yellow from a distance, like the light from lamps in kitchen windows. Her boiler valves were opened wide and her lone engine roared to full throttle as she slipped out over the night sea. Aboard the vessel, bells rang and doors slammed. She took the first roll of a surprisingly calm sea in a gentle tilt. The wind on her starboard quarter was from the northeast by the time she hauled to port after clearing the city walls. The city didn't fade away in the darkness astern of the ship. It simply disappeared as if by magic when the *Newfoundland* closed the door to The Notch behind her.

Wes Kean knew why the seas were calm in the face of a brisk wind out of the northeast. The ice pack was near, keeping the seas down. Stepping out to the bridge rail, he could smell the fresh bite of it in the air. He ordered his lookouts to "keep an eye fer ice." The *Newfoundland*'s navigator, Charles Green, made the first entry in his log.

> Monday, March 9th, 1914. From Saint Johns towards Wesleyville. Got underway at midnight. 12:30 Am steamed through narrows. Wind NNE force 3. Direction NE. Lookout---carefully attended to.

Green entered meticulous notes in his personal log and kept it private. To calculate wind speed he used the Beaufort scale. A method of accurately determining wind speeds had been in use as early as 1705, when Daniel Defoe, author of the novel *Robinson Crusoe*, had spent considerable time working at it. But it was Irish Royal Navy Officer Francis Beaufort, serving on the HMS *Woolwich* in 1805, who perfected the method.

* * * * *

JOHN ANTLE KNEW THE SHIP was leaving. The throb of her engines reverberated through his hiding place. His hand on her hull trembled with the pulse of it. John wasn't especially afraid of the dark but he hadn't known until now he didn't like close quarters. He squirmed and crawled over boxes and barrels in the dark until he found himself on the floor. There he found a door in the bulkhead with a dull light showing around its edges. Surprisingly, the hold was nearly empty. Apart from the provisions—he was sure one of the boxes smelled like prunes— the smell of the ship's bilge was overwhelming. Then he heard a low hissing sound that increased to a screeching whine. The boiler valves were being gradually opened to the engine. After a few more minutes of vented steam came a throbbing sound that he could feel up through his boots. The propeller shaft was turning. They were under way. The big shaft, turning slowly in its tunnel, had stirred up months of stagnant bilge water. The smell was putrid. Young Antle staggered in the dark until his hands found the bulkhead near the closed door. He retched until his stomach emptied itself somewhere in the dark. He felt better right away, but no matter the consequences, he needed fresh air, and had to get out. The door latch worked noisily but easy enough. The door was unlocked and, fearing he would vomit again, he stepped through.

He was standing in a small, shadowy passageway at the end of which, through an open door, he could see two men with bared arms shovelling coal into a blazing furnace. Beyond that, a ladder led above. He climbed up and entered a room crowded with noisy men. No one noticed him. Antle made his way through the crowd to the open deck to stand beside a young man who looked no older than himself. The other man was leaning over the rail as if trying to keep the fading city lights in view.

"Away to the hunt at last!" said John Antle, proud as you please.

The other man turned with the last of the city lights illuminating his yellow hair.

"Not quite yet," said Albert Crewe. "We've a stop in Wesleyville to pick up the b'ys from Bonavist' North."

*   *   *   *   *

THE WINTER STORMS OF 1914—especially the ones that brought the whelping batch of early March—were some of the worst on record. All through the winter the north winds had prevailed, piling snows in layers until inland valleys were filled level. Only the lofty barrens, their tops swept clean by the relentless winds, showed any promise of a warmer season to come. In the outports, only the scattered ends of picket fences showed in lanes packed with snow. The inner bays and coves, and even some of the outer edges of them, were still in the full grip of winter.

On one such broad, frozen cove on the morning of March 9,

just north of the little fishing village of Pound Cove, a group was struggling south through the snow. They were all sealers from the Newtown-Templeman area and were making their way to the port of Wesleyville to board their appointed sealing vessels. Boulders jutting up out of the shallow cove had their tide level marked with baddy catters. The bay ice in this area, surrounded by many communities, was fairly well-travelled, but a steady fall of new snow with strong northeast winds all day yesterday and into last night had now covered all signs of tracks. The land that stretched to the west was flat and barren save for scattered bunches of tuckamore. The low trees were bent over with the strain of a lifetime of wind and winter snowfall.

"Not much need fer hurryin', b'ys," George Tuff said. "There'll be nar ship comin' in Wesleyville harbour this day. Or t'morrow, either, I'm 'lowin', be the looks of it." He directed his speech to a few of the younger men who went walking briskly ahead of the others.

At Tuff's words they looked left to seaward, where the Arctic ice was jammed against the landwash, and understood his meaning. They had seen the ice coming for days with the constant "in-winds" pressing the ice floes onto the land. Still, they were hopeful. The SS *Newfoundland* was due in Wesleyville late this evening and they had no intention of missing her entry into the harbour. It was part of the excitement of the voyage, watching the ship they would soon board steam into view. After all, it was coming for them.

"I don't know, Jarge b'y," one of the young men said. "There's a few big swatches of water off our place and 'tis bound to be the same off Wesleyville. So being, 'tis sure Skipper Wes will find a way t'rough," he added eagerly. "'Sides, when we come down off that high knob of land before we got on the ice, I was sure I seen a scud of smoke off to the south'ard."

"'Tis only a few lakes of water made be the big pans grounded solid on shoal ground," Tuff replied, "an' not to be mistaken fer open sea leads."

"Ha ha! P'raps the smoke you seen was a louse on yer eyebrow," said one fellow, causing a ripple of laughter from the others.

"Nar louse ever crossed my brow, I'll 'ave 'e know," came the indignant reply.

"Jest wait till you sleeps with the weight of the ship's curvies drawn tight under yer chin to keep warm an' the morning glories are bitin'," laughed one of the older sealers.

The young man made to reply but realized he was being made fun of and wisely laughed with the others.

By now the sealers had crossed the quiet cove and were on the snowy land again. The lead man was already breaking trail in the deep snow, the last man walking up over the baddy catters, when they were hailed by loud voices from behind. The shouts were accompanied by the barking of dogs. They all turned as one and looked across the cove they had just crossed. Several dark-clad men with packs slung over their shoulders and hauling sleds behind them were just walking onto the ice on the other side. Behind them came another group of men led by two teams of dogs pulling komatiks loaded with seamen's bags. Despite the laborious travel, the dogs barked excitedly upon seeing the strangers across the cove.

"Swilers from beyond the cape, by God!" The men stopped walking and decided to wait for the others to cross the cove.

"Farder north than that," said another. "I recognize a couple from Dotin' Cove among 'em."

He was right. The men who had caught up with them were sealers from north of Cape Freels, where Bonavista Bay ended and Notre Dame Bay began. It happened every spring without any communication between them. When it was time for the sealers to meet their ships in different ports, they would invariably meet on the trails. Now the groups exchanged rough, hardy greetings. Old friends and relatives were welcomed, and newcomers like young Cecil Mouland and his cousin Ralph Mouland were introduced.

Some were hardened sealers meeting other vessels in Wesleyville. Word had come by wireless to the different post offices that another ship, the *Eagle*, would also pick up the last of her crew at Wesleyville this year. Most had secured their berths to the ice by this late date, but there were also a few among them who were hopeful there would be sealers who would fail to make the sailing time, or who "dropped berths" for them to fill at the last minute.

They started off again after a while and the dogs stopped barking. The last leg of their journey was silent as the ice hunters crossed the wintry barrens to Wesleyville in the gathering wind.

* * * * *

LATER THAT SAME DAY THE brewing wind from the northeast whipped up the snow-covered land again. Drifting in open places was severe. On the highest hill on the north side of Newport, a group of men stood peering into the wind. They were trying to see any sign of a ship steaming north toward them, but there was none. No ship hull down on the horizon, no smear of smoke against the grey sky. Nothing. The sea stretched white with ice as far as their vantage point allowed them to see.

Jesse Collins and his cousin Fred Collins and the two brothers Phillip and Joshua Holloway were headed for Wesleyville. With them were Jonas Pickett and Robert Brown from Fair Island. These two had crossed the bight between Silver Fox Island and Newport late yesterday evening, spent the night with friends in Newport, and had now joined the others. The wooden ship they had secured berths aboard, the SS *Newfoundland*, was supposed to have left St. John's harbour at the stroke of midnight last night and should be in sight by now. But there was no sign of the *Newfoundland* or any other ship in that immense icefield.

"She might have stood farder to sea. She could be makin' her way in open water farder nort' an' be comin' around that way," Jesse stated, ever the optimist, answering the others' unspoken question.

"You could be right, though it appears to be jammed solid in that direction, too," Fred added.

"There are always open leads to be seen from a ship's barrel as can never be seen from the land, an' Skipper Wes is the man to find 'em," Jesse commented, sounding more hopeful than convinced.

"I don't know, b'ys," said Joshua. "The ice is jammed right up the bay as far as it can go, be the looks of it. Sure, 'tis no wonder with all the in winds we've been 'avin." Still an' all, we must go to Wesleyville. She could come in the night after the wind drops or the tide slacks and loosens the ice. Wes Kean won't wait fer no man when 'e's ready to go."

"Better get on the trail, then," said Phil Holloway in his practical, no-nonsense manner. "We've a ways to go."

He and the others from Newport were wearing snowshoes that clacked on their feet as they moved away from the hills and entered the forest heading north. The two from Fair Island followed behind, grateful for their newly beaten trail. They stayed on trackless trails inland until they came down out of the hills among the scattered houses at Shamblers Cove, where they walked out on the frozen bay at Greenspond Tickle. They crossed the ice inside Pool's Island, where friends waved at them as they passed. Leaving the bay at Valleyfield, they removed their snowshoes.

Late that evening, just before dark, they walked into Wesleyville. They were the last of the ice hunters to arrive. The wind had not dropped as they had expected. In fact, it blew harder out of the northeast, and with the dark came more snow, but no ships came into the frozen harbour.

9

*I*N OPEN WATER AND FREE of ice, the *Newfoundland* could have made Wesleyville in ten hours or so. But by 8:00 a.m. she was slowed as she entered heavy pack ice. The wind was a force three out of the northeast. All day her captain twisted and turned his vessel into open leads of water, trying to claw his way northward. He was losing valuable time, but he was powerless to do more. Later that evening the wind dropped, the ice slacked, it started to rain, and the ship was making slow progress north. But by midnight of her first day at sea the wind had increased to force-five out of the northeast again and brought with it a plaster mix of snow and rain. The press of ice on her bows was impossible to get past. The *Newfoundland* was jammed solid and surrounded by a white, tumbled sea of ice. She was going nowhere. The engine was burned down for the night.

On the edge of the northern sea roads, Wesleyville was dressed in its winter glory. It is a flat land for the most part, with many outcroppings of granite rising bleakly out of the landscape. Its harbour approach from the open sea is a formidable one and not to be taken lightly. This coast to Cape Freels and points farther north is plagued with a sailor's dread: shallow water and reefs. Dozens of rocks mar the coast for miles. Small islands of all shapes, some of them inhabited, rise above the sea without rhyme nor reason. When wind and sea are in full spate, there appears to be no entrance to such a place. The ocean all around is a seething roil of foaming white water.

As fearsome as it looks, it is one of the better times to enter, for now the reefs and dangers of shallow water are exposed by the breaking seas. For those who know, there are deep, safe channels that pass between the angry-looking breakers.

But for the most part the Arctic ice floes hide it all. They calm the seas, smooth the breakers, and cover the heaving grey-green shoals. After a night of drifting ice, people awaken to silence. The ice has silenced the rote of the sea. For a huge ship tacking from one place to another looking for leads of open water, it is a dangerous time. The dangers, though hidden, are still there.

* * * * *

CHARLES GREEN HAD BEEN WATCHING Wes Kean covertly, half hoping for the young skipper to make a mistake. But he had made none. It was one thing to clear harbour in the dead of night and lay down a course for hours on end, but one needed a different set of skills entirely when confronted with ice. Charles knew this all too well. During the day, two barrelmen shouted down the sightings from their lofty view in both masts of the *Newfoundland*. Their findings were passed to the captain.

"There's a long lead to the nar'west, sir! I'll see more when we gets there, I speck."

"The only one I can see is off to the south'ard, sir! Big swatches to the east of that, and black water, looks like."

"A rent—bit narry—off to the east! She'll wedge t'rough, though, I 'lows, sir."

But most dreaded of all to come from the barrelmen: "Nar drop o' water to be seen, sir! Tighter'n a water gully, she is!"

At times like these, Wes Kean climbed the rigging like a cat and entered the barrel himself. He ordered someone else to take his place as wheelman in his absence, but not the experienced navigator, Charles Green.

One of the most feared places at sea when sailing from St. John's is northeast of Cape Bonavista, where deadly rocks lie in wait miles out to sea. Standing farthest to sea in this chain of shoal water is a rocky area the local fishermen call Young Harry. The closest obstruction is called Branchy Rock and in the centre is Old Harry. At ebb spring tide, less than two fathoms of water cover its spine. Collectively, the rocks are called Harry's Ground, but to seafarers who know them, they are called The Old Harrys.

Green, ever methodical, had carried charts of his own aboard the *Newfoundland* and plotted the course taken by Kean all the way. When they had encountered the ice floes there was little use for a direct course. A way had to be found through ice by knowledge and experience and not by compass or chart. Grudgingly, Charles Green had to give Wes Kean his respect. The man had skilfully tacked his ship back and forth across the icebound ocean, following the shouts of the barrelmen for hours trying to beat north to the seals. And the heaviest ice had been off The Old Harrys. Once, Green was about to warn Kean that he was too close to the rocks, but Kean was in full control. He heaved the wheel over, the ship turned toward a lake of black water, and they moved slowly away from the reef.

They were punching and weaving midway across Bonavista Bay. The morning had begun with thick snow and a force-five wind still out of the northeast. The Offer Gooseberry Islands were in sight. Seabirds by the thousands rose up from hidden leads as they passed. Eider ducks and old squaws—called hounds by the locals—flew over the ice in long, rapidly twisting formations. Their numbers showed as pale ribbons winging across the sky until they suddenly veered down and disappeared below the ice edge into some unseen swatch of water.

Just past noon the wind dropped and the weather cleared. The ice was heavy and tight and the ship was still barely making headway. Then they saw smoke rising astern. A ship standing to sea from them was making good way through the ice. It was the steel ship *Sagona*. She came on steadily, weaving her way through the ice, until she loomed up less than a mile to the starboard of the *Newfoundland*. As she passed, the booming and pounding of the loose ice beneath her steel hull rang out to the anxious sealers lining the rail of the *Newfoundland*.

Wes Kean silently cursed the old ship under his feet. He wished he could give the order to plough through the ice, but he knew his ship was incapable of such a thing. He watched in envy as the new ship made her way past him. The *Newfoundland* could not withstand anywhere near the beating the captain was giving the *Sagona*. By 10:00 p.m. Wes was jammed solid again and he had the engine stopped and the boilers burned down for their second night in the ice. The lights of distant islands twinkled, most notably those of the island of Greenspond, just south of Wesleyville, his final port before he would leave for the hunt. The lights mocked him. He was painfully aware that his wooden vessel no longer had an edge in this new age of steel.

* * * * *

THE SEALERS WHO POURED INTO Wesleyville from communities near and far had doubled its population. Some of them occupied the same houses they had stayed in the year before. There were no hotels and only one boarding house. After a few days with the ships delayed by heavy ice conditions, these people with simple means found it hard to provide for the hungry sealers. Nevertheless, the ice hunters were welcome at every door for as long as it took.

The long and hungry month of March was the most dreaded of all months in outport Newfoundland. Provisions gathered in the fall from land and sea were rapidly depleted. Fish, berries, and game, the staples of these hunter-gatherers, were dwindling. Store-bought foods were the hardest to replace. The flour barrel got deeper with each mixing of bread. Most of the fishermen lived by the truck system, organized by the merchants, and it was little better than indentured servitude. An entire summer's catch of fish was never large enough for them to receive money. The merchants and chandlers carried the fishermen and their families through the fishing season on their ledgers, but when it came time to settle accounts, the businessmen were the only ones who seemed to make a profit.

If in the rare event a few dollars were due, the fisherman was reminded, "The long and hungry month of March will come and then you'll need the credit. I'll keep a count on me books fer ya." But the counts were not always accurate. For example, a merchant in Wesleyville once credited a Cape Ann hat to one of his customers. Unsure as to whom it was, he pencilled on all of his customers' bills: *One Cape Ann—not sure.*

The sealers were well aware of these trying times and did what they could to help. Few of them had any cash, but while they waited for their ships they offered their labour. They grabbed bucksaws and cut junks of firewood, they carried buckets of water from wells and poured them into pork barrel water gullies, and helped with the fashioning of killicks (sometimes called old grannies). Sections of torn nets hung in every twine loft. With nimble fingers and needles flying, the sealers helped with the mending. While they worked they talked and gossiped about news from other communities: who had married, or into which family a child had been born, and who had died. Yarns were spun and great stories were told. Amazingly the most popular yarns were the ones involving disasters at the seal hunt.

Then, at 8:00 a.m. on the morning of March 11, the SS *Newfoundland* pushed her way into Wesleyville harbour with a force-four wind from the north-northeast astern and with snow falling all around her. At 4:00 p.m., another wooden sealer, the SS *Eagle*, entered port through the swirling snow. That night the winds roared out of the northeast, bringing even more snow and jamming the ice more tightly against the land, blocking the way to open water.

Aboard the *Newfoundland*, the sealers were talking about this "winter of starms" and the terrible ice conditions. Crewmen from the *Eagle* came aboard visiting and the two skippers discussed their options with their officers. Charles Green was not asked to take part in the discussion, nor did he offer his opinion. While the men talked, he stood in the background on the bridge and stared at the scarred wood from which the wireless apparatus had been removed. Wes Kean pointed to a chart of Bonavista Bay. His fingernails needed trimming.

"Dere lies the problem!" he began, indicating the long finger of the Bonavista Peninsula. "With the constant winds from the northerly point, the ice is fillin' Bonavist' Bay, as is plain fer any man to see." The other men nodded their heads and murmured their agreement. "The 'arder the ice is pressed ag'in the souther' part of the bay, it only stands to reason that the more the bloody stuff as keeps comin' is spewed back ag'in the nort' side of the bay. We must get away from the strain of the lan'. The open sea, ice or no, is our best bet."

Again the others agreed with the young captain. As soon as the weather broke, day or night, they would make for the outer reaches, where they expected great lakes of open water would carry them to the seals. Time was not on their side. Someone pointed out that the official date for the killing of seals was March 15, only a couple of days away. To that Wes Kean said, "When a man's at sea aboard his own ship, the laws made on the land seldom apply!" For a moment the brash young Kean sounded like his father, who followed no rule but his own when at sea.

The story had been told for years of an incident involving old man Kean and the theft of sealskins at the ice. It was during the spring of 1898. The crew of the SS *Greenland* had been killing a large herd of seals for days. The crew panned the seals, thousands of them, flagged them with their ship's own distinctive flag, and moved on. But when their ship returned to pick them up, they were all gone! Abram Kean's *Aurora*, loaded down with sealskins was the only ship near, and he was blamed for the missing pelts. He was confronted by an angry Captain George Barbour of the *Greenland*. George Barbour had no fear of Kean. But Kean merely shrugged his shoulders, stroked his steely beard, and with ice in his blue eyes said, "My men 'ave arders to take seals. I've no control over where they finds 'em." The matter was closed.

The *Greenland*'s crew were now hard-pressed to find and kill seals to replace the ones that were stolen. They worked by day and at night under the smoky light of torches. With their guard down, the sealers got caught away from their ship in the most horrific of storms and forty-eight of them died. Twenty-three of them were never found.

∗ ∗ ∗ ∗ ∗

THE *EAGLE* LED THE *NEWFOUNDLAND* out of Wesleyville harbour at eight o'clock the next morning. The winds had settled down to a fresh breeze, the snow stopped with the ebb tide, and the ice slacked enough from the land for them to get away. The two vessels sounded their steam whistles as they made their way out the harbour. The people who had gathered to see them off cheered and waved as the sound echoed around the cliffs of the snug little harbour. Fishermen who watched the ships lumbering out through the ice thought their chances of getting to open water were slim. The black smoke that came from the struggling ships clung to their wake, and when the day ended, it could still be seen by everyone on the coast, from Greenspond to Newtown, who were looking out their kitchen windows.

Cabot Island and Little Cabot are two islands rising out of the sea just under seven miles southeast of Newtown. The larger of the two islands was dominated by a magnificent white lighthouse. Built like a fortress, of wood, brick, and cast iron, it had nine rooms and was designed to house two separate lighthouse keepers and their families. It boasted a bright light and was equipped with a kerosene engine steam-driven foghorn. But during the winter months, which was considered the close of shipping, the lighthouse was as barren of life as the granite rock on which it stood.

The two ships made it to the relative protection of the tickle between the two islands. The ice, under the force-five northeast wind, was moving through the tickle itself at an alarming speed. They were presently joined in the tickle by the SS *Sagona*, which, despite her icebreaking capabilities, had been unable to push through the heavy ice.

She was a fairly new ship, 175 feet long, built in 1912 in Scotland by the Dundee Shipbuilding Company. Her hull was of thick pitch pine overlaid with steel. The *Sagona* was owned by Crosbies of St. John's. She had first arrived in that harbour two years previous, on March 14, 1912, and the very next day had steamed back out of the harbour to her very first seal hunt. She was captained by Sam Barbour.

The three ships reconnoitred with each other in the tickle. They had to use signals to communicate with the *Newfoundland*. It was obvious to all three skippers, even with the icebreaking power of the *Sagona*, that they could not proceed north. The ice was surging through the Cabot Islands tickle like a white river. They could not stay here. The decision was made, and all three ships turned around. And with the wind now coming force-five out of the north-northwest, they steamed south with the ice floes to Flowers Island, where Wes Kean had been born twenty-nine years before. Swinging on their hooks in the Flowers Island tickle, they burned down for another night, miles from where they wanted to be.

Charles W. Green's log:

> From Wesleyville towards Seal Fishery. March 12th 1914. Left Wesleyville at 8 AM. Ice running strong. 4:30 PM (Cabot Island) hove up anchor and steamed to Flowers Island in

company with *Eagle* and *Sagona* and anchored. Lanterns out—sunset to sunrise. So ends this day.

The two islands that make up Flowers Island looked even blacker than usual and appeared to be sitting on top of the ice as the three ships approached. All around the bleak islands and far out to sea was a plain of white. The two wooden vessels keeping close in the *Sagona's* wake looked to be under tow as they entered the tickle between the two islands.

At the time of Westbury Kean's birth here on April 29, 1886, on Kean's Island—smaller than the other, Sturge's Island—the population of Flowers Island had been just shy of 100 people. In 1911, the last time Wes had entered this harbour, there were only eight people left. Looking from the bridge of the *Newfoundland* as he steamed below the land of his ancestors, he saw the few scattered homes that remained. Despite their harsh look, the islands sprout colourful flowers in summer which some say are so fragrant their scent is carried to the mainland more than five miles away. Abram Kean, who always boasted of his birth island, claimed, "It has provided a place for wildflowers to grow and birds to build their nests and hatch their young as nature and grace intended."

Wes Kean allowed the *Newfoundland* to drift close before ordering the anchor away. The chain rattled and clanked in the still harbour when it was released from its chocks. He gave strict orders to the watch to keep him informed of any change in the wind, no matter how slight. Then he called his master watches to the bridge along with his second hand, George Tuff. Kean decided to use the time to divide the sealers into groups called watches. He was scheduled to stop for more seal hunters farther north at the fishing villages of Fogo and Seldom on Fogo Island. These men would be added to the watches as they came aboard.

The men in charge of the watches were called master watches, and these were chosen by the skipper. This year, Wes had chosen Arthur Mouland from Bonavista, Thomas Dawson of Bay Roberts, and Sidney Jones and Jacob Bungay from Newtown to lead the sealers to the hunt. These men were chosen after careful consideration. They had to be experienced in the hunt and the ways of the ice as well as being capable of dealing with sometimes angry and unruly sealers. All four stepped on the bridge. George Tuff was present, as well as the navigator, Charles Green. The master watches were instructed to choose their sealers from those aboard, bearing in mind there were more to board at Fogo. For the most part, the master watches had already made up their minds who they would pick. Seasoned hunters were always prized. The watch that brought the most seals aboard was noted by the captains, and the master watch of such a group was assured a berth next year. The sealers' names were shouted out and noted in a book.

Then John Antle, the stowaway, was discovered.

Wes Kean was furious. Like his father, Wes considered stowaways to be a bad omen aboard ship. Antle, normally with the bravado of youth on his side, stood shaking in front of the angry young captain.

"'Ow the 'ell could you 'ave hid in my ship these many days? An' you a mere slip of a boy!" Kean roared at the frightened boy before him. "Stealing grub from her, was ya? Well, by God, ar sheckle found in yer pockets will be took from 'e to pay fer it!"

Antle tried to blurt out that he hadn't stolen anything. He was given food along with the others. But Kean wasn't finished with the boy yet.

"You'll be cast ashore on Fogo Isle. Ah, didn't know we was puttin' in there, did 'e!" yelled Kean, seeing the look of defeat in Antle's eyes. It gave Kean some satisfaction.

"Bad luck. The lot of 'e's hidin' away like a thief aboard a man's vessel. I'd like to put 'e over the side now and make 'e walk ashore! God knows the bloody ice is 'eavy enough. Get below, sir! And be day you'll muck coal fer the stokers and dump slops

as is fit. And be night you can crawl back into yer hidey hole."
And with that, John Antle was dismissed.

Charles Green, standing in the shadows, pitied the boy. *Well,
well,* he thought, *a streak from the old lion showing in the young
cub, too!*

But time and circumstance have a way of changing all things.
Two days later, the *Newfoundland* had barely made it past Cape
Freels. At mid-morning of that day the huge ship *Stephano,*
captained by Wes Kean's father, and the *Florizel,* under the
helm of Wes's older brother, Joe Kean, loomed up astern of the
Newfoundland. The *Florizel* was the flagship of her owners. She
was also one of the world's first icebreakers. Each ship had a
black smokestack with a wide white border, and painted in the
centre was the red cross of St. Andrew. In a short time the entire
fleet was ahead of the lumbering *Newfoundland.*

By 8:00 p.m. she was jammed in ice again. With hood seals
on the ice and in the swatches of water around her, she burned
down for the night. Wes Kean consulted with George Tuff and
decided he would not stop at Fogo Island to pick up the rest of
the seal hunters waiting there. The ice was just too heavy, and
the closer they ran to the coast, the heavier it got. He would
continue to the hunt without them. His ship would be short-
handed by close to forty men, but he had no choice. John Antle
didn't know it yet, but he would be remaining aboard.

* * * * *

THEN ANOTHER STOWAWAY WAS DISCOVERED, or,
rather, decided to reveal himself.

Theophilus Chalk had managed to elude discovery all this
time. He was a tough-looking young man of seventeen from
Little Catalina, just north of the bigger town of Catalina, in
Trinity Bay. Theophilus rarely heard anyone use his Greek name,
which meant "loved by God." A few called him Theo, but he was
better known as Offie.

Theophilus had a more earthly friend, though, Jacob Dalton, also from Little Catalina. At twenty-four years old, Jake had been to the ice two years and was quickly earning a good name. Jacob was a bit devil-may-care and unafraid of any challenge. When Theophilus had failed to obtain a berth to the ice, and because the two men were friends, Jacob had agreed to help smuggle him aboard the *Newfoundland*.

Their friendship, however, had another, much more binding element to it. Jacob Dalton was seeing young Offie's pretty sister Delilah. Offie had walked with Jake and many others all the way to the city of St. John's. He had walked aboard the vessel in full daylight, laughing and shouting with the others from the Catalina and Elliston area. Everyone loved young Offie and had covered for him right up to this day. Hearing Wes Kean's tirade against the frightened stowaway John Antle had dampened Chalk's spirit, and learning the ship was to stop at Fogo added to his fear of being put ashore. Now, emboldened with the knowledge that the ship would not make any more ports due to heavy ice conditions, Offie felt better. In any event, the well-liked Jake Dalton was his friend, and Jake Dalton had a good friend aboard, too—George Tuff.

It was Tuff who brought the news of the second stowaway to Captain Kean. George found Wes Kean staring out the forward window on the bridge.

"Another one? God almighty! Am I to be beset with treachery for the length of this voyage? Who the 'ell is 'e? Still suckin' milk, I s'pose, is 'e?"

"Chalk, sir, from Little Catalina. Seventeen years old, sir. Looks to be a good man. Strong-lookin' and quick, like. 'E's wit' Jake Dalton."

"Dalton, eh? Catalina?"

"Little Catalina, sir. One of the best o' swilers. Been to the ice along wit' me before. Tough as a gad an' twice as strong! Dalton speaks well fer Chalk, sir. As do I, if Jake says so."

Kean's anger quieted some. Dalton's expertise and fearless attitude at the hunt had reached Kean's ears before.

"Still an' all, we can't have men sneakin' aboard ship as they pleases, George b'y."

"No, sir."

"An example must be made, as ye know."

"Aye, sir."

"Send Chalk below with the other stowaway fer now an' have 'im worked."

"Aye, sir." Tuff turned to carry out the skipper's order.

"George! We'll see about Dalton's friend when the time comes. The young Antle, though, from S'n John's, is to bide aboard. Is that clear?" Kean had heard the recommendation in Tuff's words concerning the new stowaway. He knew George Tuff did not give his approval lightly.

"Aye, sir," Tuff said, and exited the bridge.

10

*I*T WAS A FINE, CLEAR, moonlit night. Dark clouds fled across the white plain like flaws of wind scudding over a summer sea. The engine was shut down and the ship coasted with the ice floes. The night was quiet and still except for the sound of the moving ice. And then, unexpectedly, the moon darkened and the men aboard the *Newfoundland* were watching the lunar eclipse of March 12, 1914. For some of the younger sealers it was their first. The shadow of night descended like a cloak over the Great White Plain, but the silent ship was still faintly illuminated in a strange glow of light. Some of the older sealers were heard to whisper it was a bad omen.

Cecil Mouland would never forget his first night aboard the *Newfoundland*. It was not at all like anything he had pictured it to be. He had cheered with the others when the ship entered Wesleyville harbour. She looked aged and unkempt but somehow reliable and dependable to him. At first sight he liked the old ship, at least from the outside. Proof of his berth was established and he went aboard with the others from the area. When he stepped on the deck of the *Newfoundland* for the first time, his cousin Ralph Mouland was with him. Also standing nearby was Cecil's good friend from Doting Cove, Daniel Cuff. At twenty-nine years old, Daniel had just started a family with a child barely a month old. He was going to the hunt, he told Cecil, "to farden meself with a few dollars."

Before long Cecil grew to dislike the *Newfoundland*. She was overcrowded and filthy. He had not expected that at all. Men milled about her decks in confusion. Her 'tween deck wasn't high enough to walk in a fully upright position; a man had to walk bent over. Below this deck he could stretch to his full height again but the smell was worse. Cecil Mouland and many of the younger sealers ended up here. The bunks were built of rough lumber and appeared to be fastened to whatever space was available below the ship's main deck. The upper bunks were so close to the ceiling and the bottom ones so close to the top ones, the men felt imprisoned when lying in them.

The curvies handed to them were rough and smelled old and unclean, not at all like the clean quilts at home. No pillows were provided. When one of the men asked about them, he was scoffed at. "Pillows? Did ya t'ink you was shippin' out aboard a bloody liner? Ya pillow is on yer back, b'y. Yer duffle."

Scattered all over were short, fat little coal-burning bogies for cooking, their funnels leading upwards, dangerously close through the seasoned wood. Hung near the bogies was one big bo'sun kettle capable of holding four or five gallons of water, to be used for the making of tea or for cooking food. Hung on the wall by rusty nails near each stove was a large, cast-iron frying pan. Cups and plates—there were no bowls—were made of tin, some that looked rusty. There was one cook assigned for the captain and officers, who ate forward and separate from the sealers. The sealers had to cook for themselves or designate a cook among them. They weren't provided with any towels or soap or fresh water for washing their dishes or even themselves.

No heads, either. The sealers were expected to urinate above deck. They defecated in galvanized buckets with long ropes attached and tossed them over the side of the ship, where they were sluiced clean and brought up to be used again and again.

Mouland could handle everything except the unclean feel of it all. No spoons of silver had ever crossed his mother's table, nor did she make beds with satin sheets, but she was clean. From her scrubbed wooden floor to the shine of her prized Crystal Crown stove in the kitchen, everything was spotless. But young Cecil was not a complainer and he figured he could endure it like the rest. Besides, he was going to the seal hunt, and when he returned he would be an ice hunter.

Soon, Cecil met and walked the decks of the ship with men his own age. The young are always drawn to each other, and aboard the ship the living conditions were not forgotten but soon accepted. It was a time of wonder for them. They were away to the greatest hunt in the world. They knew nothing of the captain's concern about heavy ice. For them it was a time of adventure. Every time the ship lurched to open water or bore her way through loose ice trying to make her way to the seals, they experienced revived excitement. They paced the ship and explored her every recess. They sucked the biting wind deep into their lungs like drink, and strained their eyes to see their first herd of seals. They revelled at the adventure they were embarking on. And there was something else that drove them: the expectation of making real money.

"Nigh on two hundred dollars was what they made that year. Heard it a dozen times," said one of them with yellow hair.

"A fartune o' money, that is, b'y," came from another.

"I heard 'twas a hundred and seventy-eight dollars, and the crop o' fifteen or so dollars had to come out of that. Still a good dollar fer a man to have jinglin' in his pocket," ventured Cecil Mouland. "Never saw money like that where I come from."

"An' where is that?" asked the blond one.

"Dotin' Cove. Jest nart' o' 'ere be the coast. Cecil's my name. You?"

"Elliston. Sout' around the bill of Bonavist' Cape a bit. Albert be name. First time fer me."

"Me too."

"Peet—er, I mean John, John is my name," said Peter Lamb. "John Lundrigan. From Red Island in Placentia Bay, I am."

"Eh! My name's John, too! John Antle. From S'n John's, I am," another joined in. He looked younger than any of them. "Never 'eard about no one making that kind o' money at the seals meself."

"Oh, they done it, all right. In one of ol' man Kean's ships, it was. Four years ago. A bumper year, it was."

"What a feller could do wit' that kind of money!"

"I'd buy my sweetheart a ring," said Mouland.

"Spend a hundred and seventy-eight dollars on a ring? Must be a looker! What's 'er name?"

"Naw, b'y, I wouldn't spend all of it on a ring. Jessie Collins is her name. I'd 'ave marryin' money left over. That's what's in me mind."

"I'd buy a brand new 'armonica," said Lamb. "Loves music, I do."

"Can play the mout' organ, can ya?"

"Well, I'm learnin'. 'Armonica. I got one. Smaller'n a mout' organ, she is. 'Er sound is off a bit. Cowed, I 'lows."

"Play a tune fer us, will ya?"

"Naw, b'y. I only plays fer meself. Not good enough fer people to be listenin' to. P'raps if I had a new one, though."

"The price of a wedding ring, now! What d'you figure that could run a man? Never did see one in the shop in Dotin' Cove," Mouland interjected thoughtfully.

"You never been to S'n John's!" Antle chimed in. "Got everything a man could want in the stores in town. Lots of places to buy women's stuff, too," he boasted.

At this Albert and a couple of others standing around laughed aloud, remembering one woman's store in town.

The boys talked on, about big plans and little ones, about home and family and sweethearts. About life. About living.

The fortune of money the young sealers were referring to was actually just under $150. That was the amount due as the sealer's share in 1910 aboard Kean's ship, before the crop was deducted. It was still a great deal of money, though it had been an exceptional year. It all made little difference to the young hunters, who were sure this year would be even better.

That night, Cecil Mouland turned in with all of his clothes on, or, as it was known, turned in 'round. Secretly he had a concern he shared with no one. He had been told that baby seals cried real tears just before you killed them and bawled like human babies. He didn't know if he could actually kill one. He would worry about that when the time came. Despite the living conditions aboard the old *Newfoundland*, he liked her. When he got used to her smell there was a feel from the old vessel that stirred something in him. It was hard to explain. He just knew he felt secure and sheltered within her and believed she would keep him safe.

*　*　*　*　*

WESTBURY KEAN DID NOT SHARE Cecil Mouland's love for the wooden ship he commanded. He hated her. She was sluggish and cumbersome, hard to handle and slow to answer by the helm. Four years ago he had walked aboard the *Newfoundland* his first time as captain. Back then he thought she was the best ship afloat. He had been bursting with pride of having his very own command, but now it was his fourth year and he knew her limitations, and they were many.

She was waterlogged after the salty Atlantic Ocean had soaked into her body for forty-two years. Her once powerful engine, which had been repaired many times, could no longer keep up with her burgeoning weight. She was underpowered. Compared to all the others of the fleet, she was also outdated. Wes envied his brother Joe's *Florizel* and the sleek *Stephano*. Steel ships were the future and he wanted one. Aboard the *Newfoundland*, his ambitions for a career that mirrored his father's were stymied. He caught glimpses of them now as they butted their powerful way through the ice looking for seals. The search was on, and out here it was every ship for herself, though they would all communicate with each other at times. All but him. He cursed under his breath his company's decision to take away the wireless set. It had been aboard the vessel all summer as she went about her business, but when the *Newfoundland* was stripped down to her bare essentials for the seal hunt, her wireless set was not considered vital.

Harvey and Company, headed by Alick J. Harvey, kept a strict set of ledgers. One of Newfoundland's biggest firms, it had tried their tongs in many fires. They started the island's first pulp and paper company at Black River in Placentia Bay as early as 1898. They owned and operated a slate quarry on Newfoundland's biggest island, Random Island at Britannia. Their ships sailed all over the world. They were involved in everything from tar to tobacco, soaps to satins, and from fish to furs. Their bottom line was never in the red.

The cost of the wireless apparatus had been minimal to Harvey's. It had been long paid for, but the cost of paying a qualified person to run such a machine was a different matter altogether. It was common practice for everyone aboard a sealing vessel to take part in the hunt: the cook, the stokers, the boiler men, and even the captain. No one was exempt once the killing began. A man needed credentials to run a ship's wireless. He would have to be a college man, and they did not come cheap. And they certainly would not be seal hunters. They would have to be paid on the dead. For Harvey's, it would never do.

Guglielmo Marconi was an Italian inventor who pioneered the concept of wireless transmission and was credited with the invention of radio. On December 12, 1901, he received a message relayed from Cornwall, England, to Signal Hill, Newfoundland. It changed history. It was invaluable to ships at sea. In 1909, Marconi won the Nobel Prize for his work. But one of Marconi's best achievements, the greatest invention of the twentieth century—invented just beyond the roofs of Harvey and Company warehouses—had been pulled from Wes Kean's vessel.

* * * * *

IN THE GREY DAWN OF March 16, the *Newfoundland* was making her way through heavy ice east of Cape Freels and south of Funk Island. Wes Kean had never seen ice conditions so severe. It kept flowing down out of the north in a stream of white, and now, to make matters worse, the winds had shifted to the west. It bore the floes away from the land and slowed his ship's progress even more.

Scattered seals were in view. Some were in the swatches of water between the moving pans while others were on the ice. They were hood seals, old ones with their young. The ones in the water bobbed their heads up and down as the ship neared. The adults on the ice reared up to impress, barking in defiance. Kean decided it was time for his men to get a taste of blood. They had been grumbling all day, wondering why they weren't killing the seals they were passing, so now he would give them their chance at a rally. The ship was moving so slowly, he had no intention of stopping. They would have no trouble catching up. They could leap onto the ice, kill the seals, and tow them with ropes behind them. He ordered George Tuff to select only seasoned men. Tuff chose forty or so experienced hunters to go over the side.

Hood seals were vicious, fighting animals with flipper ends as sharp as razors. Unlike the harp seals, they would defend their young. They could turn as swiftly as a lynx and their roar was blood-curdling.

It was a dangerous game. The broad wooden side sticks were lowered over the ship's gunnels from port and starboard, falling short of the ice by four feet or more. They swayed and twisted under the men's weight. At the same instant the men let go of the rickety steps, they would have to jump over the churning moat of ice and water.

Once chosen, they readied themselves quickly. With gaff in hand, a tow rope coiled around their shoulders, and with shouts of pleasure, they jumped over the sides of the ship. They threw their gaffs away from the ship and rappelled backwards like warriors from a castle wall, springing like madmen upon the shifting ice. Those who hadn't been selected watched and shouted encouragement from the ship's gunnels. A couple of the sealers going over the side tripped and half fell onto the ice but quickly regained their footing and their dignity, to the delight of the onlookers. They grabbed their gaffs and raced away toward the seals with cries from the other sealers:

"Get dat big bugger off the nar'wes'! Never min' 'e's bark. 'Tis 'e's bite you should look out fer. Ha!"

"Bring back a meal o' young 'earts. Don't dawdle! Step lively, b'y!"

"Flippers we wants, b'ys! Lots of 'em! Starved fer a meal, we are!"

"'Ave a good rally, now, b'ys. 'Tis a great day fer flipsyin' in the cove! Min' yer mom now and don't get yer feet wet. Ha!"

"Never min' the cowardly dog. 'Tis the smutty bitch as will rip into yer legs! Snarly, she is." This was the sealers' name for a female seal with its first pup.

But the sealers on the ice ran on without answering, jumping between pans and over ridges of ice. Among them were a few "gunners" and "dogs." One of the gunners raised his rifle and fired at a huge hood seal coming toward him. A puff of smoke flew out of the long gun before one side of the seal's head disintegrated and the animal fell over in a lump of fatty flesh. The men cheered. The dog passed the gunner another bullet and he aimed again. Suddenly, a small black animal ran into view and stopped to stare at the seal hunters.

"Would ya look at dat now, b'ys!" shouted one of the sealers aboard the ship. "A fox, by God! An' a black one, too! Miles from lan', 'e is, poor t'ing. A pity, dat is!" The sealer, who was longing to kill seals, didn't appreciate the irony of his pitying another animal so far from safety.

The animal had wandered out onto the ice floe and was now close to forty miles from land. The gunner fired again and another female hood dropped. The black fox raced away, disappearing and reappearing again among ridges of white. Soon it was out of sight, heading away from the land.

Behind the gunner and his dog ran the sealers. The gunner, picked for his marksmanship, felled the females and ran on. The hood pups were now defenceless and the sealers eagerly moved in. A single swift, vicious blow to the young animals' heads, still tender from birth, killed them instantly. Sculping knives were drawn. The seal's charcoal skin was sliced open from vent to throat with one skilled swipe, revealing the throbbing, steaming, dark red innards.

Only a few of the sealers followed the gunners. The rest of them hunted the pups among the dangerous adult hoods on their own.

The seal herd was not a large one. They were scattered all over the place, some at the ice edge in the water. These the gunners fired at, most of which promptly sank before they could be recovered. It was said that for every adult seal retrieved from the water, twenty of them sank. Sealers and sealing skippers alike frowned upon this practice; they considered the shooting of seals in open water a waste of bullets.

But the killing of seals with bullets was insignificant compared to the slaughter carried out by skilled sealers and their gaffs. They approached the seal hood pups with caution if the mothers were nearby. They held their gaffs perpendicular to their bodies, ready to poke at the adults with the pointed end should the irate animals lunge. They taunted the females with shouts and feints of their own, and by doing so lured them away from their young. Quick as lamplighters, the sealers sprang toward the bawling pups and they were quickly dispatched before the mothers could react. With their sudden lunges, the huge adult hoods were deadly in close quarters but slow to outrun a fleet-footed sealer.

Many of the seals were alone on the ice. Though hard by a bobbing hole, they simply cried and waited for their deaths.

The hood seals were not what the sealers were looking for. They didn't want old fat, but the skins of young whitecoats, which brought the best money. However, today's slaughter had whetted the appetite of some of them, as their captain intended. On the bridge of the *Newfoundland*, ever vigilant in his search for seals, the captain spotted four of the fleet making slow progress through the ice. Though they were far ahead of him, he could tell the vessels were not on the hunt. It gave him comfort to know he wasn't the only one who hadn't found the harp seal herds. Still, if only he could communicate with them!

One of the barrelmen shouted down directions to a favourable lead of water and Wes ordered the helm over. The ship's bow turned more slowly then ever, then suddenly stopped turning altogether. Her port wheel chain had parted. Kean cursed the old gear he was forced to deal with. He shouted for men to go aft and see to the repair before ordering Tuff to get the sealers aboard while the chains were fixed.

The ship's whistle was sounded and the sealers started returning from far astern. They towed the skins, carcasses, and viscera of hood seals behind them, staining the virgin ice with blood. A hard hiss of steam came from the ship's windlass and her derrick swung outboard with a squeal. The hook, called the seal dog, was lowered down and passed through the tow rope bights, and the seals were slung aboard. They had killed less than 200. The men made quick work of loading. The wheel chain was repaired and the ship moved on again.

The last of the sealers with their loads still on the ice had to walk fast to catch up. Ice was crushed and pushed aside of the *Newfoundland*'s hull, some of it thrown onto the ice with her movement. Great slabs of ice, four to five feet thick, overturned to expose their clear blue undersides. They could easily bury and kill a man. The sealers on the ice yelled and cursed, but the ship steamed on. Her young skipper stared out the bridge window, apparently more concerned with finding the herds of harp seals than the loading of a few paltry hood pelts.

Crewmen jumped down the side sticks and handed ends of ropes to the men running alongside. They laughed and cursed as they hauled the seals up, the blood from the blubbery hides painting a path up the ship's hull. The last of the sealers clambered aboard. And the *Newfoundland* had tasted her first blood of the season.

11

*F*UNK ISLAND IS ANOTHER POINT of land that suddenly appears far out to sea. To sailors it looks as though it doesn't belong, a full thirty-eight miles northeast of Cape Freels. It is a flat, barren, desolate island that resembles a badly drawn triangle, rising to no more than forty-six feet above sea level. It is intrusive igneous with alkaline feldspar properties: in other words, granite rock. Its ancient past is a violent one, as its two faults lines, which run parallel to each other, can attest. The island is no more than a half-mile long and at its widest point is one-fifth of a mile. Off the southwestern end of the island, two rocks that appear to have been flung away from the bigger island are constantly awash by the seas.

Sailors call the area The Funks. There is no safe landing place, even with moderate seas. However, over the years, daring people have taken their chances on calm days—rare events here, indeed—and left their names. Landing Rock. Escape Point. Indian Gulch. Artifacts of Beothuk Indians have been found here: spearheads and arrowheads dated for their age, and a broken paddle, the remains of what appears to be a simple birchbark canoe.

These natives from the island of Newfoundland had paddled here in their small crafts to gather eggs and birds. It must have taken superhuman nerve and intelligence to come over the mysterious sea aboard a frail canoe whose gunnels were just inches above the water. The low-lying Funks are not easily seen from afar. The Beothuk would have had to venture far from land in their quest for food. But then, water is only a barrier for those who fear it. The only thing the Beothuk feared were the white-skinned Europeans who came in their great ships, marauding, stealing their lands, and killing them.

The great auk was the Northern Hemisphere's largest seabird. They could not fly, and so they were easily killed. Their only nesting place in the world was The Funks. Tales are recorded of the early Europeans killing them by the thousands. Jacques Cartier, in his book *Navigations of Newe Fraunce*:

> In lesse than halfe an houre we filled two boates ful of them, as if they had beene with stones: So that besides them which we did eate fresh, every ship did powder and salt five or tene barrels ful of them.

Tales abound of the early sailors cooking them alive, and driving them up over gangways to waiting crews. The bird's fat was used in lamps, its feathers for stuffing, its flesh and eggs for food. They were hunted and killed without mercy. Between the years 1800 and 1844, the great auk, hunted beyond recovery by the discoverers of Newfoundland, disappeared from the world. During the same period, these men ended another native species, too. On June 6, 1829, the last living Beothuk woman, Shanawdithit, died in captivity.

The name Funk means vapour or evil smell. The nitrate- and phosphate-laced guano of one of the world's most important seabird colonies can be easily detected from miles to its lee. Many species of seabirds, including the great auk, have nested and lived there: Arctic tern; northern gannet; northern fulmar; great black-backed gull; herring gull; black-legged kittiwake; razorbill; thick-billed murre; Atlantic puffin; and the most plentiful of them all, the common murre, which Newfoundlanders call turrs.

On March 17, the sealers aboard the SS *Newfoundland* smelled the island long before it came abeam. Even in winter and still months away from the breeding season, The Funks lived up to their name. Two other ships, the SS *Diana* and the *Ranger*, worked their way toward the *Newfoundland*. They were all headed for the same stretch of open leads. Long before they reached the open water, all three vessels became jammed in heavy ice and in easy walking distance of each other. There were no seals to be seen, so the sealers went bird hunting.

They had boiled and fried the hood seal carcasses, though they didn't like it much. The hood seal meat was strong, coarse, and fishy. Even the meat from the young wasn't tender like the meat from a young harp seal. The sealers especially relished the thin tenderloin that grew along the spine of the harp seal. Fried in an iron skillet with pork fat and onions for just a few minutes, it was delicious. However, for many of these hard-working men, this was the first fresh meat they had tasted for months.

"Beds o' turrs in the leads ahead, b'ys," shouted the barrelman. "Millions of 'em! More'n that, boys, dey're by the t'ousan's! Ducks, too, by God!",

"Someone run far'd, b'ys, an' see if th' second 'and will 'low us to go fer a meal o' turrs."

George Tuff went to the captain and passed on the sealers' request. Kean was not in a good mood and was about to dismiss the idea outright when he reconsidered. His men had been aboard ship for days with little to do and morale was low. His ship was jammed solid in close proximity to the other ships, and he planned on conferring with their captains.

"'Ave the b'ys take a few shells from the lazaret and try fer a meal o' turrs fer the men. None o' them young gaffers, mind, pick our best gunners. No need to be wastin' shot. 'Sides, a few meals o' turrs will save on ship's stores."

Tuff was pleased with Kean's permission but not his reasons. He turned to arrange the bird hunting trip when Kean spoke to him again.

"Tell 'em to 'ave an eye fer a duck or two while they're out dere."

"Aye, sir!" Tuff said, and exited the bridge.

It was a dull day, mild with a misty rain. With a fresh breeze out of the southwest, the temperature had warmed up some. Just about all the sealers from the ships were on the ice. The talk was about seals and where they expected to find the main patch. The sealers and their captains always believed there was a massive herd of seals out there, the elusive main patch.

The five or six gunners started off. Each man carried a long-barrelled, breech-loading musket on his shoulder and a bag with cartridges in his hand. The lead of water the lookouts had directed them to was nearly a mile away over very rough ice. It was hard going. They had to weave around ice formations and jump across small rents in the floes to get there. As they neared the water, the raft of eider ducks saw them coming and flew off. Some of the turrs did, too, but most of them just dived and appeared again farther away from the ice edge. The sealers figured the lead was no more than two gunshots across and half a mile long. They approached from the leeward side so that any birds they killed would float toward them. A few feet from the lead of water, they hid behind high clumps of ice and began firing. The turrs dived and emerged again on the surface, swimming by the dozens. The skilled gunners waited for the birds to line up before shooting, often killing several with one shot.

The three skippers met on the ice between their vessels. The ships looked out of place, black and useless, embedded in the Great White Plain. The sealing captains all voiced their concerns and agreed these were the worst ice conditions they had seen for years. None of them had seen any of the harp herds yet. They had only a few hundred seal pelts aboard. The time for killing whitecoats was now at its prime; in a few more days the young seals would be taking to the water and the opportunity for a good harvest would be lost. Every spring it was a game of hide and seek: they steamed north to the ice and searched for the birthing seals. It was a tedious game, always risky and forever dangerous.

From a distance came a popping noise as the captains talked and smoked. "'Avin' target practice, is dey, Wes?" one of the captains said with a grin.

"Ya knows 'ow 'tis now, b'ys", Wes Kean drawled. "My fellers from Bonavist' Bay can't pass up a chance fer a good meal o' turrs. Saltwater ducks is my table, though. Slim chance of dat today, though, I 'lows."

"The steel fleet are all headin' fer the bottom of Notre Dame Bay, right up into Green Bay," the skipper interjected, getting their conversation back on track. "Me wireless man got a word from 'em. The breeze out of the sou'wes' has loosened the ice a bit. Makes fer better steamin' be the lan'. Damn and bugger the luck, to be caught out 'ere!"

"Dat's right enough. My feller picked it up on our set, too. Wonderful t'ing to 'ave aboard a vessel, dat is," came from the other skipper.

Wes kept his head down and said little. He suddenly felt distanced from the rest of the sealing fleet.

"Got stowaways aboard, 'ave 'e?" one of the skippers queried Kean.

Wes's dark eyes flashed. "Snuck aboard in S'n John's, the shaggers did. Kept wit' the rest of me men large as life fer days, they did!"

"Found one on me own ship," another captain said with a grin. "What odds, I say. 'Tis what I done meself. Little 'arm in it, I says." He was a good-natured man.

"They are all bad luck, sir," Wes replied. "The lot of 'em. Jammed in ice since the day we found 'em! I'd like to put the young buggers ashore on The Funks!"

"Ah! A man's a man, young er ol', I says. Wit' no say of the way wit' wind and tide, er ice, either. The young feller found aboard our vessel is comin' along smart, like. Stowaway dis year, swiler the next, I says!"

The captains soon parted with rough goodbyes and returned to their respective ships.

Later, the gunners returned laden with plump turrs. They tossed them up aboard the *Newfoundland*, where eager hands began to pluck them. The captain's cook appeared, grabbed several of the birds, and walked forward. That evening the sealers below decks feasted on dark turr meat boiled in pots on their bogies. They preferred to have them baked, but the bogies were not equipped with ovens. Some of the men had the birds cooked with salt beef, some with fat pork, while others had them cooked with both. Others added vegetables to the pot, making a rich turr soup.

On the bridge, the captain of the *Newfoundland* was in a dour mood. It stung him that he couldn't communicate news of the ice conditions and the seals with the other ships in the fleet. Not only that, while his officers were eating succulent turrs baked in pork rinds and onions from his galley oven, he was dining on salt beef, with more fat than beef, and cabbage—again!

* * * * *

"TALKIN' 'BOUT ME TODAY, THEY was, ya know," said John Antle. "The skippers, I mean. Some of the men, too. Calls me the stowaway, even though they knows me name. I heard 'em call me bad luck. Funny, though, they never says a word about Offie Chalk. He hid aboard, same as me!"

Night had come. The ship was burned down for the night and Antle and a few others were gathered at the rail. Thin smoke trailed across from the two nearby ships. They too had their boilers banked for the night. Lights glimmered from their rigging, and now and then the sound of men laughing reached them. Stars appeared in the heavens and reached down over the slope of the sky, some of them so low they appeared to be dangling from the rigging of the sealing ships. Against the night sky, the ships appeared to be resting on the ice like great beasts that had risen up out of the sea only to become stranded on the Great White Plain.

"Bah! Sealers and skippers're always blamin' their luck on somet'ing," said Cecil Mouland from his place next to Albert Crewe. "If 'twasn't you it'd be somet'ing else, John b'y. A rope coiled agin' the sun, or someone steppin' across a gun, or settin' sail on Friday the thirteenth! Which, as we all knows, was the day we left Flowers Island, the skipper's ol' home. All superstition, it is, and dere's no mind to be paid to it."

A door opened and light bathed the deck. The cook appeared, wearing a filthy apron. He was carrying two buckets filled with slops from the forward galley. Smoke from a short-stemmed pipe blew out through his clenched teeth. He promptly emptied both buckets over the side and onto the ice, then entered without speaking and slammed the door behind him.

"Sure, yer almost as ol' as me", said Albert. "I 'lows I would've stowed away meself this year if I 'adn't a bert', I was that set on swilin."

"Yer no worse than me, John. Snuck aboard wit' another man's name on me ticket, fer God's sake," Peter Lamb said in a low voice. "You could say I'm standin' in another man's shoes." He had shared his secret with the others days ago. They were all good friends now.

"When we finds the seals there'll be no talk of stowaways or names on tickets, either. We'll load this one, we will! We're all ice hunters now. 'Twill be a spring to remember!"

12

THE FIRST DAY OF SPRING came on a Saturday and, according to Green's log, it began with a raw, force three wind from the east. The wind changed and had become a moderate gale from the northwest by nightfall, turning even colder. The barometer was 29.55 and rising. Green didn't know what the actual temperature was; the *Newfoundland* had no thermometer aboard.

The spring equinox occurs when the earth's invisible line at the equator crosses the sun's centre. It is a time when the earth is in a neutral position on its axis, leaning neither toward nor away from the sun. Day and night are of equal length everywhere on the planet. It is the harbinger of warming days for the Northern Hemisphere.

But on this spring day the only warmth aboard the *Newfoundland* was from the smoke tumbling out of her stack as she pummelled against the ice. She was making little headway and there were no seals to be seen anywhere. The wind was too blustery and laced with snow for the sealers to be on deck. Most of them were below, the smell of more than 150 unwashed bodies blending with the odour of the ship's bilge. But by now no one seemed to notice it. Despite the presence of several storm lanterns hung from the ceiling, the hold of the ship was still dark and filled with shadows.

The sealers were lounging on their lumber bunks or standing around in groups. Some were gathered around the bogies. A pot called "the slut," big enough to cover most of the top of the stove, was burbling. At intervals the men poured scalding black tea into tin mugs. Some were leaning against the hull of the ship. There were no chairs or tables. They were sitting on kegs, boxes, or buckets, whatever was available. A dirty pack of coalies, or playing cards—even called the Devil's picture books by some of the churchgoing sealers—was produced. The cards were torn and thick with use. Before he shuffled them, the dealer flicked a handful of flour over the cards to make them slippery and easier to deal out.

At times the sound of the ship being forced through the heavy ice was deafening. Sometimes it came as a loud scraping sound, as if the wooden hull were being cut open, a rumbling, pounding noise as the broken ice pans were turned over, an explosive din as the ship's weight suddenly broke apart a particularly heavy pan. The engine pounded out its might. The propeller shaft sent a tremble throughout the ship. Sometimes the ship leaned back as her bows were driven onto the ice, where it rode smoothly for a short distance before falling down again, lurching and listing. It had become a monotonous, day in, day out, getting nowhere routine.

Their boredom was relieved only by the daily task of gathering ice to throw into the pinnacle tanks situated on the ship's mid-deck. The boiler below, fed by pipes running down from the tanks while the ship's engine was powered up, was at a constant boil. It drank water at an amazing rate and had to be replenished constantly. The men were sent over the side every day, while the ship was moving or stopped, to cut ice from the ridges to fill the tank. The tops, or pinnacles, of the ice pans were the easiest to gather. They chopped large clumps of ice with axes and lugged them to the ship's side, where cargo netting was waiting. The loaded net was winched aboard and its contents dropped into the tanks. The water was always warm and the ice promptly melted. The tops of the tanks were wide open, and smoke from the stack rose overhead, only to settle on the water in a grimy scum of coal ash. The water from the same tanks was used for cooking as well as for tea. A large pot or kettle was skimmed over the filthy, rusty surface to brush aside the film, and then it was dipped and filled. Pinnacle tea, made from water obtained from clumpers of ice melted atop the bogies, was what the sealers used at every opportunity.

Periodically the sealers bent over the hot bogie and poked long, thin wooden spills they had made themselves into its drafter. The spills quickly caught fire and were placed against the tobacco-packed pipes clenched between the men's teeth. The smokers' jaws contracted and their lips made a puffing sound until they exhaled a blue smoke. As is usually the way with smokers, when one started, it triggered the urge of all. The room was cloudy with smoke. The slanted beams of lantern light defined wide bands of thin smoke that moved toward the heat rising from the stove.

Many of the sealers preferred to chew their tobacco, spitting the juice on the floor at the base of the hot stove, where the floor was spattered and stained a reddish brown. But the aim of the chewers was not always true, and their spittle sometimes landed on the hot stove. It sizzled and gave off a heady smell that added to the room's cloudy vapours. Again, no one seemed to mind.

The ship gave a sudden lurch and the men staggered to keep their balance. The hull rocked back and forth for a minute or so and then stopped dead.

"Jammed tight ag'in, b'ys," someone said.

A door above was opened and slammed shut again. A man climbed down the companionway and confirmed the speaker's comment.

"Jammed tight as a bloody drum, we is, and the riggin' is singin' the same ol' tune! The h'ice is riftered half up 'er sides. Give her a good go that time, the skipper did. Never worked, though! She mounted the h'ice like a black ram on a white

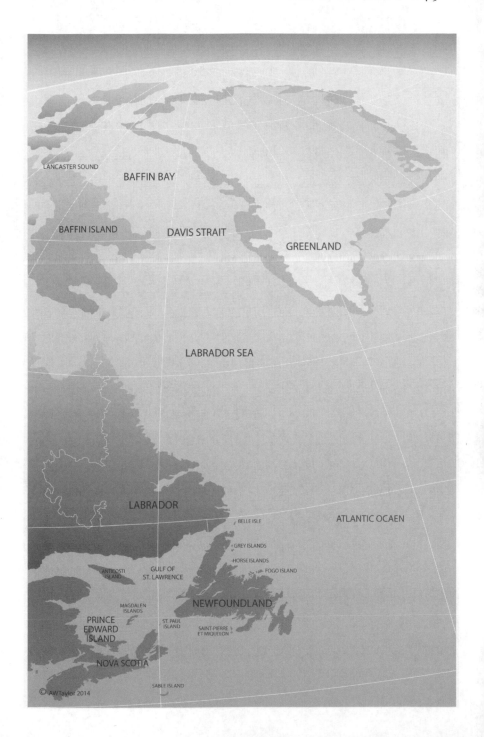

LANCASTER SOUND

BAFFIN BAY

BAFFIN ISLAND

DAVIS STRAIT

GREENLAND

LABRADOR SEA

LABRADOR

BELLE ISLE

ATLANTIC OCAEN

GREY ISLANDS

HORSE ISLANDS

ANTICOSTI ISLAND

GULF OF ST. LAWRENCE

FOGO ISLAND

MAGDALEN ISLANDS

NEWFOUNDLAND

PRINCE EDWARD ISLAND

ST. PAUL ISLAND

SAINT-PIERRE ET MIQUELON

NOVA SCOTIA

SABLE ISLAND

© AWTaylor 2014

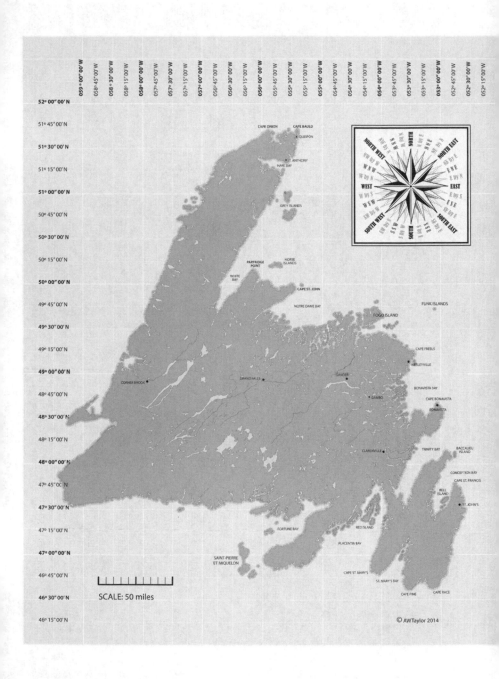

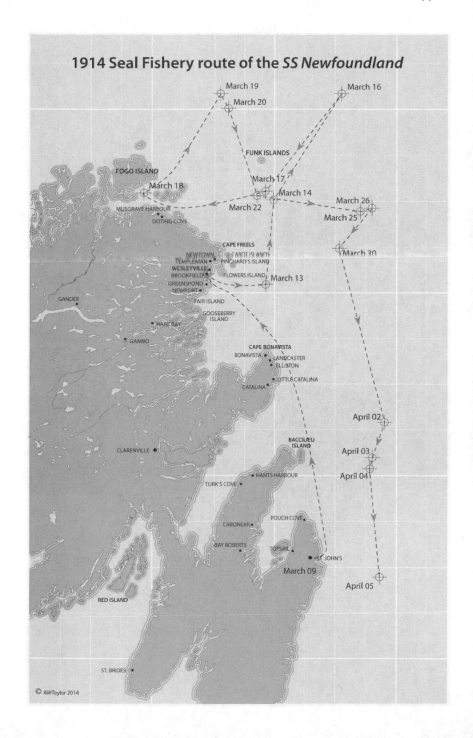

1914 Seal Fishery route of the *SS Newfoundland*

Cecil Mouland as a young man. (Photo courtesty of the Centre for Newfoundland Studies Archives Coll-115 Memorial University of Newfoundland)

Left: Cecil and Jessie Mouland travelling by ship. Right: Cecil Mouland working as crew on a Pastor Billy Graham crusade. (Photos courtesy of Jerdon Collins)

Cecil and Jessie Mouland. (Photo courtesty of the Centre for Newfoundland Studies Archives Coll-115 Memorial University of Newfoundland)

Clockwise from top left: Three men aboard the SS *Newfoundland*: Jesse Collins from Hare Bay, considered a hero on the ice; Second Hand George Tuff; and Jacob "Jake" Dalton from Little Catalina. (Jesse Collins photo courtesy of Jesse "Jed" Collins III; George Tuff photo courtesy of the Centre for Newfoundland Studies Archives Coll-115, Memorial University of Newfoundland; Jacob Dalton photo courtesy of Jake Dalton, Jr.)

Abram Kean. Captain of the *Stephano* during the SS *Newfoundland* disaster, he was considered a villain by most. (Photo courtesy of The Rooms Provincial Archives Division, VA 164-7/R.P. Holloway)

SS *Newfoundland*, with Captain Westbury Kean insert. (Photo courtesy of the Centre for Newfoundland Studies Archives Coll-115 Memorial University of Newfoundland)

William J. Tippett, crew on the SS *Newfoundland*, rigged out in his Loyal Orange Order regalia. Brother to Norman Tippett, lost in the disaster. (Photo courtesy of Wilbert Goodyear)

Top left: Norman Tippett, sealer, victim of the SS *Newfoundland* disaster. Top right: John Antle from St. John's in 1959. In 1914, he stowed away aboard the SS *Newfoundland* at fifteen years old. (Photo courtesy of Margaret Antle) Bottom (L-R): Brothers William and Norman Tippett. (Tippett photos courtesy of Wilbert Goodyear)

Clockwise from top left: Edward Tippett, lost in the *Newfoundland* disaster; Wes Collins, crew on the *Newfoundland*; SS *Bellaventure* with inset of Captain Robert Randell; Captain Joseph Kean of the SS *Florizel*, brother to Westbury Kean.

(Edward Tippett photo courtesy of Wilbert Goodyear; Wes Collins photo courtesty of Craig Parsons; SS *Bellaventure* photo courtesy of the Centre for Newfoundland Studies Archives Coll-115 Memorial University of Newfoundland; Joseph Kean photo courtesy of T. C. Badcock)

The SS *Newfoundland* at the icefields. Note the dangerous open leads of water. (Photo courtesy of the Centre for Newfoundland Studies Archives Coll-115 Memorial University of Newfoundland)

With adrenalin pumping, sealers wait for the order to go over the side. (Photo courtesy of the Centre for Newfoundland Studies Archives Coll-115 Memorial University of Newfoundland)

Sealers with their gaffs walking over the ice. Note the open water between the pans, making falling in a common, life-threatening occurrence. (Photo courtesy of The Rooms Provincial Archives Division, VA 137-27/R.P. Holloway)

After the kill, the warm walk back to the ship with bundles of seal carcasses. (Photo courtesy of the Centre for Newfoundland Studies Archives Coll-115 Memorial University of Newfoundland)

After two days and nights of storms, frozen bodies and survivors of the crew of the SS *Newfoundland* are brought aboard ship. (Photo courtesy of the Centre for Newfoundland Studies Archives Coll-115 Memorial University of Newfoundland)

sheep! Fell back just as quick, too." His vivid description brought uproarious laughter.

"I 'lows the seals will all be dipped be the time we finds 'em," came from one of the sealers. Dipped was the word the sealers used to describe a seal pup's first time in the water. After they took to the water, hunting them was all but futile.

Evening fell around them. The ship was wrapped in snow and cloaked with winter night and the snow kept coming. The wind howled out of the northwest, and the night was more like the first of winter than the last. After a time the snow had disguised the ship until she looked more a part of the Great White Plain than she did an old and brittle intruder.

The sealers dined on salt fish cooked in the same pot with onions and potatoes. The fish was not watered and still held enough salt to burn their lips. They drizzled melted butter all over it and ate their fill. After the meal they lounged around the stoves again. The talk was all about seals, the ice, the contrary winds, and skippers they had sailed with before. They talked about their wives and girlfriends and the money they hoped to earn.

"Cecil is buyin' a ring fer his girl wit' his money!" one of the men stated.

Some of the others laughed at him and Cecil Mouland was embarrassed. Then a firm, commanding voice spoke out of the shadows and no one laughed.

"Noble t'ing it is fer a young man to be pledgin' his love to a woman. Powerful t'ing, a ring is. Silver is my favourite colour, but 'twas a gold one I slipped over my Mary's ring finger. Dat was a while ago. Still loves 'er, I do. Misses her, too," said Reuben Crewe.

Sitting on the floor with the stove between him and his father, Albert Crewe couldn't believe his ears. He knew his father loved his mother dearly, but he had never heard him say he loved anyone. Albert loved his mother, too. The day he had left for St. John's, she had slipped some money in his hand. "Every man needs a few jingles in his pocket," she had said, smiling up at him. It was $7 in coin. He remembered how the coins were warm from his mother's hand, as if she had held them for a long time. He knew it was the last cent his mother owned. Later, after he had been long gone from her, heading toward St. John's, he was sorry for taking the money. While in St. John's the boy had gone alone to one of the stores that sold jewellery and trinkets. It took him a while to decide what to buy for his mother. He finally settled on a matching pair of combs to hold her full head of hair in place. They were a glassy brown with a cloudy white inlay, which the merchant had told him was pearl. Albert paid $5.60 for the set of combs and kept them hidden in his bunk.

The sealers' talk came around, as it always did, to hard times at sea, and especially of seal hunts and the method of killing them.

"'Eard last year a feller aboard the *Stephano* was caught skinnin' a seal pup alive," said one man.

"Damn an' bugger right down on top of 'im," another sealer responded angrily. "Why would a man do sech a t'ing? 'Tis not human to be tarturin' dumb animals."

"'Tis one t'ing to be killin' 'em fer a man's livin'. Skinnin' 'em alive is somet'ing else altogether. A man as'd do sech a t'ing should be blacklisted!"

"Can't see 'ow 'tis possible to do. Dey wriggles like a bloody eel," said one logical-sounding voice. "Don't 'old wit' it a'tall. 'Taint right," he finished.

"I've 'eard of sech t'ings afore," said another. "But in all me days of swilin' I never seen it done."

"Should 'ave 'is bloody knees broke!" came a vehement voice from the shadows.

"Talk is, ol' man Kean, bad as 'e is, banned him from his ship fer life," said the first sealer.

"Aye, an' so 'e should," came from another.

And the sealers all murmured their disgust at such a cruel activity. These men were, by necessity, involved in a brutal trade.

But they killed as humanely as was possible and despised acts of barbarism. Behind their rough facade, most of them were a caring breed of men.

Sitting under one of the lanterns, the men with the cards were playing stud poker. They were using matches for ante and listening to the talk around them. The time most loved by the sealers had come, as it did every night—for cuffers. Some of the men didn't tell them well, but others were masters at it. Or, as one fellow was heard to say, "Dey kin tell a cuffer as'd make a man's eyes water fer the want of it."

Some of the yarns were short and funny.

"'Ad an ol' muzzleloader dat used to snick every time afore she fired, he did. Never failed. Always hung fire the first time he pulled the trigger. Was out on Norder 'Ead one fine marnin' waitin' fer a shot o' ducks. 'Ad four fingers in 'er! When dey come in shot, he pulled the trigger. The bloody gun went off and knocked 'im back on 'e's ass. Ah! Bloody gert man 'e was, too. Could pick a king eider and keep all the fedders in one 'and!"

"Tell the one about the trappers from Brookfield, Phil," said Jesse Collins.

Furrin' Phil leaned against the hull. He was usually a shy man, but because the room was deep in shadow and he sensed the timing was right for his story, he began.

"Dere were two fishermen from Brookfield, as Jess said. They done a bit of trappin' in the fall time, much as meself, after the cod was over and done wit'. Furs were fetchin' a pretty good price dat year, especially long fur, like fox an' lynx an' beaver an' such."

Here Phil shifted uneasily, seeing they were all paying rapt attention to him. But he continued.

"They left a bit early in the year, before freeze-up. 'Twas a damp ol' fall, been rainin' off an' on fer a week or more. One of 'em, can't min' 'is name—Jake, I t'ink—asked the doctor in Brookfield, who were a friend of 'is, fer a few doses of poison to take along wit' 'im. Don't 'ardly know why doctors 'ave poison all the time, but they do. 'Twas in powder form and the doctor told 'im 'twas tasteless.

"The b'ys set off inlan' fer a fortnight of trapping. Gone fer t'ree weeks, they was, an' still no sign of 'em." Here Phil paused long enough to fill his pipe. He had the audience's full attention by now. "A party o' men was got up to go an' look fer 'em. Not easy to fin' a man in the deep woods with nar tree cut nor trail blazed. By a bit of good fartune, it had snowed a bit shortly after the trappers had left. Not much, but enough fer good tracking. And dat's 'ow they found 'em." He stopped to light his pipe.

"Never min' yer bloody pipe, b'y! What 'appened to the two trappers?"

The sealers were well into Phil's yarn by now and were eager to learn the outcome. Phil patiently bent back from the stove, flaming spill in hand, and lit his pipe. He stepped back to his place while getting it fired good, then continued. He was enjoying it now.

"'Tweren't a pretty sight they found. Dead, they were, the two of 'em. All nunnied up in a ball, they was, like a rabbit in a snare. Wit' nar cap on their 'eads, their eyes all bloodshot an' bulgin' out of their sockets an' their mout's all jawed open, as if they died screamin'. The front of their clothes was ripped to shreds from neck to gut. The fellers who found 'em figured 'twas wil' animals 'ad done it first. Then they seen pieces of cotton and wool gripped in their dead 'ands. The poor fellers' flesh was ripped and torn open, too, like 'twas done be a cat! An' pieces of their own flesh was hanging from their fingernails. 'Ad tore open their own flesh, they did!"

It took a while to figure out what had happened to the trappers, Phil explained, but the mystery was soon solved. Inside their two packs, all that remained of their food were a few crumbs of bread wrapped in paper. Next to it was what was left of the poisons, also wrapped in paper. The deadly powder had leached into the bread. They had eaten the food not knowing it had been poisoned; the doctor's poison was tasteless. The men had died slow, horrible deaths. The toxin had acted like a fire in their digestive tracts, so severe they had tried to rip it out of their bodies.

"There was more," said Phil. "That early winter, I was trappin' the same area. I found a lovely red fox, dead. His jaws was filled wit red fur an' bits of his own flesh. 'Twas pitiful to see. An' the next day I was b'ilin' me kettle over a crackling fire when a jay pitched on a limb above me. He was tremblin' all over and begun to pick at 'is chest wit' his bill, fedders flyin'. Never stopped peckin' at his chest till he fluttered down dead at me feet!

"Bad t'ing to use poison on innocent animals. Don't 'old wit' it, I don't. Nor sculpin' seals wit'out killin' 'em, either. Many said the trappers got what they deserved, a taste of their own medicine, like." Again the sealers cried out their disgust against men who would torture animals. Many of them agreed the two trappers had gotten just what they deserved.

The yellow flame from one of the lanterns began guttering for more fuel. Someone found a two-gallon can half filled with coal oil and removed the lantern from its hook. He removed the stopper and poured oil from a short spout in the can, and the flame brightened as the wick absorbed the fuel. The sealer returned the lantern to its hook.

The wind outside the imprisoned ship gave a distant, moaning sound dulled by her wooden hull. The rushing of it past the masts and through the rigging was a higher pitch that rose and fell with the flaws. The sound of the ship's timbers creaking and straining as they tried to resist the pressure of the ice on them was thunderous. She was so tightly wedged into the ice, even with the force of the wind on her superstructure she moved but little. One of the sealers placed his hand on the lower hull as if to test her strength and to reassure himself they were safe. He pulled his hand away in surprise. The ship felt as cold as ice.

"I 'ope this one's strengt' has 'ardened wit' age an' not weakened!"

"Oh, she's still strong yet," ventured young Cecil Mouland, not yet secure when talking with the sealers but trying to be a part of them. "I feels safe nuff aboard this one."

The *Newfoundland* seemed to settle deeper into her icy cradle, as if to remind the men that between them and certain death from freezing were but her aged walls . . . and below them the waiting depths of the sea.

The air was pregnant with silence for a moment. The bogie pinged its heat. The boiling kettle on its top gave off a faint bubbling sound. The ship's timbers rasped again. The wind from above came in howling gusts upon her deck, swirling with snow. Someone coughed, then spoke the minds of them all.

"By God, ol' er not, I'm glad to be wrapped in her arms dis night! A man wouldn't survive wit'out 'em, dat's fer damn sure."

A sealer who had been standing with his back against the hull suddenly walked toward the bogie. He turned his back to the stove, relishing in its warmth. "Still an' all," he said, "wood rots after a time, b'ys. Dem steel ships o' the fleet, now, they're safe enough."

"Dere's men aboard this one who've survived sech a night as this out on the ice away from deir ship," one man said. "Maybe worse. The secon' 'an', Tuff, now, he was cast into the starm o' the *Greenlan'*. Survived it, too. 'E won't talk much about it, though. 'Appened not far from 'ere, too, alongside The Funks, I 'ear."

"Uncle Reuben knows all about survivin' a gale at the ice. In a steel ship, too! Tell us about it, Uncle Reub."

Amazingly, these men, who were inches away from what could be their own watery grave, wanted to hear about other men who had faced their own perils at sea. Reuben Crewe had to be persuaded again, but after a while he shifted his weight to a half-sitting position on the bunk where he had been lounging. The wooden boards creaked under his weight. His face came half into the lamplight. Not yet fifty years old, Crewe's body was bent. His features were rough and creased, more from years of toil and exposure to wind and weather than from some trait of his ancestors.

"Iron, she were, not steel! Big difference, dey tells me," he began. His voice was deep and strong, a voice men listened to without interrupting. "SS *Harlaw* be name. She was built in Scotland in 1881, shorter than dis one, only a hundred and sixty-five foot long, she was. Owned be the New York, Newfoundland and Halifax Steamship Company. As sturdy-looking a cargo ship as a man ever sailed in. She was slow, though, wit' only a seventy-one-'arsepower steam motor into 'er."

Crewe was a born storyteller and was laying the foundation of his tale. He had everyone's attention, including his son's. Albert had heard his father tell the story of the *Harlaw* before, but only in bits and pieces and never with such passion. It was as if his father was speaking directly to him, warning him how things could be. Albert shrank deeper into the darkness of the ship and listened.

"We sailed from S'n John's that spring, down along be the souther' part of the island and out into the Gulf of St. Lawrence. Made good time, too, we did, no ice a'tall till we got to the wester side o' the Gulf that year. We struck the young 'arps be the t'ousands jest nart' o' the Magdeline Islands. We killed 'em fer days, workin' back and forth through the ice, pannin' seals young an' ol' as we went. Ah, b'ys! Bloodied 'er decks, we did! Fat, too! She was as slippery as a barrel of eels in a gallon of snot!"

The sealers laughed with glee at Uncle Reuben's description.

"Wit' the steady flow of ice bearin' down t'rough the Gulf, we was off Cape Nort' near St. Paul Island on April 7, a day I'll never ferget as long as I lives."

Here Reuben paused and leaned farther out into the light. His unshaven face looked harsh and grizzled. Flecks of grey in his scraggly beard were picked up by the dull light, and his entire countenance looked sad.

"The morning begun civil enough, not much wind, and we started huntin' swiles early. We seen two sun galls on either side of the sun jest after it rose, an' we figured a blow was comin'. We took no worry o' it, though. Our skipper was a good man and warned us to bide close to the ship. Dere was a good many seals all around. The ice was running along be the island pretty good, an' a man had to be quick dodgin' the pans!

"We killed seals all dat marnin'. The wind backed from the nort'east wit'out our noticin', so deep into the slaughter we was. It was comin' on snow, too, when we heard t'ree blasts from the *Harlaw*'s whistle. A signal to return to ship in a 'urry, dat was. All shroudy-lookin', she was, wit' the wind and snow comin' on. We made her, though, wit' not much trouble, not being too far from 'er.

"But makin' the ship was not the safe 'aven we t'ought it was a'tall. We couldn't get aboard 'er! She was all listed out on her port side like a draft 'arse scratchin' against a picket fence. The gale o' win' had pressed the ice against 'er sides wit'out warnin' an' she looked like she was to tip over."

Most of the sealers had never heard the story of the *Harlaw* before and sat gasping with amazement.

"Be now the win' was howlin' like dat new freight train comin' down over the Trinity barrens," Reuben went on. "The skipper was shouting orders like a madman. He was aboard of the *Harlaw* along wit' a few men an' was orderin' grub and blankets and stuff hove over her side. We fellers on the ice scrambled fer it and put it in a pile. Still didn't believe she was goin' to go. We'd never seen anyt'ing like it! Didn't t'ink 'twas possible! Oh, b'ys, it were a terrible t'ing to witness! A man's refuge bein' destroyed afore 'e's very eyes, for dat's what it was. The ol' *Harlaw* was being devoured be the ice! It bulged against 'er and leaned 'er out on 'er port side with the press of it, till she slowly settled in the water.

"Her rigging gear clanked and clinked when she tipped over and we could 'ear the rumble of her innards fallin' out o' place. Scaldin' 'ot water poured out o' 'er boilers and sent a cloud of steam rising up from her doors. Now dat the ship was heeled over, the ice pans large an' small slid up over her sides. Like a pack o' white dogs on a downed black sheep, it was! An' we fellers stood all around stunned with the look of it, an' nowhere to go but down into the blue drop!"

Crewe stopped talking long enough to lean forward and pull a dirty handkerchief out of his back pocket. He sat back down and blew loudly from his nose. No one said a word. The man had them enthralled.

"Then the skipper bawled out to us. 'Fill yer pockets with grub, grab a few blankets, and make fer the goddamn islan'!' 'Twas the first time we fellers'd 'eard the man curse, he was dat excited, you see. Kept 'is 'ead, though, the man did. Shouted fer us to get goin'. Stayed be'ind us like a shepherd, driving us on toward the island. 'E was the last to leave 'is ship, you see, in a way as 'tis fittin' fer a skipper to be doin'. We bore off fer St. Paul Island, only a black shadow rising out o' the driftin' snow!

"Betimes we looked back to see if 'twas real. It was true enough, all right. The *Harlaw* was down an' the ice was pouring over her. We could 'ear plain the sounds of dat awful ice bein' forced over her metal frame. She groaned in pain, b'ys, I swear to God she did. Then she was out o' our sight an' the island was near. My God, the speed of the ice was somet'ing to see. We had no way of tellin', you see, out on the floe. But when we came in under the land and saw 'ow fast it was rushin', b'y, we was shocked! Don't forget now, b'ys, we was on dat ice an' 'ad to jump off!

"The tide from the Gulf along with the force of the nodeast wind was forcing it along be dat island like a house afire! A man wouldn't be able to row a punt wit' it! The cliffs loomed above us, but along the shoreline the ice was bein' crushed to pummy. Not only dat, the bloody ice was risin' an' fallin' with the swell. We had our gaffs and used 'em to jump from pan to pan at times. And once when a feller fell through, two o' us hooked 'im into 'is jacket an' hauled 'im out!"

By now they were spellbound with Crewe's story, and though they were eager to turn the page, they hated to read the last one. Their greatest fear, Reuben told them, was that the ice might run out. Visibility was poor by now, and the swell that was running could mean the tail end of the ice. They had no way of knowing if it was miles long or there was just a string left of it. The ice was very rough and difficult to walk on. Most of it was very hard ice that had accumulated over many years. Approaching St. Paul Island, the sound of the ice bearing upon the rocks was terrifying. It cracked and snopped like gunfire; it squeaked like wood and groaned with the pain of being forced onto the land. It split and cracked and was pummelled to slush against that terrible shore. But, thank God, the ice kept coming out of the drifting snow.

The sealers now looked like black-clad hobos scrambling to jump off a train. They had to walk quickly, parallel to the island, watch their chance, and then jump onto the slippery baddy catters. And behind them their captain kept yelling his support.

"Run, by God, run! Jump ashore! We're ice hunters, by God, not a bunch of bloody schoolb'ys!"

And run and jump they did. Singly and in groups, they leaped ashore. They used their gaffs to haul themselves up and to find holds in the ice-encased shoreline. They shouted and yelled and cursed. A few of them fell through to their knees, some to their waists, but they were hauled back up to the dry land by their friends. At last, all but one was safe on St. Paul Island. The captain who had urged his men to safety was still out on the ice. He was weak from exertion. Now it was his men's turn to yell their support to him, and soon, exhausted, he was hauled to the shore. The crew of the *Harlaw* had escaped death and were safe.

"Safe from the ice, we were. But a good lot o' us was wet and numb wit' the cold. St. Paul Island, as you may not know, is no more'n t'ree miles long, I 'lows, all growed over with tuckamore. Well, we all knows under the tuckamore trees can be found piles of dry crunnicks and wood good fer firin'. We still 'ad our gaffs, as I tol' 'e. An' we rooted out enough o' dat dry, snarly wood wit' 'em to get a fire goin'. We burned a 'ole in dat place, I can tell 'e. Still see it, I 'lows! We stood aroun' the fire fer hours like a troop o' mummers.

"We gnawed on 'ardtack and canned stuff froze solid till a ship seen our fire and hove in view out in the ice. The wind 'ad died be then and the tides slacked wit' it. We still 'ad to get out on the ice to go aboard the rescue ship, but 'twas easy enough. Only a few fellers got wet, as is common. We was saved, but wit' all o' our 'ard work gone to the bottom of the Gulf. Not a penny fer us dat spring. 'Twas a 'ard blow, b'ys. I swore to me woman, Mary's 'er name, I would come a-swilin' no more. But 'ere I am again, trapped in the bowels of another one."

Reuben finished his poignant tale and told no one why he had really come on this trip. He would not embarrass his boy by telling the others he had come to protect him. He knew Albert had been listening. He had seen the glow of his yellow hair in the dim light afforded by the smoky lantern. The boy sat drawing on a pipe, the flare from the spill falling on his eager young face.

For a while the sealers discussed in low tones what he had told them. It was an amazing yarn, and they realized the same could happen to any of them. But, as was their way, they soon dismissed that possibility. After all, they reasoned, there were two men aboard who had survived disasters on the ice. The chance of such a thing happening to them again was slim.

The night was deep now and the wind seemed to be subsiding. The sealers had a last mug-up and sought their hard bunks. The men with the cards were still playing; one of them had a pile of matches and pipe spills gathered on the head of the keg on which they were playing.

From deep in the shadows came a growly voice directed at the card players: "If ya stays up wit' the boys da night, ya still got to git up wit' the men in the marnin.'"

The card players took the hint and stopped playing.

They talked for a while in the dark rows among their makeshift beds until they quieted down.

"Dere's a fedder on its edge in me bunk, b'ys!" yelled someone from the dimness of the place.

The men laughed at the joke. The ship creaked as before.

Someone started snoring. There came a faint sound of music from somewhere among the crude bunks. It was Peter Lamb practising on his cowed harmonica. Cecil Mouland knew the song the young man was playing was called "Hard Times." He knew the song well.

"Stop the racket, b'y, an' save yer breat' fer snorin'!" shouted a sealer with a sleepy voice.

"Ah, leave the boy alone. A lullaby is jest the t'ing aboard o' dis one!"

Cecil hummed silently, "Hard times, hard times come again no more," and waited for the music to continue, but the sweet music didn't come again.

And tucked tightly in its bed of ice, the *Newfoundland* slept.

George Tuff, standing in the shadows, had been listening. He had heard Crewe's yarn, and he had heard the men speak of George's own reluctance to tell of his ordeal aboard the *Greenland*. They were right. He seldom spoke of it. Unlike Reuben Crewe, who seemed to draw strength from the telling of his tale, George knew he would take no similar comfort. Walking forward, he went away to find his own bunk. He wasn't used to living apart from the sealers. He didn't consider himself an officer at all and secretly wished to be just one of the men again. He removed his outer clothing and, after a while, nodded off under the heavy quilts in his own berth. And then the cruel dreams of death, which he had relived for more sleepless nights than he could remember, came flooding back.

13

$\mathcal{F}$OR FIVE MORE DAYS THE *Newfoundland* tacked her way across endless fields of ice. The scunners aloft in their barrels called down directions toward countless leads of water that led them nowhere. With powerful binoculars they scanned the ice for a way through for seals. Lining the port and starboard rails, the sealers kept their vigil, anxious to spot the harps. But they found nothing. The upper deck of the *Newfoundland*, covered with snow, was tracked by a thousand footprints. Snow had piled against her doors and her upper works and drifted tight to her hatch coamings. And on the bridge of the ship, her restless young skipper strode back and forth like Ahab seeking his white whale.

The ice became heavy and tight again and the ship slowed to a crawl. The weather was clear with a light breeze out of the northwest. In frustration, Kean sent a few men off to the windward in the early morning to search for seals. They returned and reported having seen whitecoats—but only five of them.

Later on that day they saw more, and just before dark they had killed a total of fifteen whitecoats. Wes Kean was not pleased. The following day proved better, but not by much. They killed 300 young harps. For men who expected to kill thousands of seals, it merely whetted their appetite. And during all that time they saw no other ship, no high mast with a crow's nest etching the sky, no sign of smoke abroad on the horizon—nothing. They were alone on a white sea.

The next day was just as bad, and Kean could not contain himself to his ship any more. He jumped over her side before noon and strode away to the west-southwest in the company of three other sealers. A swell came up, and after a while the men looked to be walking up and down on sloping, snowy hills, until they walked out of sight.

With Kean gone for the time being, Charles Green directed the *Newfoundland*'s course, when she could move at all. It was the first time Green gave an order on the ship.

Wes Kean and the others were gone for nearly five hours. They were first seen in the distance like tiny specks that might have been low-flying seabirds. Coming aboard the ship, Kean merely growled a greeting to any man who spoke to him. They had not found the seals, but others in the fleet had.

* * * * *

THREE DAYS EARLIER, ICE OBSERVERS on the northern part of the island of Newfoundland, just south of St. Anthony, had spotted a herd of seals riding on the ice far out to sea. The ice was black with their numbers, and the herd was so big it took the whole day for them to pass. The seal herd was estimated to be as long as sixty miles. The ice was speeding south. Wireless operators sent the exciting news south by the coast and it reached the operator in Twillingate, and he passed it on to the ships at the front.

Abram Kean had better luck than his youngest son. The holds of the *Stephano* were well soaked with the blood and fat of seals. But, despite all his efforts, the old man had not found what he was looking for. Kean was well aware of the advantage of having a wireless set aboard. Not for any reasons regarding safety, but for finding seals. His wireless officer was ordered to stand by the set day and night for as long as he could keep awake. Kean would have the worth of the man's dead wages, by God! The man was also under strict orders to keep him informed of any messages from the other ships regarding open water, and especially seal sightings. He was further told not to return the same courtesy to any other ship.

Then his wireless operator, paper in hand, came bursting through the bridge door and reported the news he had just received from the operator in Twillingate. Kean roared out his orders almost before the man had finished reading his report.

"The main patch, by God! Nart', by Chris'! Nart' be the wheel!" He continued bellowing to the helmsman,

"Full steam a'ead," he roared down the pipe that connected him to the engine room. "Give 'er all she will bear, sir! Melt the boilers! Never mind yer bloody gauges! Tell the stokers to bare their bloody buffs, my man! The main patch is mine!"

"What will I send to the rest of the fleet, sir?" asked the wireless operator.

Kean hauled his face away from the pipe and turned on him as if he were insane.

"Send, sir? Nutting, sir, dat's what you'll send! Back to your post, sir. And report to me any more clackin's you 'ear from your machine!"

The wireless operator trembled as he left the bridge.

A great rumbling sound came from deep in the *Stephano*'s bosom, accompanied by a vibration throughout the ship as her energy was released. Valves were spun wide open and pent-up steam startled her mighty engine into life. Black smoke shot out of her stack and billowed skyward. From beneath her stern came a violent roil of white water and ice churned to powder by her massive bronze screw. The pride of the steel fleet went plunging away through the ice in search of the main patch.

Far astern of the mighty *Stephano*, smoke appeared like the bluster from cannons. Others of the sealing fleet had heard the news and they came charging. The huge seal herd would not be Abe Kean's alone. When they came upon the seals, the ships found the animals had drifted farther south than they had anticipated. As far as the barrelmen could see, the Great White Plain was delivering the lambs and the slaughter began.

The killing went on by day and far into the night. Framed by torches, the pelts were hoisted aboard. The ice was streaked with trails of blood leading to the ships as the men dragged their harvest behind them. Windlasses hissed and clattered as their long cables hefted strings of bloody seal pelts onto the vessels. The men were in their glee. They worked until they could barely stand on their feet. They tripped and fell as they sprang among the little ice hills, they fell through the ice in their haste to kill the seals, and still they laughed and some of them sang ditties.

The work was far from easy, a back-breaking hunt on an unforgiving sea of ice. They had to leap over treacherous pans and navigate over and around pressure ridges. Their feet were seldom dry. But the harp pups were prime and plentiful. A single blow with a heavy gaff was all it took.

Far away from these fields of plenty, Wes Kean was unaware of the success of the rest of the sealing fleet. The *Newfoundland* was still marling its way through heavy ice with not a seal in sight. There were no ships to be seen, either, and he wondered where they had gone. North and a bit west, he figured. He was held back as much by the lack of modern technology aboard his ship as he was by the restraints of the tired old vessel.

* * * * *

THE *NEWFOUNDLAND* HAD BEEN OUT of her home port for twenty-one days with barely 400 seal pelts aboard. The harp seal pups would be taking to the water any day now and the time for prime hunting nearly done. The sealers crowded the deck daily, searching in vain for their quarry. They were restless and all too aware that they were losing time at the hunt; they still made little headway, stuck in the ice as they were.

In the wheelhouse of the ship, Wes Kean paced the deck as he had done for days. Never had he seen ice conditions so severe nor the seals so scarce. His men hadn't taken enough pelts to pay for their grub, but it wasn't their fault. Any failure in the hunt would be blamed on the skipper, and he knew it. The reputation he was trying to make for himself was at stake. Then at 8:00 a.m. on March 30, he saw the *Stephano* and the *Florizel* rise up, black and smoking, on the distant white swells. As if by some homing skill, some ability that even he wasn't aware of, the young skipper had found his father and brother. Despite his lack of success with the hunt, Wes took some comfort in the sure knowledge that his hunting instincts had been right. Without any form of communication in all that expanse of white ocean, he had found the fleet, and with them would surely be seals. Maybe there was still time for a successful hunt.

On the starboard rail of the *Newfoundland*, Cecil Mouland stood with many of the other sealers. The ship lifted ponderously with the might of unseen water. One of the young sealers was starting to feel the results of the rolling deck. He was seasick and embarrassed. The others laughed at him.

Mouland had heard the excited shout from the barrelman who had spotted the two ships. The news ran through the ship like electricity. Skipper Wes had found the fleet, by God! Not only that, he had come upon the old man himself. Their luck was about to change, for sure. Mouland was not a complaining man, but after days of searching the seas without result, the feelings of his fellow sealers were beginning to wear on him. He had listened to their disgruntled talk for days, mostly without comment:

"What's fer supper t'day, b'ys? Fousty beef er smatchy fish? Lumpy bread an' fatback! Not flipper pie, fer damn sure."

"The next time we spots one of the fleet, we'll dart across to 'er and carry back a load o' flippers and a few young carcasses!"

"Raisin duff wit' currant jam smothered in custard fer the skipper's table, I 'ear."

"The young crackie can't smell the swiles like the ol' dog."

"Why don't 'e run far'd an' tell that to the skipper's face, b'y?"

"'Tis the stowaway's fault! Bad luck, the lot of 'em."

"The bloody stowaway's got nothin' to do wit' it, b'ys. 'Tis the ungodly ice dis spring. Dere's never been such a spring! 'Tis riftered up like rocks below a cliff."

"The skipper's tried to bore 'er t'rough, God knows. We've all seen 'im ram 'er bows into the ice so 'ard, at times she's trembled all over like a flattie on a prong wit' the strain of it."

"More like a horny bobby sheep butting against a barn door, if you ask me."

And so the talk among the sealers had gone on for days. The men, who had come to hunt seals and found none, vented their frustration the only way they knew how. Then the two ships hove in view and the past days were forgotten. The sight of the ships bolstered their spirits anew. They had another chance to make a go of it.

Before noon the *Florizel* came boring through the ice toward the *Newfoundland*, her steel bows pushing the ice aside in thunderous roars. She stopped within easy speaking distance and Wes Kean talked to his brother, Joe. The sealers lining the rails of both ships shouted across to each other, too. Despite the power of his steel ship, Joe Kean had not had much luck, either. He had only a few hundred seal pelts on board. Joe had heard the news of the gigantic herd of seals on his own wireless and had gone steaming after them in his father's wake, but neither he nor the old man had found them. But Billy Winsor, skipper of the *Beothic*, had. Joe told Wes that the seals had scattered, and with the gale of wind and snow out of the north on Saturday night, they had moved farther south than anyone had anticipated. They were now well south and east of The Funks again and closer to Cape Bonavista.

Billy Winsor had been broadcasting to the fleet that he had over 25,000 sealskins in his holds. Heading for St. John's in a couple of days, he would be getting all the glory for being the first ship through The Notch with a full load this year. Abe Kean was fuming. He would not be head jowler this year.

"There's a good lot o' seals around here, though, Wes b'y," Joe told his brother. "If you can get t'rough! 'Tis the worst ice conditions I've witnessed. Over towards the *Stephano* now, there's a string o' lighter ice. That's where the seals are, seems like."

Wes told Joe of his trouble dealing with his aged ship and his inability to contact the rest of the fleet. Joe reminded his brother that he had found some seals without help from anyone.

"Well, yes, dere's that, I s'pose!" agreed Wes, his spirits lifted.

Joe waved goodbye to his younger brother and shouted an order through the open bridge door. The *Florizel* was smoking his command out of her stack and moving away slowly when Joe shouted back to his brother again.

"Don't ferget Father's signal, Wes b'y!"

Wes waved to his brother without comment. He had heard and knew what his brother meant. The parting shout was plainly heard by some of the sealers, too, though few of them knew its meaning. Wes Kean ordered the *Newfoundland* hard over into the cleared wake of the *Florizel*. He followed close in his brother's trail until it closed solid behind him and his ship was mired in the ice again.

* * * * *

THE ROLLING SEAS OF THE open Atlantic Ocean come in contact with the outer edges of the Great White Plain and steal under it, making the ice floe ripple like a quilt spread out to dry on a grassy meadow. It raises the ice in powerful swells and brings it gently down without breaking it, moving on into its white heart. Restless mistrals, winds of the north, bear across the width of the plain and steal snow away in streaming white drifts. As far as the eye can see, the ice is spotted with forms of life, both new and old. The largest population of nomads in the world has finally come to rest. The harp seal herds had come into their own in nature's greatest display of reproduction.

Unlike desert vultures, which circle high and wait for carrion, ravens fly out from the land in a straight line, pitch near the herd, and wait. They are drawn here by the scent of blood of birth and of death, for these legions of seals leave their spoor to the winds.

On rare evenings when the winds have died and the sea air is calm, the warm breath from millions of mammals rises above. It creates a pall-like mist that follows them and hangs just over them, stagnant. The ice and seals are now combined and the hunters are afield.

Soon there will be another presence among them. The fiercest storm of the century is coming and bringing with it a time of great challenge.

Nowhere in the Northern Hemisphere is a place more situated to attract the storms of winter than the ragged east coast of Newfoundland. Jutting out into the Atlantic Sea, its shores mark the farthest reach of the Americas toward the European continent. Far below these rugged shores and spreading away from its watery foundation, hidden canyons fall into vast depths between mountain ranges that rise up. They are responsible for changing, turning, and otherwise mixing two of the ocean's greatest currents. From up out of the Gulf of Mexico comes the world's largest and warmest current, and spawned from the Greenland glaciers and pouring down from the polar seas comes the Labrador Current. Their confluence is off the east coast of Newfoundland.

So powerful are the reach and pull and influence of these immense currents, they dwarf the earth's mightiest rivers. High above and forever following are created other currents which are the cause of terrible atmospheric upheavals.

But there is more. Away from the winter Atlantic and far to the balmy south, unbearable heat waves rise above the world's most barren and hottest deserts. Borne south out of the Dark

Continent and flowing seaward past the bulge of Africa, the heat from the Sahara is carried on the Northeast Trades. South from the Cape Verde Islands they are deflected at the imaginary line at the earth's waist, the equator, and turned west to South America. North from that land, which ancient cartographers called the "Great Leg O' Mutton," and up past Hispaniola and the slave islands, the warm expanse of tropic air finally forms over the swiftly flowing Gulf Stream. Now it is carried north and east to its death. It will not die easy.

The northlands of the entire American continent are covered in winter. Every stream, pond, lake, and river is frozen solid. Air masses from the continent's greatest mountain range, the Rockies, pour down across the winter lands. Like the Gulf Stream, they too are headed northeast. And not to be outdone, down from the frozen regions come sweeping blasts clothed with winter.

The warm air coming north will not go unchallenged. A winter gale of unbelievable proportions is in the womb. The end of its gestation is at hand. Without cold it cannot survive, and it will suckle on the breast of the Great White Plain. Like all great events, timing is everything for it to reach its full effect.

And now its time is at hand.

14

*U*NTIL NOW, CHARLES GREEN HAD never been on a vessel that didn't carry a thermometer. The *Newfoundland* had an aneroid barometer on board, but that was it. He checked it every four hours, tapped the glass with his finger, and recorded its reading in his log, in accordance with the Board of Trade regulations. Thermometer readings were also required, but there was nothing he could do about that. Even so, the barometer was far from modern.

The aneroid barometer was designed in 1842 by Lucien Vidi, a French scientist. It was little more than a small box beneath a glass face with a hidden cell, or aneroid, holding metal alloys of beryllium and copper that expanded or contracted when it came in contact with external air pressure. It was designed to be stiff so that a slight tapping on the outer glass would cause the needle to jump, thus indicating barometric pressure. But for accurate forecast of impending weather, Green knew it had to be used in conjunction with a thermometer. With a thermometer reading high and barometric pressure dropping, a hard wind from the south or east could be expected; with both barometer and thermometer dropping at the same time, especially during the winter, hard, cold winds were feared from a northerly point along with freezing conditions.

On March 30, Green recorded:

> Begins with fine clear weather and heavy swell, moderate breeze from N.W. Ship steaming to W.N.W. 8: am the *Florizel* and *Stephano* in sight: 10am spoke to *Florizel*: noon, fresh breeze and dull sky: 4: pm, fine clear weather, wind light from the n. two more steamers in sight: 6pm ice very tight and heavy swell, wind light and variable. Barometer 30.60. standing. Funks bore N45W. Dist. 42 miles. So ends this day.

The barometer was at the highest point Green had seen for the year, but he had no way of telling the temperature. Neither could he consult with Captain Kean. They barely spoke to each other. Wes spent almost as much time aloft in the barrel as did the scunners. The young captain was desperate to find seals. Late that evening, Green heard him shout from the mast.

"The *Stephano*'s in the seals, b'ys!"

His voice sounded hopeful yet frustrated. The *Newfoundland* was working very slowly toward the distant *Stephano* through some of the heaviest ice she had encountered. Even with powerful glasses, the *Stephano* was too far away for Wes Kean to see seals around her. Green stood on the bridge and raised his own binoculars, training them on the *Stephano*. There were no seals or men to be seen. He knew all about the signal pre-arranged between Abe Kean and his son to let him know when he had found seals. He had heard Wes and George Tuff talking about it in the wheelhouse.

Green adjusted his glasses to better see the *Stephano*'s rigging. The ship was broadside and looked grand against the evening sky. He started at the bow and slowly worked his vision aft. The forward derrick was raised vertically against the foremast. Slowly, he trained the powerful glasses toward the ship's stern. Past the fat stack encircled with the white border and the red cross of St. Andrew, her company's logo stood out. The stack was emitting little smoke; the ship was stopped. Her white superstructure was framed against the grey sky, her high castle, or bridge, rising over it.

Then he saw it. Standing obliquely from the *Stephano*'s mizzen-mast, her after derrick was pointed over the ship's stern. Green kept his glasses on the derrick for a while to make sure the boom wasn't just halted in the process of working. The grappling hook was tight against the tip of the spar. It was not in use. Wes had his father's signal. Now, if he could just get his old ship through the ice!

Despite the tension between them, Green pitied the young skipper. No one aboard had worked as hard to find the seals as Kean. Green had watched him pore over the charts day and night. He had ordered the barrelman down and had climbed up the ratlines himself again and again. Several times Green had seen Kean suddenly dash out onto the windward side of the bridge and sniff the breeze.

And again, Green, who was a reader, likened him to Captain Ahab.

Knowing his quarry was within his reach, Kean ordered the *Newfoundland* even harder into the ice. He rammed her bows up against it until the sealers who were watching thought they would break. The heavy greenheart fastened to her bows and strapped at intervals with steel plating gave her reinforcement, but Wes Kean was pushing her limits.

Wes knew very well the tried-and-true method of two men rallying a punt through heavy slob ice. While a man in the stern warped as hard as he could against the long sculling oar, the other man threw his weight from gunnel to gunnel. The violent motion caused the punt to roll from side to side, creating a lateral wave that separated the slob. This allowed the punt's bows to ride up over the grey mess and her weight to open up her own channel. He tried this now with the *Newfoundland*.

Backing astern in her churned slobby channel for several lengths, he powered her forward. At the same time he ordered her helm hard over, hoping the ship would wallow to one side in the ice channel and her hull would rise above the ice. But her rudder was cumbersome to answer. Her engine had lost compression with age, and for his efforts the ship responded with a slight tilting of her uppermost riggings. Still, the skipper ordered the ship back and forth, forcing his way toward the seals. The sealers walking the deck leaned out over the gunnels and shouted encouragement to the ship as if she were a schoolboy trying to sprint across a ditch or chasm. Each time the ship came to a stop, they threw lumps of coal out onto the ice to see how far she had progressed. Jesse Collins decided to give the old ship some help.

"Let's give the ol' girl a 'and, b'ys! All 'ands rally back and fort' as she goes. 'Twill give us somet'in' to do, if nothin' else."

It took a while for Collins to make himself understood. Some of them thought he was crazy. However, Collins was not only a likeable fellow but very persistent, and he succeeded in getting his way.

"'Tis simple, b'ys. When the skipper runs astarn, we'll run far'd! And when 'e arders 'er far'd, we'll run astern. Over a hundred and fifty of we fellers runnin' astarn will lift 'er bow, fer sure!" The men now knew what he meant and got into the game.

It was a spectacle never before seen on a sealing vessel. Each time the ship moved astern or forward, the sealers raced along her gunnels in the opposite direction. They shouted and yelled as they ran.

"Come on, ya ol' bugger! Go fer it! Run 'er up on the bloody ice, Skipper! Rally 'er, b'ys! Rally 'er!"

The sealers roared with laughter. They piled into and sometimes tripped over each other, cursing and laughing as they ran on. Their commotion alarmed Wes Kean, who ran to the bridge rail. At first he thought his men had mutinied—he had dealt with such a thing before. He was about to yell the wrath of God down upon them when he realized what his men were doing.

"They're tryin' to rally her, by God! Like a punt! Never have I seen men like it! Did you ever see such a t'ing before, sir?" Wes had addressed Green without noticing. The excitement of the seeing his swilers racing up and down the decks like madmen made him forget where he was for a moment.

"I never have, sir!" replied Green, also caught up in the excitement.

The men's efforts were rewarded for a little while as the tired old steamer tossed back and forth in her roads. At times she rode almost half her length upon the ice with the weight of so many men in her stern, before giving way and foundering under her dead weight. And when the men dashed forward, their combined weight in the ship's bows caused her prop to cavitate and claw for water. But soon the efforts of both ship and men proved to be in vain. Ahead of the *Newfoundland,* ice-rocks stretched like rows of eskers. The sealers grew tired of their game. They slowed and then stopped. The lumps of black coal on the ice were separated by only a few feet.

Night came and the sealers went below.

* * * * *

BEFORE MIDNIGHT, CHARLES GREEN WALKED off the bridge and headed for his berth. He removed his heavy coat, his hat, and his boots before lying down on his bed and pulling the heavy quilts over him. Lulled by the throb and vibration of the ship's overworked engine as she tried to make her way forward, he fell fast asleep.

Wes Kean prowled the bridge and stared into the darkness at the twinkling lights of his father's ship.

Of George Tuff's seventeen years to the icefields, ten of them had been as master watch. Now at thirty-two years old, he was first mate of the *Newfoundland*. He could not write. The only thing he could read was the compass rose. He was an excellent helmsman and could follow a chart. But his old habit of bowing to authority was still with him. His role as master watch had been an easy one. Though he had been in charge of a group of men, out on the ice he still killed seals with the best of them. He was one of them. He was a worker. But now he was not a part of them anymore. He could feel it when they spoke to him. He knew many of them well, yet they rarely spoke to him. As ship's officer he was considered above them, and Tuff did not like it.

After Kean came down from the barrel that evening, he consulted with his first mate. He told George he estimated the *Stephano* to be six miles or so to the south-southwest. Tuff hadn't seen old man Kean's signal yet. He knew that the son would also signal the father with a raised staysail if he found seals.

From the bridge, George had shared in the joy of his comrades as they tried to rally the big ship. He had known Jesse Collins a long time. There was no one who could raise the morale of men like he could. Kean expressed his all too real concern about the lateness of the month. The seals were ready to moult, if they weren't already doing so. Any day now, without warning, the females would abandon their young. The pups would take to water and their chances of a good hunt would be gone. Kean told Tuff he would order his men over the side in the morning and send them across the ice toward his father's ship. The position of the *Stephano*'s derrick was the signal he had been waiting for. Tuff agreed. He would not be expected to go with them. He was not a sealer now but an officer. The sealers would be led by the four master watches.

Kean assured Tuff he would keep working his ship toward

the *Stephano* for as long as he could during the night, to shorten the men's walk. Tuff stayed beside Kean on the bridge until his watch ended. He walked back to his berth, removed his heavy coat and hat, and fell into a troubled sleep.

It was an uplifting sight for the *Newfoundland* sealers to see the lights of other vessels near them. Standing on the deck of the ship, they had watched the distant lights come on, a welcome relief after seeing nothing but ice for days. They recognized the long, spaced lights of the *Florizel*, the flagship of Bowring Brothers. She was specifically designed to navigate ice. Two other ships, well ahead of the *Florizel*, were also showing lights, though faintly. At intervals faint sounds came over the bed of ice: a ringing bell, a muffled shout, and, once, a single shot, as if a gunner were testing his rifle for tomorrow's hunt. But it was the *Stephano*'s lights that drew the attention of the *Newfoundland*'s sealers. Though she was the farthest away from them, her lights shone brighter than the others. Barely three years old, the world's newest icebreaker was the pride of the Red Cross fleet. Her steam-driven generating plant had the most modern design and gave off the brightest light.

"'Lectric lights all over dat one, I 'ear. Burns 'em day an' night, they says."

"Every man 'as 'is own bunk, too!"

"Ol' man Kean sleeps in what dey calls a stateroom. Drapes hung over 'is bed, and cow'ide ledder on the walls to keep the noise o' the ship from the almighty when he sleeps!"

"Got his own personal cook, too! He roasts a fat chicken wit' gravy fer the ol' man's supper every evenin'. Kean won't eat swile meat. Gives 'im the runs, they says."

"Toilets on 'er, too! Even fer the sealers. Heads, they call 'em."

"I don't believe it! Never seen a toilet on a ship, nor in a house, neither, fer that matter."

"Maybe that's why the *Stephano*'s got toilets on 'er, eh b'ys? To take care of the ol' man's runs! Ha ha!"

Cecil Mouland, Albert Crewe, John Antle, and Peter Lamb were crowding the ship's rail and listening to the talk. Everyone was staring toward the light from the *Stephano*. With the lights of the sealing fleet all around them, their hopes for a hunt as early as tomorrow ran high.

"The scuttlebutt is we fellers will be walkin' aboard that one tomorrow! The skipper saw the signal!"

"Signal? What signal?"

"Where 'ave you been, b'y? You must 'ave yer ears stopped up. Everyone knows about the ol' man's secret signal to let 'is boy know when there's seals about."

"T'ree puffs of smoke from her stack at the stroke of four dis evenin', it was! The *Stephano*'s funnel is equipped wit' a damper what allows 'er to blow smoke rings."

"Naw, b'y, you're wrong. 'Twas dem 'lectric lights. The mast'ead one blinked five times jest as dark come on! Seen it meself."

Regardless of the nature of the signal and how it was presented, rumour travelled throughout the ship that they would be sent toward the *Stephano* in the morning and that Wes Kean would keep butting the ice all night.

"Maybe you'll get that ring fer Jessie after all, Cec b'y," said Peter Lamb. "We'll be in the fat tomorrow, fer sure."

"You could've walked ashore a few days ago when we was off The Funks, sneaked a kiss from yer girl, an' caught up wit' us again. We was goin' slow enough, fer sure!"

"One kiss from my Jessie would do me just fine right now," Cecil replied. He shifted his eyes from the *Stephano*'s beckoning lights and looked west toward his home.

"A good ways sout' of The Funks now, we are," said Albert. "Closer to the cape at Bonavista, I 'lows. I knows a girl in Bonavista. Real pretty she is, too. I spoke to 'er dis fall when Father an' I was dere yafflin' our fish fer weighin'."

John Antle's voice was high in anticipation of the hunt. "'Tis not girls that should be on yer minds, but seals, b'ys! I can't wait fer t'marrow to come. Jest t'ink, when I walks down the gangway o' this one in S'n John's I'll be one o' the ice hunters!"

"Clear 'eads and not sleepy ones is what's needed fer flipsyin' pans," growled Jesse Collins.

The young sealers grinned at him and walked off the deck. Collins knocked his pipe against the scarred gunnel to clear out the dead dottle, spat over the rail, and walked off the deck.

Stepping out of the shadows where he had been standing, Reuben Crewe smiled with pride and wondered who the pretty girl in Bonavista was. He couldn't wait to tell Mary that their boy was becoming a man.

* * * * *

THE WIND DIED DOWN AND the temperature went up several degrees. A few stars shone through seams in the clouds. Overall, it was a pleasant night at sea. The dense smoke from the *Newfoundland* fell slowly from her stack as she tried to make her way through the ice. The wind, what little there was, bore the smoke down toward the water instead of up in the air. The lines of the ship's rigging dissected the smoke; the ship's lanterns illuminated the smoke, creating an eerie effect, like dark curtains on either side of the vessel.

The ice became thicker and heavier. Westbury Kean figured he might as well try and butt his way through the cliffs of Baccalieu. He ordered the engines stopped. The *Newfoundland*'s lights dimmed while the lights aboard the *Stephano* shone as bright as ever. Wes Kean was dead tired. He staggered to his berth and, without removing one garment of clothing, lay down on his back. He pulled his hat over his eyes and fell asleep.

George Tuff's face showed the misery of his nightmare. His head moved slowly from side to side and his eyes watered. He was hot but he wasn't sweating. His lips drew tight and trembled, as if trying to mumble something, but no sound came. His body, curled into a fetal position, continued twisting as if he were a small boy trying to hide from his tormentors. Then he awakened with a start.

Sitting upright on the edge of his bunk, he went over the terrible dream in his mind again. The room was dark, with a pale light showing through the lone porthole. The new day was almost here and the ship wasn't moving. The dream was not a new one for George. He had seen the images hundreds of times before. They were more frequent each spring, just before a seal hunt, and had appeared in his head so often he wasn't as afraid of them as he used to be. The dream was always the same. Visions of dead men from the long-gone sealing ship SS *Greenland* haunted his nights.

Built in Ireland in 1872, named for the world's largest island, and owned by Newfoundland sealing companies for thirty-five years, the *Greenland* had brought over 400,000 seal pelts into St. John's harbour. But she was fraught with misfortune. A fire aboard her did enough damage to sink her in September of 1884, when she was making ready for a freighting trip north to Labrador. It happened in shallow water, so she was refloated and rebuilt and continued to sail.

Owned by Baine Johnston and Company of St. John's in 1898, she left for the seal hunt on March 10 of that year. George Barbour was her skipper, and George Tuff sailed in her for his second year to the ice. It was the best year Tuff had ever experienced. The seals seemed to offer themselves to the slaughter. The hunters stained the ice blood-red in record time. To maximize the full potential of the harvest, Barbour dropped his watches in the thick of the seals at different places. They killed what seals they could before the ship returned for them. Their kills were piled, or "panned," and flagged with the company's colour for pickup at a later time. The *Greenland* then carried its hunters to other herds to continue the killing. For as long as he lived, George Tuff would never forget the day they returned to claim their harvest.

To their surprise, all that remained of their hard work were bloodstained pans and downed flags. It left a hollow feeling in the gut of every man aboard. Every last one of their seal pelts had been stolen! And the only ship nearby was the *Aurora*, captained by none other than Abram Kean. The sealers aboard the *Greenland* roared and cursed their rage. They wanted answers and they wanted revenge. So did their skipper. Barbour ordered the *Greenland* in pursuit of the *Aurora*, which was steaming away from them in a great plume of smoke. Despite all of the *Greenland*'s signals for Kean to heave to, the *Aurora* plunged on through the ice. It took hours for the *Greenland* to catch her, but soon both ships were mired in heavy ice. Barbour walked across for his pound of flesh. Abram Kean was feared by almost everyone, but George Barbour was not one of them. He feared nothing on two legs, and few on four.

Kean did not come out of the wheelhouse to greet Barbour, as was customary for captains to do. Even the crews of both sealing ships were silent: no shouted greetings, no friendly jibes thrown back and forth between the two vessels. George Barbour ran up the steps to the *Aurora*'s castle and burst through the door. The sound of the confrontation on the bridge came to the men in muffled shouts, lasting for close to thirty minutes before Barbour emerged outside again. He slammed the door as if he hoped it would destroy the whole ship. He shouted orders to his own ship while crossing the ice between them.

"Heave 'er off! Away! Away from dis den of iniquity!"

His ship started forward under his order. Barbour ran alongside her, sprang up on her side sticks as spry as a cat, and climbed aboard. The two ships went their separate ways with not a single shout of goodbye from the sealers on either deck.

Barbour told his disgruntled crew that he had accused Abe Kean of thievery right to his face and had told the man just what he thought of him. But it was no use. Kean had taken Barbour's tirade like water off a duck's back, he said.

Kean had said in no uncertain terms, "When I orders me men over the side fer swiles, I am not responsible as to where they finds 'em, sir! Every last pelt aboard o' dis ship is mine, sir!"

What infuriated Barbour all the more was that, although Kean had not admitted to stealing the pelts, he had not denied it, either.

Now the *Greenland*'s sealers were distraught, as was their captain. The time for good hunting would soon be over. The young seals would soon be in the water and then the killing would prove to be much more trying. It was doubtful they could recover their terrible loss. The *Greenland*'s sealers were now facing a bleak spring. But Barbour was a relentless man. Infuriated by the theft, he pressed his men on, and they responded with a vigour born as much from desperation as it was from anger.

They worked before dawn until far into the night. They tied seal fat to their gaffs and set it ablaze to provide a light. They ran among the seals killing young and old, oblivious to time and weather. They were off their guard, and for that they would pay a deadly price.

In the pre-dawn hours of Monday, March 21, the first day of spring, Barbour dropped off his first of four watches in the midst of a brewing storm. The sealers hunted without noticing their peril. Barbour managed to get only one of his watches aboard before the *Greenland* became hopelessly jammed in heavy ice. A storm of gale-force wind and heavy snow fell upon them like a thing possessed. Between Barbour and the rest of his sealers was a lake of water nearly three miles long. It is one of the mysteries of the ice, to hold within itself huge lakes of water, unfrozen and uncluttered with ice.

On the ice, the sealers found themselves in a dire situation. The night came early. Shrouds of snow plastered them and froze them and hid them from view. Aboard the *Greenland*, George Barbour was sick with worry. His ship was caught in the ice and swell at the ice edge. In a blow, it was the most dangerous place for a ship to be. The rising wind and wave among the heaving ice pans could crush it like matchwood. He fought the elements all night to keep the *Greenland* from being pulverized. Knowing his men were facing a far worse dilemma, Barbour kept the whistle sounding every few minutes.

The storm raged until late afternoon Tuesday. The *Greenland* had survived the gale, but many of the lost sealers had not. The rescue began. Among the ice hunters, most of them struggling and barely alive, was young George Tuff. All through that desperate night, the *Greenland* crew searched for their own and found young men dead and frozen in their tracks. With the sun closing down on another day, the *Greenland* left for open water. On her deck, covered in ship's canvas, were the bodies of twenty-five dead sealers. Left behind were twenty-three others who were never seen again. The searchers had discovered hats and woollen cuffs and even coats in the lake of water. The items of clothing were greasy and left calm streaks on its surface. The sealers had waited long enough to hook every last one of them with their gaffs.

George Barbour headed his ship for open water, away from the ice edge, to home. She rounded Fogo Island on the northeast coast of Newfoundland and bent her way south to Cape Bonavista. For as long as he lived, George Barbour blamed Abram Kean for his men's deaths.

Trying to beat her way around Baccalieu Island, the *Greenland* was caught broadside by another storm. Barbour managed to get her into the harbour of Bay de Verde, just south of the island where he thought she would be safe. He dropped her hook well into the harbour, rowed ashore, and wired the sad news to his company in St. John's before rowing back to his ship again. The storm raged on, and that night the *Greenland*'s collar chain parted. She went adrift deep into the harbour until she grounded on the rocky bottom. After the storm passed, she was refloated with help from the Bay de Verde fishermen and went on her way.

Incredibly, the *Greenland* faced yet another storm and nearly foundered off Cape St. Francis. She sailed into St. John's harbour on the evening of March 27 with her flag standing half-mast. But the polar icefields were not yet done with the *Greenland*. Her quest for seals ended in 1907 when she became jammed in the ice. In the end, the ice bore her under with not one splinter left to show where she had been. Fortunately, all of her crew were rescued.

George Tuff didn't want to believe Abe Kean had stooped to stealing pelts to be top dog. Still, Kean's ship was the only one near enough to do the deed. He could tell her story better than anyone. There were times when he wished he could talk about it. He somehow believed the telling of it would help him, would release him from the nightmare of it.

In his tormented dreams, sealers appeared, rising up from narrow cracks in the ice and trying to squeeze through. They never once managed to do so, but were held forever at its edge, pleading. He saw sealers carried over the surface of a huge swatch of water in the arms of a kraken-like beast, whose many outstretched arms were constructed of swirling snow. Cradled mercilessly in the snowy image, the faces of the sealers screamed without sound. Despite the great, raging blizzard, the water in his dreams appeared as a brilliant summer blue. The nightmare always ended the same way. The ice fissures closed over the men until just their naked hands showed for a minute, hanging on for life. Then that image disappeared, too. The snow-kraken released its hold and the men dropped under the surface without a sound. The lake of water remained blue except for a few calm, greasy streaks in the shapes of men.

Now daylight was pouring in through the porthole. There didn't appear to be much wind and the air felt warmer. The ship was not moving. The skipper would be eager to put last night's plan into action. Tuff turned toward the door and opened it partway when he realized something was different about this dream. His legs grew weak and he trembled all over. He leaned against the door frame for support. In all of the other dreams, the faces of the dead sealers, though lustreless and without feeling, were known to him. But in this one they had no faces at all, and there were three times as many.

15

*T*UFF DRANK A HOT CUP of tea on the bridge with Wes Kean. After speaking to the captain, he left the wheelhouse without eating. He climbed the rigging without stopping and entered the barrel. Through his glasses he spotted the *Stephano*, still four or five miles away; the *Newfoundland* had not travelled far during the night. He also identified the *Bonaventure* and the *Florizel*. Although the day was dawning, he could see men killing seals between the *Stephano* and the *Florizel*. Tuff hurried down from the mast and reported his sightings to Kean, who climbed the rigging to see for himself.

Tuff, suddenly feeling hungry, went forward and poured another cup of tea, which he drank without sugar. He smeared jam on a thick slice of bread and ate a hurried breakfast. In less than ten minutes he was back on the bridge and standing below the mainmast just as Kean was exiting the barrel. Tuff scrambled up the ratlines and met the captain at mid-mast. Below them, every sealer aboard was on deck and waiting in anticipation, sensing that something was about to happen.

"Have you come to the same reasonin' as me, Skipper? The *Florizel* and the *Stephano* are killin' seals!"

"I have, George b'y. You've made no mistake 'bout that. 'Tis 'ard to watch. The others in the fat and dis one stuck solid, an' it lookin' to be a wonderful warm day, too. The time is advancin' fer good huntin', as ye well know. Still, there's nothin' we can do about it, I s'pose." Kean sounded wistful as he spoke to his second hand.

"Nothin' we can do, sir? Why, by heavens there is one t'ing that can be done! The men can walk across to the *Stephano*, sir, as we talked about!" Tuff looked up at his captain, but he didn't notice the way Kean was looking at him.

"You're right again, of course. Still, I would want a good man to lead them."

"I'll go wit' them, sir. If you t'ink I'm the man fer 'em."

"You, George? You the man to lead the men? Dere's not a man aboard o' dis one I'd trust more'n yourself. Now, bear in mind, George, in case you get in the seals good and are panning for any length of time, you must reckon on Father's ship for the night and not the *Newfoundland*. Will you go and lead them?"

"Yes I will, Skipper."

George Tuff willingly volunteered, but it had little to do with his lifelong propensity for obeying the wishes of authority without question. It had more to do with him getting back on the same level as the other sealers.

"Let's get below," shouted Kean. He was more than pleased with his second hand's answer.

The two men scrambled down the rigging, with Tuff hard-pressed to descend fast enough to prevent Kean from stepping on his fingers.

"Master watches, ready yer men! Rally 'em! Rally 'em! Over the sides, b'ys, there's seals fer the killin'!" Kean shouted over his shoulder before he reached the deck, his voice hoarse with excitement.

A collective shout went up from the sealers below him. The skipper's order electrified them.

At 6:00 a.m. the sun was shining and the spring day was warm. A faint breeze came from the southeast, lifting the smoke straight up from the banked engine. It was a prime day for a rally at the seals.

Now the deck of the *Newfoundland* was in a general state of excitement. The captain shouted directions at Tuff and to the master watches, who in turn yelled to the men. Most of the sealers had already dressed for the crossing to the *Stephano*. Those who were not ran below and dashed back on deck, hauling on coats and hats in a hurry. The watches were as eager to walk five miles to the seals as they would have been if the animals were only a few hundred feet from the ship. They grabbed gaffs from the racks and fetched tow ropes to drape diagonally across their shoulders. Some of them hurried to the ship's stores and stuffed their pockets with small cakes of bread as hard as glacier ice. Big wooden spoons doled out black molasses into small thick bottles for them. With their hands they took a lumpy, gelatinous mixture of sugar, oatmeal, and raisins from a galvanized tub filled to the brim, placed it in cloth bags, and stuffed them into coat pockets. A few took clear bottles of a type of liniment filled with essence of sweet spirit of niter, commonly used to ease the pain of seal finger or seal hand, an infection that sometimes set into minor cuts after exposure to seal fat. Seal finger was known to cause tiny cuts on the skin to become tender, festering boils. Sweet spirit of niter was a nauseating yellow blend of distilled nitric acid and saltpetre, or niter, and alcohol and water. The sealers believed it could cure anything. They inhaled it for headaches, drank it for stomach aches, or applied it to their skin as their ailment required. Many of the men took nothing more than extra tobacco and matches.

All of the pent-up frustration the sealers felt after having been confined to ship for days on end was released in a flurry of activity as they prepared to go over the side. Their master watches gave the order, "Over the side, b'ys!" No other persuasion was needed. They began scrambling down the side sticks like schoolboys leaving a one-room schoolhouse on the last day of school. They went like men hurrying to get their part of a great treasure. The side sticks on both sides of the *Newfoundland* were crowded with men shouting as they scurried to the ice. The men on the lower steps of the makeshift ladder could not hold on an instant too long, for fear of having their hands trampled on by hobnailed boots.

"Jump wit' the men or be left aboard wit' the b'ys!"

"Come on, b'ys, 'bout time fer us to get into the fat!"

"We'll show ol' man Kean 'ow to kill swiles, by God!"

"Crack on 'er, b'ys!"

"Keep off me bloody fingers, b'y!"

"Min' yer bloody gaff! You damn near stabbed me!"

In their hurry, some men got their tow ropes tangled in the ends of the side sticks. Others dropped their gaffs and struck men below, who bellowed out curses.

"Save yer blows fer the seals! You've bruised me pate, b'y!"

"You men below there! Don't stand around bobbin' like a bunch of twillicks on a rock! Step away afore you sinks the pan! Make room fer yer mates," shouted Arthur Mouland of Lancaster, near Bonavista. He was one of the master watches.

After a short period of confusion, the scaling down over the sides of the ship was going well. Some of the men were carrying tall poles with the ship's flag fastened to their tops, giving the whole procedure a regal look. Wes Kean was watching from the bridge. The side sticks did not reach all the way to the ice and the men had to jump the last few feet. Cecil Mouland had jumped from the sticks and was sprinting away from the ship, when suddenly the captain's voice thundered overhead.

"You there! The young stowaway from S'n John's! Where the 'ell do you thing you're going?"

John Antle was on the side sticks and he was about to jump onto the ice where Cecil Mouland and his new-found friends waited for him. Antle stopped, as did everyone else, arrested by Wes Kean's angry voice.

"Why—we—I—I'm goin' a-sealin' wit' the b'ys, sir!"

"Sealin'? Sealin', sir? Wi' the b'ys, sir? An' that you are not, sir! Git back aboard an' tend to your duties, sir, as is fittin' fer a man who steals 'board my ship!"

Antle was devastated, humiliated, and hurt beyond speech. The men allowed him room to climb back up. Some of them who had resented his presence now pitied the boy. Dejected, Antle made his way up and stood on the deck. Staring down at his friends, he looked like a boy put out of a game by his chums. The sealers started yelling again and their dismount continued.

Antle slunk away out of Kean's sight. Though shaken, he was still set on going, as he called it, a-sealin'. He was hoping to sneak away from the ship with the men on the other side. As if reading the boy's mind, Wes Kean roared again.

"Furder to my orders!"

The sealers stopped again.

"If the young stowaway is found in any o' the watches, the master will answer to me!"

Kean's anger toward Antle was evident to all who listened.

Jacob Dalton was standing on the ice next to Theophilus Chalk. Chalk had climbed down over the ship along with the others, and now he looked at Jake nervously, waiting for the skipper to turn his wrath upon him. But it never came. Jake, ever ready to seize an opportunity, quickly pushed Chalk ahead and away from the ship. They walked past many of the men and merged into their ranks, losing themselves in the milling crowd.

* * * * *

THE STORM IS FOLLOWING ITS track up the coast of North America. Huge cold masses of air forced down from the northern plains region hold it at the outer rim of the continent. It licks at the Carolinas and the southern spit of Chesapeake Bay, tearing across the land and dropping torrents of rain. It rages northward, reaching inland to Philadelphia and through the canyons of New York City. It mixes with a plastering snow and shatters windows and strips the roofs off skyscrapers standing in its way.

North past the divide between America and Canada, it bears for the maw of the Bay of Fundy. Here the circulation of air bearing down from the Canadian northland stops fighting with the upward-reaching wind from the south. Now it merges with the storm and adds to its terrible might. Pulling it north and east, searching, a winter gale is born.

The storm reaches to sea hundreds of miles east of Cape Sable. It buries Nova Scotia and most of New Brunswick with heavy snow. Roaring out over Cape North, at the end of Cape Breton's highlands, it engulfs St. Paul Island and the Îles de la Madeleine in its ferocious grip. Here, at the end of the St. Lawrence, it finds what it is looking for: the southern edge of the Great White Plain. It feeds on the cold air rising from the icefield and for a time stalls over it.

North and east it bends its way over the frigid plain, toward the unsuspecting island of Newfoundland and the ice floes beyond. Driving ahead of the maelstrom is a deceivingly pleasant spring day. It is a warning of what is yet to come for those who know, and men ignore it at their peril.

* * * * *

AT 7:00 A.M., GEORGE TUFF took the point position and led northwest toward the *Stephano*. He wore thick, round-eyed goggles to protect his eyes from snow blindness, and when he turned around to look at the sealers behind him he saw that only a few wore sunglasses. The ice was heavy and extremely rough. There were ridges to get over, and some of them were so uneven they had to be circumnavigated. Judging distance from the *Newfoundland*'s barrel, or even from her deck, and trying to see their goal from a man's height on the ice surface, was entirely different. There was no way to walk in a straight line, and it was only when they topped the ice ridges that the *Stephano* could be seen at all. There was a low, heavy swell that lifted the ice surface like a living, breathing thing, and sometimes the *Stephano*'s masts could be seen against the sky. She was still hull down in the ice, but the morning was pleasant enough, the sun warmed as it rose, and the sealers were in great spirits as they started out. They were fresh and well-rested after days of inactivity. It took a while for the master watches to get their men organized, but they were soon following behind Tuff four and five abreast.

The ice was fused together in pans of all sizes. The weight of so many men jumping and landing in the same spot often weakened the edges of the pans, and sometimes they broke and a man fell through to his knees—to the delight of the others. When this happened, the sealers behind would stop and hurriedly looked for a way around the slushy hole. Many of them, especially the young and experienced, considered their walk a lark and made fun of it. One man, who suddenly broke through a pan edge, recovered so swiftly from his fall he claimed he had not gotten wet. The others piled to a stop behind him. Scrambling to his feet and seeing the men behind him hesitate to follow, he shouted with glee, "Ah! I got yas duffed, b'ys!"

Duff was a popular game among the boys in the outport communities on the northeast coast of Newfoundland. It was a game of challenge and could involve as many boys as were willing to play. The game was simple enough. All that was needed was for someone to claim he could leap over the highest rock, across the deepest gulch, or even from the highest outhouse roof than anyone else. But the best challenge of all was flipsying, or copying, across coves on pans of ice. The smaller ones presented the greatest challenge. A boy would run with outspread arms and, like a log driver on a river, cross dozens of ice pans too small to bear his weight, with five feet or more of icy water under the pans. If he made it across without falling through, and if the others would not try it, he had successfully duffed his opponents. However, if he fell through and had to wade ashore, his duff had failed. The innocent games of duff that boys played in sea coves choked with ice were good practice for the deadly game of hunting on the shifting ice floes.

Soon the walk ahead of them became a hard and trying journey over miles of sea ice. The men strung out into a long, single line behind George Tuff. Wide cracks and chasms appeared between the thick pans. Small lakes of water drew them up short, but the slob between the pans was what the sealers feared most. From a distance the ice looked to be stable and unmoving, but it was not. Aside from its constant drift, which went largely unnoticed without some landmark to judge it by, there was the constant movement of the individual pans. They rose and fell with the roll of the deep ocean swells beneath. Their serrated edges, miniature headlands, and countless pointed ends rubbed against each other, grating off tons of ice into the fissures between them. The sealers called it slob. The cold emanating from the ice surface sometimes fused the slob to the harder pans, but it was a deceptive weld that could never be trusted. It would rarely hold a man's weight.

Along the way, some of them fell through knee deep. A few men stopped to wring out wet stockings, but most of them carried on. The walk was now an exercise of burning muscles and dwindling energy. There were few level patches of ice. Most of their trail went over a rocky, icy plain. Men had to climb over ice formations taller than themselves. In places they squeezed through openings to save distance. They were in constant motion, leaping, jumping, climbing, and sometimes stumbling.

George Tuff slowed the pace. Some of the older men were tired. The morning was warm and the sealers were warming up further with the exertion. The men were sweating. They sucked on handfuls of snow and clumps of ice to quench their thirst. They had breakfasted on salt codfish and carried no water with them.

Toward the rear of the column, some stopped for a rest. They began to remove their heavy hats and coats, and a few decided to leave them behind.

Reuben Crewe spoke to a young man who had removed his coat and placed it on a pinnacle of ice to retrieve on the way back. "Don't be leavin' yer coats behind, b'ys. Better on than off. Remember where yer to, b'ys."

"Ah, Skipper, 'tis a warm day. I'm sweatin' like a bull. The *Stephano* is no more than another hour away, so I'll pick up me coat when we comes back."

"Aye, 'tis a bit warm, me son. No buttercups showin' yet, though, I 'low. Yer coat is better on than off," Jesse Collins said.

"Dere's no guarantee we'll get back dis day, my b'y," Reuben continued, looking at the cloud cover as he spoke. "I don't like the looks of the marnin'. 'Tis already closin' in, an' I saw a sun hound when I come on the ice. A wedder breeder, dis day is, I'm 'lowin'."

"Two, I saw!" said another sealer. "One on the souther side and one on the nart' side. Close up, too! Which we all knows means wedder is 'longside! An' two of 'em means the debt will be paid back double." He too was studying the sky, and there was concern in his voice.

Sun hounds are pinkish, reddish images of light, usually rectangular, which sometimes appear to one side of the rising sun, or sometimes on both sides. Fishermen swore by their presence and believed that the closer they were to the sun, the closer an impending windstorm. Two sun hounds meant there would be two winds. The second wind would shift around from the opposite direction of the first one and blow back twice as hard.

Though the morning was warm with little wind, the sun had indeed clouded over and the sky was lowering. The men talked about the weather and about the *Stephano*, which was still a hard walk to the northwest; in fact, she looked even farther away now than when they had started, as if the ship was steaming away from them. But mostly they discussed the absence of seals. Then one of the sealers voiced his opinion openly.

"I'm goin' back to the *Newfoundland*, b'ys!" It was Tobias Cooper, a tough, experienced fisherman from Bonavista Bay.

"Back? We can't go back! We've no orders to go back!"

"Orders? I don't need orders from no man to return to ship wit' nar seal in sight and a starm comin' on," Cooper replied.

"What about the signal the skipper got from ol' man Kean tellin' 'im 'e's found a patch of seals fer us?"

"Signal? Bah! I never heard anyt'ing about no signal, b'y. An' ol' man Kean sharin' his seals wit' us? I don't believe it!"

Not all of the sealers had heard about the signal between Wes Kean and his father. With no master watches near them, they talked about what they should do. Cooper's mind was made up, and he issued the challenge.

"I'm goin' back to our ship, b'ys. I'll go be meself if I 'ave to! Who's got guts enough to jine me?"

Reuben Crewe looked all around for his son, Albert John. He was nowhere in sight.

"I'll be goin' on," he said, and without further comment he strode away after the scraggly line of sealers now well ahead of him.

Joshua Holloway was having second thoughts, too. He looked for his brother, Phillip, but didn't see him. He consulted with his friend Jesse Collins.

"Don't much matter to me one way or the other, Josh b'y. What do you 'ave in mind?"

Josh stepped up on a high point of ice, searching for his brother. "Naw, Jess b'y, I'll be goin' on."

"Me too, then," said Jesse.

Jacob Dalton was listening to the argument without speaking. He was standing with Theophilus Chalk apart from the milling men. Dalton was warm and clutched his salt and pepper hat in his big hands. He had stuffed his mitts inside his coat pockets.

"I'm not goin' back, Offie," he said quietly to his friend.

"I'm goin' wherever you goes, Jake b'y."

Jacob turned and followed the sealers headed toward the *Stephano*, with Offie following close behind. Cooper was walking back the way they had come. He spoke again to the men who were undecided.

"I don't like it, b'ys. I see all the makin's of a bad starm comin'. The sky was blood red dis marnin'. Before dis day is over, you'll wish yer cake was dough."

Thirty-three others joined him. Their leader, George Tuff, was close to a mile ahead, unaware that his ranks had broken.

The *Bellaventure* took the lead in the recovery efforts. Here, her crew bring the living and the dead back to their ship. (Photo courtesy of the Centre for Newfoundland Studies Archives Coll-115 Memorial University of Newfoundland)

The dead and injured sealers of the SS *Newfoundland* continue to be brought aboard the SS *Bellaventure*. (Photo courtesy of the Maritime History Archives)

After two days and nights on the ice, a survivor is assisted aboard the SS *Bellaventure*. (Photo courtesy of the Centre for Newfoundland Studies Archives Coll-115 Memorial University of Newfoundland)

A gruesome sight on the deck of the SS *Bellaventure*. Frozen bodies lay side by side. (Photo courtesy of the Centre for Newfoundland Studies Archives Coll-115 Memorial University of Newfoundland)

The SS *Bellaventure*, shown here with a dangerous buildup of ice on her hull and decking. (Photo courtesy of the Maritime History Archives)

By telegraph, citizens of St. John's learned of the SS *Newfoundland* disaster. Friends, families, and curiosity seekers crowd on the waterfront to await the arrival of the rescue ship SS *Bellaventure*. (Photo courtesy of The Rooms Provincial Archives Division, VA 164-7/R.P. Holloway)

Thousands of people line the St. John's waterfront to get news of their relatives and friends. (Photo courtesy of the Centre for Newfoundland Studies Archives Coll-115 Memorial University of Newfoundland)

Stockpiles of coffins awaiting the dead of the SS *Newfoundland*. (Photo courtesy of the Centre for Newfoundland Studies Archives Coll-115 Memorial University of Newfoundland)

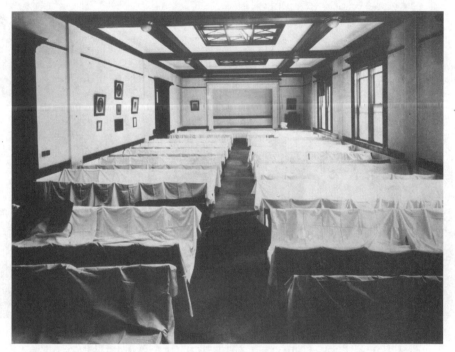

White sheets laid over chairs. Bodies were placed under the sheets in order to thaw before being identified and placed in coffins. (Photo courtesy of the Centre for Newfoundland Studies Archives Coll-115 Memorial University of Newfoundland)

At the Harvey and Company wharf, a survivor is transferred to shore by stretcher. (Photo courtesy of the Centre for Newfoundland Studies Archives Coll-115 Memorial University of Newfoundland)

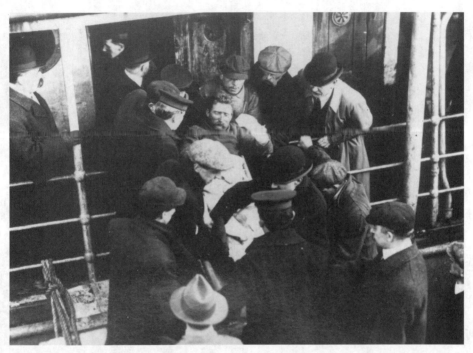

Thomas Dawson survived the *Newfoundland* disaster. Here he is being brought ashore from the rescue vessel SS *Bellaventure*. (Photo courtesy of the Centre for Newfoundland Studies Archives Coll-115 Memorial University of Newfoundland)

Cecil Mouland's cousin, Ralph Mouland, being landed from the SS *Bellaventure*. (Photo courtesy of the Centre for Newfoundland Studies Archives Coll-115 Memorial University of Newfoundland)

Landing survivors of the SS *Newfoundland* disaster.
(Photo courtesy of the Maritime History Archives)

The naval reserve was seconded to assist in transferring injured men to hospitals. Here, a survivor of the SS *Newfoundland* is being taken to an ambulance to care for his frostbitten limbs. (Photo courtesy of the Maritime History Archives)

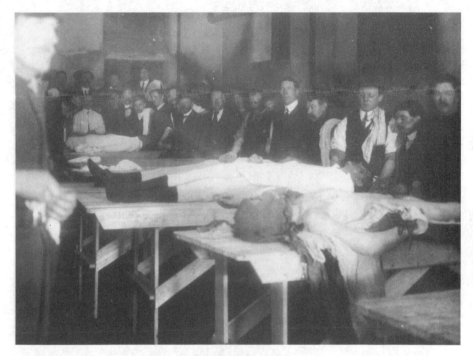

Bodies laid out for thawing. There seems to be little dignity, with so many people allowed in the room to satisfy their morbid curiosity. (Photo courtesy of the Centre for Newfoundland Studies Archives Coll-115 Memorial University of Newfoundland)

Top and bottom: A long funeral procession through the streets of St. John's. (Photos courtesy of the Maritime History Archives)

16

W HEN HIS CREW LEFT THE side of his ship, Wes
Kean climbed the rigging and entered the barrel of the
mainmast and stayed there all morning. With glasses in hand he
watched every move his men made. They had left a smutty trail
at first. After walking for days on the deck of the *Newfoundland*,
their heavy boots were caked with coal dust. Kean had watched
the sealers run and jump with apparent glee as their trek began.
He smiled to himself, remembering his own forays for seals.
Their broad column narrowed to a twisting single file after a
few hundred feet. From his vantage point the men looked
like a gigantic black eel meandering over the white plain. The
company flags scattered throughout the troop appeared plain in
his glass as the sealers fell into the march they were famous for:
the sealers' walk. Now they appeared as they had weeks before,
when crossing the harbours to join their ships, a tough breed of
men walking into history.

Some of the men in the rear stopped and bunched together.
At first he thought they were killing seals, but soon, even at
that distance Kean could tell they were deep in discussion over
something. He kept his glasses trained on them and waited.
Finally, they broke up and began walking again.

Kean pulled the glasses from his burning eyes. He thought

he must have been mistaken. He wiped his eyes with a dirty handkerchief, raised his glasses again, adjusted them for a better view, and dropped them again in disbelief. It couldn't be! He raised them again and stared long. There was no mistake. A group of his men were returning!

At first he reasoned that one of them had fallen through and was returning to dry his clothes—a rare thing for any sealer to do. They usually pressed on, wet or no. Then he feared someone had broken a foot or even a leg. He had seen that happen before. In such an event he could see a couple of men returning with the injured man. But as he stared through his glass, he counted twenty-nine of them coming his way.

Wes stayed in the barrel until he saw clearly the head of the group of sealers boarding his father's ship. Shortly after it began snowing, the returning sealers were near and he was angry.

He left the barrel and scampered down the ratlines. His glasses bounced on their lanyard around his neck as he went. He strode across the empty deck of his ship and burst through the bridge door, announcing his frustration to no one in particular.

"A bunch of the men are returning! Twenty-nine of 'em, by God!"

Bo'sun John Tizzard and Charles Green the navigation officer were there. Green had his own glasses trained on the men. "Thirty-four of them, sir!" he corrected Kean.

"Worse again, then!" said Kean, picking up his glasses again.

Kean stormed away from the bridge and glowered down at the sealers as they approached the side sticks.

"What is the meanin' of you men comin' back aboard ship in the middle of a fine day?"

"We didn't see anyt'ing to go on fer, sir," ventured Tobias Cooper. "We saw the crowd a'ead of us climbin' the pinnacles looking fer seals an' findin' none, sir. Then we was outdistanced be the others. 'Twas plain wedder was coming on, so we come back, sir," he finished, hoping for some agreement from the skipper. None came.

Wes Kean took his text and spoke strongly. "Well b'ys, I'm purely disappointed in ye! If ye came back along wit' yer master watch, I wouldn't blame ye. I would blame 'im, though. I saw the sealers who went on board the *Stephano* an hour ago. Saw 'em do so wit' me own eyes. Here's the rub now, b'ys. The men who went aboard the *Stephano* are now in the seals, that I am sure of. You lot are not. You 'ave divided me crew and our chances fer a good hunt be twenty-nine men!"

"Thirty-four men," Charles Green said. He had appeared on deck unbeknownst to Kean.

"A'right, then, dammit, thirty-four!" Kean glared at his navigator. Green was not helping their relationship much. Kean hated being corrected by anyone. "You are not supposed to be makin' decisions o' yer own accord," he continued. "You must listen to yer master watch an' no one else when on the ice. B'ys, 'twas by no means a 'ard walk, an' you had the right to go along wit' the master watch an' return when he s'id so an' not before. If a couple of fellers come back in company wit' a buddy who'd fallen in the water or was crippled, or a man after a spell, figured he was not up to the walk, I'd 'ave no objection. But to give up the hunt when yer comrades 'ave gone on? I would not 'ave believed it!"

The young skipper walked away as the sealers, looking just as dejected as they felt, made their way aboard the *Newfoundland* in the fast falling snow. John Antle, who was standing to one side, had heard all of the talk between the sealers and the skipper. He looked for his friends among the sealers who had returned, but they were not among them. Antle wished he had the courage to tell the captain that if he had been allowed to go a-sealing, they would be short by only thirty-three men.

*   *   *   *   *

NEWS OF THE DEFECTION TRICKLED up the line and finally reached George Tuff at around 11:30 a.m. He was surprised to hear it and said so. Tuff was thinking that by now Wes Kean had drawn a black line through the name of every one of those who had gone back. Looking back to the southeast, he couldn't see the *Newfoundland* through the falling snow. However, the *Stephano* loomed over the ice in all of its modern splendour.

"Oh, ain't she a beaut, b'ys! First time I seen her up close. Big as Wester' 'Ead, she is!"

"The b'ys was right. All o' her lights burning and 'tis not even nigh dark!"

"I hope dey got the kettle on. I'm starved fer some of the good grub aboard of that one."

"She's steamin' towards us, by God! Jest listen to the sound of the ice rumblin' under her bows!"

"We'll be sleepin' in the lap o' luxury dis night, b'ys. An' ol' man Kean hisself will tuck us in our blankies, ha ha!"

"She looks like she's skiddin' over the ice. Dere's power fer 'e, b'ys!"

The *Stephano* was indeed steaming toward them. For a group of men standing on a sea of ice, the huge, grey ship pounding toward them at full power was a formidable sight. She foundered the ice away from her sides in huge broken pieces as she came. The ship was steaming through an area of thinner ice, or what the sealers called young ice, creating a dull booming noise that rattled their ears. Suddenly, one of the sealers cried out in disbelief.

"Look at 'er, b'ys! She's turnin' away from us, by God!"

The sealer was right: the *Stephano* was swinging around.

* * * * *

THE SECOND HAND OF THE *Stephano* was Fred Yetman from Brookfield, Bonavista Bay. Yetman had been going to the seal hunt for thirty-four springs, six of them as second hand with Abe Kean. From the barrel, Yetman had seen the sealers from the *Newfoundland* on the ice earlier in the morning. At

9:00 a.m., he reported to Abram Kean that it looked like they were walking toward them.

An hour later, Kean came out on the bridge from his private quarters. He was freshly groomed, looking as though he had just stepped out of a barber's chair. Kean spoke to his first mate, walked forward to the window, and picked up a pair of binoculars. They were his personal pair, always adjusted to his preference, and no one else was allowed to use them. Abram Kean called the glasses "hoppers." He studied the *Newfoundland* sealers wending their way toward his ship for a while and wondered who was leading them. As he watched, the line of men showed small and black against the ice as they rose up and settled back down again on the gentle swells. With the standard of their ship standing tall in their midst, they looked like crusaders forging their way across the frozen plains of Europe.

The line curved and swung as the man leading them negotiated the many barriers in their path. Kean was all too familiar with the terrain of the icefields. He had been there before and had earned his captain's stripe well.

Abram Kean was born on Flowers Island, on the north side of Bonavista Bay, on July 8, 1855, at the very edge of the sea, where he had spent his entire life. At seventeen he was married to his father's maid and went to the ice for the first time. From the beginning, Kean loved the physical act of seal hunting and possessed an innate understanding of the animal's migration habits. Just ten years later, he had achieved such a reputation that Baine Johnston, the St. John's sealing company, hired him as captain of their ship the *Hannie and Bennie*. Despite his bravado and bursting confidence, his first years at the ice had not been very successful. However, failure merely strengthened the man's resolve. Now, at fifty-eight years old, he was a grizzled veteran of the hunt and had acquired a reputation for finding and killing seals few skippers could match. Some men respected him, even looked up to him, but most feared him.

Kean watched the struggling *Newfoundland* sealers make

their way for a while. Finally, forty-five minutes later, he ordered the *Stephano* to power up and her helm over to intercept them. He called his chief cook to the bridge.

"Have the kettle b'iled and prepare a mug-up fer the crew of the *Newfoundland*, who will be comin' aboard shortly. Be snappy, min'! There will be no time fer dallyin'!"

"Aye aye, Skipper," the cook said.

"And tell the b'ys on deck to show the *Newfoundland* sealers where to go to get their dinner. Advise them to make quick work of it and eat on their feet! 'Twill go down faster, as the sayin' goes."

"Aye, Skipper." The cook left the bridge.

Soon, Kean could see the men clearly without the aid of his hoppers. His eyes were sharp and he knew the stride of the man leading them.

"Westbury has chosen well, as I knew 'e would," he thought out loud. "George Tuff in the van, as spry as you please, one of the finest men who ever came out of Bonavist' Bay. Port the wheel!" he shouted. "'Ard over! Clum her way back into her wake!"

"Aye, sir," came from the first mate as he spun the big wheel to port.

The ship heeled over like a racehorse that had been kicked in the ribs, and huge sheets of ice crumbled in her wake. Her engine was ordered stopped when she got close, and by 11:30 a.m. the *Stephano* was docked on the Great White Plain in the falling snow, waiting for the tired visitors.

*　　*　　*　　*　　*

THE CREW FROM THE *NEWFOUNDLAND* hurried alongside the *Stephano* and began to climb up the ladders that had been lowered for them. They had just walked over the worst of terrains for five hours without rest or food. Many of the sealers had fallen through, leaving them with wet feet.

The men who had turned back were right. The *Stephano* had been moving away from them. Abram Kean had steamed farther to the northwest from where Wes Kean had spotted the ship at five o'clock. When they finally reached her, she was more than a mile away from her earlier position.

As quickly as the men came up over the side of the *Stephano*, Kean roared from the bridge, "Hurry up and get yer dinner!" He also asked George Tuff to come to the bridge. Just before he walked inside with Kean, Tuff noticed Thomas Dawson. Dawson from Bay Roberts was one of the master watches of the *Newfoundland*. He was on deck with his crowd, looking confused as to where he and his men were supposed to go.

"'Urry below and get some grub fer yer men, Tom," Tuff yelled.

"No, damned if I will! I'm no officer aboard o' this one and got no orders to fetch prog fer meself nor me men, sir."

Dawson hurried his men below, where he found a mug and water. He gave it to one of his thirsty men. Dawson walked back up on deck without eating or taking food with him, sat down on the after hatch, filled his pipe, and waited for the rest. It wasn't a long wait.

Phillip and Joshua Holloway stood on the deck with Jesse and Fred Collins. Snow was falling and they couldn't see the *Newfoundland*. They didn't know why the old man was rushing them. Surely they would be staying aboard for a rest, and with weather coming on, probably for the night. They were the last to go below, and as they were going down, others of their group were coming back up, some with cakes of hard bread in their hands.

Abe had already ordered his ship away by the time Tuff sat down to dinner with the captain in Kean's private dining room. He ate quickly while the old skipper talked.

"Now, George b'y, I'll tell 'e straight the way of it. Early this marnin' I put my men on a string of seals off to the nar'wes'. 'Tis only a narrow string of 'em and the *Florizel*'s crew have already foreled my men. The *Bonaventure*'s men are well on the hand of foreleading the *Florizel*'s crew. Be the time I could get yer crew onto that patch of seals you would be twelve or fourteen miles farther away from yer vessel. As ye know, that is not a practical t'ing to be doing."

Tuff nodded at the captain and continued eating.

"Here's me plan as regards to yer men. Yester evening I spied a fine spot of seals off to our port 'and. Dere's a t'ousand of 'em fer sure, an' if they've not taken to water there'll be fifteen hundred or more. They bear to the southwest quarter and will bring you an' yer men two miles closer to the *Newfoundland* than ye are now. When you pan the seals fer the day, you can board yer own ship. Is dat to yer likin', George?"

"Aye, it is, sir," said Tuff.

"I see ye finished yer dinner, George b'y. Best to get yer men on the go now. We 'ave to get ahead to our work quick, like, as some of my men are five or six miles away from us be now."

At 11:50 a.m., the two men left Kean's dining room and walked to the bridge. Through the windows Kean saw the men of the *Newfoundland* pouring up from the forecastle again. George's men had been aboard the *Stephano* for no more than twenty minutes.

Kean asked his second hand, Yetman, if he had seen their ship's flag, which had been left in the ice yesterday evening. Yetman replied that he did. It was in the southeast quarter, just a little off their port bow. Kean ordered the *Stephano*'s engines stopped and the wheel over to starboard, in order to press his vessel hard against the ice to facilitate easier access onto the ice from the lee or starboard side. He shouted from the bridge and *Newfoundland* men began climbing back down to the ice.

Kean approached the large binnacle and stared at the compass rose. He beckoned Tuff, who had been looking through the windows at his men, to join him.

"Here's the bearin' of yer ship, George b'y, southeast, plain as day, she is. 'Bout farty-five miles or so southeast of Bonavist' Cape, we are."

George looked down at the compass and out toward the southeast. He couldn't see for snow, but as was his way to follow orders unquestioningly, he didn't tell Kean that he couldn't see the *Newfoundland*.

"Aye, sir, southeast. Looks like weather comin', sir. Soft, though," he ventured.

"Aye, George, soft it is. The glass is fair and 'twill be mild, is my guess. 'Urry, now! I have my men to pick up."

"Aye, sir," said Tuff, and without speaking further he left the bridge and joined his men as they left the *Stephano*.

*   *   *   *   *

FOR JOSHUA HOLLOWAY AND HIS friends from Newport, dinner aboard the *Stephano* consisted of a few platefuls of leftover boiled beans, hard bread with butter just as hard, and cold tea without sugar. Jesse Collins hated cold tea, so he had none. He grabbed a cake of hard bread and shoved it in his coat pocket with the others he had taken from the *Newfoundland* that morning. The ship lurched her way through the ice while they were below. The sounds of the sheet ice brushing past her steel hull were altogether different than when the same ice flowed past the wooden walls of the *Newfoundland*. Here it was a tearing, screeching, frightening noise. The ship stopped suddenly; the noise of her movement faded away to nothing.

Someone yelled down the companionway, "All *Newfoundland* men on deck and over the side!"

"Over the side, did 'e say? My feet are froze, b'ys! I figured we would be allowed to warm up a bit."

"I got wet to me knees crossing that last rent. I was 'lowin' to dry me socks aboard dis one!"

"I've jest cracked me 'ard bread! Where's the good grub aboard we all 'eard about?"

"What's the ol' man's 'urry? There's a starm coming, anyone can see that!"

"He's steamin' to the nar'wes' to pick up his own men."

"Funny queer t'ing, dat is! The ol' man is in a tear to get 'is own men aboard because of the starm comin', and in a bigger tear to get the crew of the *Newfoundland* off!"

Despite their concerns, no one complained to his master watch. They left the hold of the *Stephano* willingly, their bellies just as empty and their feet just as wet as when they had boarded. They walked up on deck and began climbing back down to the ice. From his perch at the after bridge rail, Abram Kean supervised the off-loading of the sealers. They climbed quickly down and walked away with Tuff leading them.

"Over the side, men! Don't dally! You there, on deck! Get the rights! What are ye waitin' fer? Over the side, quick! If ye don't jump out right now, I'll carry ye away from the seals! Or I'll cut ye off before you can cross the bows o' dis vessel!"

Kean kept roaring to the last six men of the *Newfoundland*'s crew until they were gone. Powered up and ready to go, the *Stephano* moved to starboard.

The men from Newport, as well as Reuben Crewe from Elliston and Theophilus Chalk from Little Catalina, scampered down the side sticks. Jacob Dalton was waiting for his friend, Offie. Reuben stared all around for Albert John and thought he saw his son heading off in the snowy gloom with some of the other men, so he went after them. The others walked away as the big ship ploughed ahead, crushing and renting the ice as she went. Smoke poured black and thick from her mighty engines and out her stack, drifting down upon the last of the men to leave her. They hurried to catch up with the rest of the sealers in the falling snow.

Hearing the rumble of the *Stephano*, Joshua Holloway turned back for a look. The noise of her butting through the ice was loud and clear, but he couldn't make her out through the snow.

17

*T*UFF SET OFF IN A southwesterly direction without explaining his intentions to any of his master watches. Thomas Dawson wondered where Tuff was taking them. He caught up to him and asked where they were going.

"To the sou'wes', Tom, as per Skipper Kean's orders. We'll find fourteen to seventeen hundred seals in that direction. We should come up on some seal carcasses first from the *Stephano*'s kill o' yester evenin', 'bout two miles. Just past that we'll come on the seals."

"Two miles? Sure, dere's weather coming on, as ye can plainly see. Is the *Stephano* coming to pick us up dis evenin'?"

"No, we'll 'ave to board the *Newfoundland*."

"How the 'ell are we supposed to find 'er if we walk two miles and more to the sou'west?"

"We'll allow a point or two."

"George b'y, I've been to the ice fer twenty-two springs, an' you would want to run 'er pretty neat to strike a ship on a day like dis one is shapin' up fer. I couldn't see the *Newfoundland* when we left the *Stephano*, an' now 'tis much worse. 'Twill be like findin' a bull bird in the middle of Bonavist' Bay, I 'lows."

Tuff did not acknowledge him.

By now the falling snow was thick, and though it was mild with a southeast wind, drifting had begun. Visibility was no more than a few hundred feet and the sealers coming up from behind looked like shadows to Tuff. He led on anyway, in what he said was a southwesterly direction, though Dawson did not see him use a compass. They had gone a mile before they came upon approximately 200 seals. Tuff ordered Jacob Bungay and his watch to start killing them.

Bungay was from Newtown. After spending five years at the seal hunt, he was now master watch for the first time. Trying to earn a good name as leader, and being a compassionate man by nature, he had seen that his men were taken care of on the *Stephano* before himself. When the order came for all hands over the side, he had led his men topside without eating or drinking. On deck he followed Kean's further order to get out. In his pockets he carried several cakes of hard bread that he had taken from the *Newfoundland*.

The seals were skittish and hard to kill in the mild weather. Bungay's men managed to kill twenty or so before the seals disappeared in the drifting snow. They pelted and panned them, stuck a *Newfoundland* flag in the snow, and walked ahead to join the others. Tuff was behind the men and not leading. He had shouted for them to stop. They gathered around him, and he was in heated conservation with one of the sealers, Lemuel Squires of Topsail.

"Where are ye takin' us, Jarge?"

"What odds is it to you where I takes 'e?" Tuff answered angrily.

He and Squires had had a disagreement aboard the *Stephano* when Tuff shouted down from the bridge for the men to "Bolt yer prog or go wit'out it!" Squires, who had a ready temper, wasn't about to let that go. "If you was down 'ere, by Chris', I'd show you who'd be going wit'out." Tuff didn't respond.

"What odds is it to me?" Lemuel said now. "I'll tell 'e, Jarge Tuff, what odds it is to me! My life is jest as sweet as any man's on this ice, an' I wants to know what course we're goin' and where we're goin' to."

"Well, if you don't like what I'm doin', you can go off and perish be yerself!"

"That I won't be doin', by Chris'! I'll stick with the gang. An' your place is up ahead pickin' out the best leads fer we fellers an' not laggin' behind!"

"Laggin' be'ind? I can board our own buggerin' ship meself in three hours!" George Tuff was shouting now. It was as if he had chosen this venue to vent all his frustration.

"The fastest time you ever travelled, I could keep up wit' 'e, Jarge Tuff!" returned Squires. He walked away angrily.

"I knew we was in fer a night of it when I saw the *Stephano* leave," said Reuben Crewe, not liking the confrontation between the two men. He was now standing next to Albert. He sounded worried.

"The only chance we fellers got of findin' our ship is to find our trail from the marnin' and follow it back to 'er," someone said.

"The bloody trail will be snowed in be the time we reaches it, I 'lows," came from another.

"We've the best o' the day be'ind us now, b'ys, an' not a'ead o' us," said Job Easton, a burly sealer from Greenspond. "I don't like it one bit."

Hedley Payne from the same community was standing next to him. At seventeen years old, this was Payne's first time at the ice, and though he agreed with his friend, he said nothing. Payne would go wherever he was led without complaint.

"The *Greenland* disaster will only be a peck alongside o' dis one," said Jesse Collins in his matter-of-fact manner.

At this, Tuff lost his anger. The colour seemed to drain from his face, and he suddenly looked ill.

"We're 'eadin' back to our own ship right now, men," he said. With that, he ordered Thomas Dawson to lead off to the southeast, saying that was the direction Abram Kean had told him to find the *Newfoundland*.

Dawson turned and started to lead off and the men followed him without comment. Tuff spoke to him as he passed.

"Keep the wind in yer eye, Tom b'y. 'Tis from the southeast, be my reckonin', an' 'twill take ye to our path o' the marnin's walk. Stop an' wait fer all 'ands to rally up when you comes upon it. I will stay as the hinder man."

Tuff looked at Lemuel Squires, who said nothing. Dawson took the lead and walked away with the sealers in tow.

"Keep yer flagpoles an' gaffs in 'and, fellers," Tuff said as he fell in behind the last man.

When the sealers left the *Newfoundland*, each man had carried a gaff. Close to fifty of them had also carried a heavy wooden pole with the *Newfoundland*'s flag attached to it. Over the long hike, some who carried both gaff and flagpole discarded the latter. Tuff had noticed the shortage of flagpoles when they had arrived at the *Stephano*. They played an important role in identifying the pans where the seal pelts were gathered and they could not be replaced while at the hunt. While he was arguing, he had seen at least two of the men with flags wrapped around their necks as scarves. There were other reasons why Tuff wanted them to keep their gaffs and flagpoles. They would make good fires should they be caught out all night. However, he didn't want to alarm them, even though he was pretty sure they were not going to make the *Newfoundland* before dark.

William Pear was the only man aboard the *Newfoundland* who wore spectacles, and now he had lost them. Without them he was nearly blind. Pear fell to his knees in the snow and searched in vain for his glasses. A couple of the sealers who were walking past helped him for a minute or so, but soon they gave up and went on ahead. Pear was also sick. He had been ill for a couple of days but had told no one, and now it was getting worse. He stumbled and tried to stare into the blinding snow. It stung his eyes until he was forced to blink rapidly. The men who were walking away from him appeared as ghosts. He fell again, thinking he was alone, the last man in the line, when Tuff approached him. The second hand spoke words of reassurance to Pear, helped him to his feet, and pushed him ahead. Pear told him he was very sick and afraid of being left behind, but Tuff said he would stay with him.

There was a good reason for Tuff to walk at the end of the line. By his count there were 132 men in the group. All of them were walking, and sometimes jumping, over the same pans of ice and weakening the edges. As a result, men at the end of the line on a sealers' walk were more likely to fall through. Last in line was the most dangerous place to be, and it took an experienced eye to spot the dangers.

There was another, much more troubling reason why Tuff had taken up the rear position. He hated being responsible for the lives of so many men. George Tuff was a good man. He was a hard worker, conscientious and very dependable. Though it was true he had volunteered to lead the men to the *Stephano*, he had been ordered by Abram Kean to take them onto the ice in a gathering storm, and he simply could not defy the voice of authority. Now he was caught up in an ordeal that would find old man Kean wanting, and images of the *Greenland* were already crowding his head.

Jacob Dalton was with Arthur Mouland's watch. Arthur was from Lancaster, a fishing village a few miles east of Bonavista. He was known throughout the area as a seasoned ice hunter. Dawson, whom Tuff had selected to lead all of them, had called a halt. He had found one of the *Stephano*'s flags, which he believed to be the same one they had passed just one side of the path they had taken that morning. The number on it was 198. Some of the men argued that the morning's flag had the number 189 on it. Below the flag were a few seal pelts tied to a strap. They argued about the flag number for a short while, then moved on again, searching for the path.

At 2:00 p.m., shouts from the head of the line announced that Tom Dawson had found the path back to the *Newfoundland*. Now all they had to do was follow—if they could manage to stay on it in this weather. There was still time to make the *Newfoundland* before dark. Jacob's booming voice shouted back down the line of men coming up behind him.

"Dawson has found the trail, b'ys! Nothin' to it now, we'll jest backtrack to our own ship."

The sealers cheered heartily at the news.

"Never t'ought we would find the path in this weather, b'ys!"

"A night out fer sure, I 'lowed."

"Good eye, Tom Dawson's got."

"A gallon of 'ot tea fer me when I gets aboard, an' a full pan o' bread. I'm starved."

"A feed of spuds an' fish, smatchy or no, smothered in pork fat will do me."

"I'm glad we'll be gettin' aboard the *Newfoundland*. Didn't feel welcome aboard o' the *Stephano*, I didn't."

"Me neither. Wouldn't let me finish me drap o' tea afore almighty Kean was bawlin' to get out."

"Cold, my tea was, an' weak, too."

"Skipper Wes is not like 'is ol' man, dat's fer damn sure."

"Well, as dey says, b'ys, the last of the litter is always the best."

They talked on, about how good it would be to get aboard their own ship, to get warm and dry and eat a hot meal, about Abram Kean and how callously he had ordered them away from his ship. None of it mattered now. Now that the outward path had been found, they would soon be safe and sound aboard the *Newfoundland*. They moved off again through the drifting snow, their steps lighter now. They were walking home.

Tom Dawson called another halt. He and the others had lost the hard-won trail and couldn't find it in the blinding snow. They were crestfallen. It was snowing harder now, even though the wind was still in the southerly quarter and the air still had a mild feel to it. Some of the more optimistic sealers thought the snow would turn to rain. They were wrong.

*   *   *   *   *

THE TURBULENT AIR MASS, WHICH had its birthplace in far warmer climes, and which had been reaching toward the southwestern edge of the island of Newfoundland for days, had arrived. The warm and pleasant spring day that had heralded its coming was over. The confused depression of atmospheric movement had pushed the spring-like airflow out of the way to make room for a brutal gale.

The storm came in eastward from the St. Lawrence Gulf. It raced across the sandy spit of the Port au Port Peninsula and surged inland toward the forested heart of insular Newfoundland. It swept south across frozen St. George's Bay and up over the Anguille Mountains, which were cloaked with aging winter snow. It roared out past the southwestern end of the island at Cape Ray, where the sea was free of ice, engulfing all before it. It ripped over fallow fields and across frozen harbours. It slammed up against white clapboard houses and those with peeling coloured paint. It baffled down the red brick chimneys of the rich and the black funnels of the poor. It heaped more snow down on the cold white mounds of Elliston's cellars.

The wives of ice hunters all along the coasts listened to the howl and moan of the gale as it rattled single-pane windows and drifted snow through the seams under eaves. Though they fretted and stared with worried eyes and comforted their brood who sensed their concern, they were safe. But their absent hunters, some adrift and some stumbling in the storm's path, were not. The gale raged seaward, and there its all-seeing eye found the first of its innocents—the SS *Southern Cross*. The ship was well burthen and fleeing for safety from the fury bearing down.

The name carried so proudly across her broad stern was not the one of her christening. Built of thick hardwoods in Arendal, Norway, when it slid from its ways and floated free into the Skaw fjord in 1886, it was christened *Pollux*, after a star in the northern constellation of Gemini. The *Pollux* was a three-masted, barque-rigged vessel, 146 feet long and powered by coal-fired steam. For the next decade she hunted whales very successfully. Then the stout Norwegian whaler changed ownership and was fitted by ownership and was fitted by Sir George Newnes for Antarctic exploration, with the explorer C. E. Borchgrevink as leader. On December 19, 1898, she sailed into the Southern Hemisphere with Captain Bernard Jensen, her new master, at the helm. Above her was one of the earth's smallest and most distinctive constellations, the Crux or Cross of the southern nights. And under the glow of her namesake, the ship proudly wore her new name, the *Southern Cross*. The ship struggled through the Antarctic ice pack for weeks until February 11, 1899, when she broke through that formidable barrier into the Ross Sea. She was the first ship to do so. The *Southern Cross* had opened up the Antarctic sea roads for Ernest Shackleton, Robert Falcon Scott, and Roald Amundsen, the explorers who would journey across earth's southernmost land mass. This feat earned the *Southern Cross* her first page in the books of nautical history. On March 31, 1914, off the south coast of Newfoundland, the gale was sneaking up behind her. It would put the SS *Southern Cross* onto the pages of history books again.

When she left the port of St. John's, she headed for the Gulf of St. Lawrence hunt with 173 sealers and crew aboard. Her sealers were, for the most part, inexperienced men from the Conception Bay area. Most of them were young and unmarried, but what the young sealers lacked in experience they more than made up for with energy and zest for the hunt. They killed enough seals on the Gulf ice floes to load the vessel in record time. On March 29, her captain, George Clarke of Brigus, a veteran seaman in his mid-forties, ordered his vessel away from the hunt and sailed for home. Clarke figured his ship should enter port with a full load of pelts and claim the "silk flag" this year for being the first to do so.

The *Southern Cross* left the Gulf and came in under the land at Cape Ray at an oblique angle. She was spotted by a wireless operator, who passed the word on that she was coming with all flags flying, indicating a full load. The loaded ship made her way south and east in open water, past the rugged south coast communities of Newfoundland. Her young crew was jubilant. Their bunks had been removed to make room for the bumper harvest of greasy sealskins, and some of them slept on these. It was a small price to pay for being first in port fully loaded. Another vigilant wireless operator saw her as she sailed past the islands of Saint-Pierre and Miquelon, one of France's last claims in the western world. The Frenchman sent his sighting by using the telecommunication codes common to all operators in any language.

Captain Thomas Connors saw her next on the evening of Tuesday, March 31, from the bridge of the SS *Portia*. The *Portia* was taking the first deep swells of an impending storm five miles west-southwest of Cape Pine and her skipper was pushing his ship hard for the safety of St. Mary's Bay. The *Portia* was close enough to salute the *Southern Cross* with her loud steam whistle. She sounded back her proud acknowledgement. Connors noted the ship was so heavily burthen she rose but slowly on the deep rollers. He ordered his operator to pass on the news of her progress. He would have liked to congratulate Captain Clarke of the *Southern Cross*—they were old friends—but the *Southern Cross*, owned by Harvey's, had no means of communication aboard.

The *Southern Cross* was never seen again.

Sealers who had sailed in her before said the *Southern Cross* was in need of repair. Others said she carried pound boards, made from Newfoundland softwoods, to keep the slippery pelts from shifting in her holds; they were thin and weakened by years of rotting seal fat and would break in heavy seas, causing her listing cargo to capsize her. Another old seaman said, "Maybe she simply sprung a leak and could have been saved—the *Portia* was close to her—if she had a wireless aboard, but her owners saw no need for it."

But for those who wait on shore, there are no reasons. There is only loss, sorrow, and pain. All that remained to mark the spot where brave men died was a silky-smooth patch of water. It widened and calmed the seas for a time, until the source of the viscous slick simply stopped rising up out of the grey depths. The careless brush of sea water smeared over it all and hid the calm place where so many men had died, until all was as everything and yet like nothing at all.

*   *   *   *   *

ALL OF THE *NEWFOUNDLAND* SEALERS who had been put on the ice with a threat of a snowstorm clearly in the offing were now in serious trouble. Dawson had found the trail, as Tuff had hoped he would, but lost it again. The sealers at the front of the line were now searching for the path back to the *Newfoundland*, but no one could find it. Everything was against them. The coal smut from their boots when they had left their own ship, and which had clearly identified their path when they had first started, was somewhere far to the southeast. A few discarded flagpoles had been stuck by the path, but none were found. A howling wind and blinding snow were quickly covering the tracks of the 132 tramping men. Worse yet, night was nearly upon them.

The ice where they had left the *Stephano* was relatively smooth, level ice where herds of seals had whelped. Birthing seals seemed to prefer this type of ice, which the sealers called true whelping ice. They left this area and bore to the southeast, where they believed the *Newfoundland* to be, and they came upon the same heavy, thick ice they had crossed in the morning. As rough as it was to walk on, this was the only place where they could hope to find shelter if they were to spend a night on the ice.

Taking up the rear, George Tuff had gotten a couple of volunteers to help him with the ailing William Pear. Pear was a stranger to Tuff. He needed assistance to walk, and when he had to jump across narrow rents between the ice pans, he fell in more often than not and had to be pulled out. Pear was pitiful to look upon. Each time his feet went into the icy water he fell forward to his knees, not having enough strength to pull himself free.

When he was pulled out of the icy water, snow clung to his feet and calves, encrusting his lower legs in a plaster cast of snow and ice. Pear was suffering terribly. He couldn't see, he was very sick, and he was soaked to the bone with icy sea water. Moans of pain and misery came from him every few minutes. Unable to go on without help, Pear just wanted to lie down and rest.

William Pear lived by the side of the Thorburn Path that led through the stunted tuckamore forest leading into St. John's. He had obtained a ticket to the ice as much to satisfy his curiosity as for any other reason, and right now he couldn't believe he was here.

"Leave me bide, b'ys, I'm done fer," he pleaded.

But the brave men who had chosen to stay with him dragged him on. They were now alone in a fierce vortex of wind and snow. George Tuff didn't carry a compass, and on that naked plain without contrast, and with dusk falling, the wind could be coming from any direction. They held their hands above their eyes, below the bibs of their hats, but they couldn't see. To look windward, into the snow, was mesmerizing. The roar of wind was frightening. It howled and tore over, through, and around the upper edges of the ice pinnacles. It hissed and whistled through ice canyons and over pressure ridges.

A shout came out of the blizzard, muted and muffled as if from a great distance.

"Hark, b'y's, the men in the fore 'ave found our ship," said George Tuff, staring into the shroud of snow. "Sounds like Bungay and Jones. Ahoy dere! Where 'ave ye found the ship?" He yelled the last at the top of his lungs.

Silence followed for a while, then a baffled reply to Tuff's anxious query: "No ship. We've lost the trail."

"Bide steady, men, till I comes upon 'e. Keep bawlin' out to keep us fair to ye."

Shortly after 5:00 p.m., Tuff led off toward the shouts and the others followed, dragging William Pear with them. Tuff's small group joined the others, who were bunched together on a large pan. He talked with the master watches. Their conversation was grave, their prospects dire. The sealers drew close to their master watches. The weight of so many men on a single pan was dangerous, so they moved around to other pans, distributing their weight. There were few decisions to be made. Without landmarks or direction, there was nowhere to go. They knew the ships were just beyond the blinding snow, but they may as well have been a continent away.

Then, from out of the storm, bearing its sweet music from windward, came the hoarse sound of a ship's whistle. It was the unmistakable sound of their ship, the SS *Newfoundland*: a groaning, distant sound over the howling wind. It was a lifeline, a peal of hope coming out of a steeple hidden by darkness and snow.

"The *Newfoundland*'s own whistle, b'ys! Not far, either, no more'n a mile, I 'lows!"

"Aye, Skipper Wes is lookin' fer we fellers. Comin' towards us, she is!"

"Hush, b'ys, and listen, won't 'e?"

The sound of the wind rose and fell on the flaws while the snow scudded all around them. Men listened in absolute concentration. They cuffed their ears to the might of the wind, listening, straining for that sound of hope to come again. And come again it did, a long, mournful *arrummp!* from the southeast.

Instinctively, they started to march toward the sound. They would be guided all the way to safety by the sound of their ship's horn. They walked a few yards before they were ordered to stop again and listen for the next one. It should be louder, more distinct, and give them clearer direction. They waited without talking, their ears straining, bursting, longing for the next blast to come out of the storm.

But it never came.

There was nothing save for the sound of wind and driven snow. Why had their captain stopped blowing the ship's whistle? they asked aloud. Why had it sounded at all, if not for them? Why were there no shots fired from the sealers' rifles? Why weren't their fellow sealers lining the gunnels of the *Newfoundland* and bawling out to them? As to get an answer to their own question, the stricken sealers began to shout into the wind with all their might.

18

*B*O'SUN JOHN TIZZARD HAD ASKED Captain Wes Kean for permission to sound the *Newfoundland's* whistle a couple of times, just in case there were men astray on the ice. Kean told him to go ahead and do so if he wanted to. Shortly after 5:00 p.m., Tizzard sounded the whistle twice. With his mind at ease, he left the bridge and turned in for the night.

Charles W. Green's log:

> Wind force six. East south east. Barometer 29.80, falling. Strong gale and drifting snow. Ship burned down for the night. Lookout carefully attended to. So ends this day.

Kean had spent almost all day aloft in the barrel. Only for short breaks did he allow his bo'sun to take his place. He had watched his men leave the ship. He had seen thirty-four men return. He had studied the sealers who went on through the thickening snow until they boarded his father's ship. He was still in the barrel at noon when the cook called him down to dinner. When Wes stepped down from the ratlines, he had ordered his bo'sun up to take his place.

"My men are safely aboard the *Stephano*," Kean said to Green, who was seated at the table. Green looked up in surprise. It was one of the rare times Kean had spoken to him. Kean sounded relieved.

"Good news indeed, sir," said Green, sharing the captain's mood. "Just in time, too, sir. The glass is dropping. A blow comin', I fear."

"Yes, sir. No matter, though. Father will look out fer my men now."

"Very good, sir."

Kean left the table and walked outside again. Green finished his meal, went out on deck, and lit his pipe before looking up into the rigging. Wes Kean was in the barrel again, his glasses glued to his eyes. The *Newfoundland* was lurching back and forth, trying to butt through heavy ice. Kean had given the order to move as close as they could to the *Stephano* and his men. The sky was thick with snow and there was little to be seen beyond a few hundred feet. Soon, the wind breezed up and the snow fell heavier. Though it was still mild, the wind sometimes carried cold gusts from the north. The masts on the windward side were plastered with snow and the scarred hull of the *Newfoundland* had a white coat of snow painted to her exposed flank. Inside the bridge, the blinding snow came at the warm windows like swarming white moths.

When Wes came down out of the barrel, his eyes were burning from using his powerful binoculars all day. He walked onto the bridge, where Green and the bo'sun were on duty. Kean looked tired, but he was in a good mood.

"I 'lows the b'ys will be up all night cufferin' wit' the crew on Father's ship. A treat fer the men to spend a night on a modern vessel, eh, Green?"

"Indeed it will, sir, indeed it will."

Night came, thick with snow, and the *Newfoundland* was hopelessly jammed again. Kean ordered his engine burned down for the night. With the night lanterns hung and the night watches in place, he left the bridge and went to his cabin.

*   *   *   *   *

GEORGE TUFF ORDERED THE FOUR watches to group their men on pans of ice large enough to bear their weight. He also ordered them to take shelter from the cut of the wind behind snowy hummocks, to fortify them with snow and ice, and to try and get fires going with oily gaffs and flagpoles. If they could find seals they were to kill them, burn their hides, and eat their flesh. They scattered to their respective groups and began preparing for the night sweeping down upon them. The storm intensified and the sky filled with snow. It piled up and made walking difficult even as the wind began banking in colder flaws from the north.

On the pan where George Tuff stood with his men, William Pear was getting worse. Tuff asked him if he was hungry, and when he said that he was, Tuff pulled a tin of sardines from his own pocket.

"You will have to cheer up, Pear, and do the best that you can, b'y. 'Twill be every man fer himsef, I 'lows, before dis night is done."

Tuff opened the tin of oily sardines and handed them to Pear, who was sitting on the ground. He walked around the perimeter of his men, inspiring them as he went. With trembling fingers, Pear pushed the sardines into his mouth one at a time. Oil poured down over his chin and inside his coat collar without his notice. The tin empty, Pear put it to his mouth and poured the coagulated grease into his mouth. Then he curled into a fetal position and coughed a few times.

When Tuff returned, he asked the others about Pear. They told him he was sleeping. Tuff prodded Pear gently with his foot; when he got no response, he bent down and spoke his name aloud. Pear remained silent, tucked into a tight ball and facing away from him. Tuff pulled on Pear's shoulder and turned the man toward him. His face was covered with snow and his eyes were wide open and staring. William Pear was dead.

If there was a man among them who knew what was to come, it was Tuff. William Pear was the first of the blank faces of Tuff's dream. Horrible images now came into focus in his head.

"We will all die! We'll all be smuddered!" he heard himself saying.

George Tuff sat on the ice with his head in his hands and wept. He didn't weep out of fear. He wept for the terrible responsibility that had been thrust upon him, for the senselessness, the futility of it all, and for the first of many more blank faces waiting to come into focus.

*   *   *   *   *

THE *STEPHANO* LAY CROUCHING LIKE a great grey beast on the white-shrouded field of ice. The latest falling snow was quickly covering her from stem to stern, and with no water to be seen anywhere near the vessel, she looked out of place. Hard by her hull, the sound of the storm thrummed through her rigging. On her deck, which was slowly suffocating with the snow, her steel stays whined and whistled and vibrated.

Even without anchor or lines, she was wedged firmly in the ice. Her modern generators proved fruitless to penetrate the storm when they powered up the ship's big-gimballed night lights. They appeared to twinkle as the curtains of snow swept past, and the *Stephano*'s green starboard and red port lights could not be seen at all.

Suddenly a noise blared through the storm like a foghorn coming from a lighthouse hidden in mist. It was the ship's steam whistle sounding its call against the Arctic might. Unfortunately, it was miles to the lee of the men who were caught out on the ice.

William J. Martin from St. John's was a master mariner and the chief navigator on board the *Stephano*. Everyone called him

Bill, except Abram Kean, who called him William. He kept a detailed log of the ship:

> Tuesday March 31st, A.D. 1914—11:20 A.M., *Newfoundland*'s crew walked on board, had 'mug up' and went on ice again about 11:50 A.M. Noon, wind increasing from S.E. with light snow. Barometer 29.50 and falling. 3:30 P.M., wind increasing to storm with blinding snow; ships horn kept going. 4:00 P.M. wind E. S.E. with heavy snow, blizzard and turning very cold.

When the *Stephano* headed away from the *Newfoundland*'s sealers at full steam, Bill Martin grew anxious about their safety. As the day wore on and the weather worsened, he became more concerned. They picked up their own men from the ice early, as well as sealers from the *Florizel*, who were hunting in the same area. The *Stephano* and the *Florizel* were in contact by wireless, so they arranged a meeting and the *Stephano*'s men returned to their own ship.

Most of the *Stephano*'s sealers who walked back to their ship didn't see her until they were almost on top of her. Using compasses, they followed flags they had set in the ice earlier in the day and were drawn by the *Stephano*'s whistle, which sounded every five minutes. They had done well, hunting and killing seals all day, even though the area of their day's hunt was among some slack and very dangerous ice. The pans were small and loose.

One of the sealers who had walked aboard was Ambrose Conway from St. Bride's. Conway had fallen through several times and was soaked to the bone. He was standing on deck, shivering, when Abram Kean appeared. Kean was wearing his greatcoat, which was covered in snow from the brief walk from the bridge. Kean directed his attention to his ice master, James Morgan, and asked him how they had fared with the killing.

Morgan gave him his report and Kean walked away without comment while the sealers went below. Everyone was aboard and accounted for.

Below deck the sealers removed their heavy canvas jackets and jumpers and hung them to dry. Steam rose from their clothing as the heat of the ship met the cold, wet garments. After hanging his clothes to dry, Ambrose hurried to the same place at the table where he had been sitting for days. He was a neat man and always cleaned his mug and turned it bottom up after finishing a meal. Now, though, his cup was upright, its rim was stained with tea, and the bottom of it was filled with soggy tea leaves.

"Who the 'ell was using me mug?" he asked, looking around.

No one knew or cared. One of the crew members who had been on board all day said, "Maybe it was one of the *Newfoundland* men who used yer mug."

"*Newfoundland* men? What are you talkin' 'bout?" Conway asked.

"The sealers from the *Newfoundland*, b'y, they was all aboard 'ere this marnin', 'cept fer her skipper an' firemen. Walked across from their vessel, they did. Must've been seven miles from the sout'east, I 'low. I couldn't see the *Newfoundland* fer snow when they come on board."

"What was they here fer?"

"How the 'ell would I know?"

"Where's 'em to now?" Conway looked all around, as if expecting to see the *Newfoundland* sealers aboard.

"Dey're gone, b'y. The skipper ordered 'em back on the ice quick as you please. Time the last ones was below, the first ones was leavin' again. Hot tea fer some, col' fer more, and none fer most. They stuffed their pockets wit' hard bread and climbed over the side again."

"What time was the men from the *Newfoundland* put overboard?" asked Samuel Horwood, who was seated nearby. Horwood was a *Stephano* sealer from Carbonear. He had been picked up by the *Florizel* at 1:00 p.m. and had walked aboard the *Stephano* at four o'clock that evening. Horwood had been a seal hunter since 1879. This spring was his fourth one with Abe Kean. He was a hard, no-nonsense kind of man who spoke his mind.

"Jest before noon," answered the crewman.

"'Twas snowin' by then, fer God's sake! Seven miles from their ship, did you say? Sout'east? They'll never make it. The roughest of ice is off to the sout'east. Why didn't the skipper keep 'em aboard fer the night?"

"Why're ye askin' me fer?" replied the indignant crewman, as if he needed to defend himself. "I don't know, b'y. Dey come aboard an' 'ad a mug-up in jig time. The secon' 'and bawled out fer 'em to get over the side an' they went, that's all I knows about it."

"I don't like it, b'ys," said Horwood.

There came a murmur of concern from the other sealers gathered at the table. Anxious voices were heard all around. Some of them were angry: to think the *Newfoundland*'s crew had been ordered off the ship with heavy weather coming!

"Nor do I," said Mark Sheppard, who was from St. John's. He had been sealing for three years previous and this was his first time aboard the *Stephano*. "'Twas between twelve and one when we left to come back to the *Stephano*. We couldn't see 'er then. We could see along the line of flags, but not all the way. We come back mostly be the ship's whistle. Our master watch, Abram Best, was along o' the nar'west from us and didn't come back wit' us. We come back with our ice master, James Morgan." He was concerned for the crew of the *Newfoundland*. "Someone should speak to the ol' man about it."

"Dere's a good many men aboard o' this one who ent got the guts to confront the ol' man," said one man.

"I'm not one of dem," said Horwood. "I'll go and speak to him about the *Newfoundland*'s men."

He rose from the table, climbed the companionway, and

walked forward toward the bridge. The snow slammed against him as he walked and the wind howled through the rigging. He tried to face into the wind but the snow blinded him, so he hurried forward with his head down and entered the forward saloon. Crossing it to the stairs leading to the bridge, he met Samuel Kean. Samuel was Abram Kean's brother; he had worked as wheelsman all day. Talking to Samuel was as good as talking to the captain himself, even if Horwood was a stranger to him. The sealers all called him Uncle Sam. The two men introduced themselves and talked about the weather for a minute. Then Horwood asked Kean straight out if he thought the sealers from the *Newfoundland* were still out on the ice.

"If they stopped to kill seals, I'm afraid they did not get aboard," answered Uncle Sam.

"To my mind, if they stopped to kill seals or no, dey did not get aboard the *Newfoundland*," said Horwood. "Dere's a rumour 'board ship dat the glass is gone bottom up, which means the wind will come 'round from the nar'west and freeze like guns. Dat being the case, the men o' the *Newfoundland* will perish on the ice, sir."

"I'm afraid so," said Samuel Kean.

"You can depend on it, Uncle Sam. 'Tis goin' to be a bad job. These men will perish on the ice!"

The two men wished each other a good night's rest and departed the saloon. Uncle Sam headed toward the bridge to find the captain, while Horwood went below to join the rest of the sealers.

When Uncle Sam walked on the bridge, Garland Gaulton was addressing Abram Kean about the *Newfoundland* men. Gaulton was one of the master watches of the *Stephano* who knew the Keans well. He was from Brookfield, Bonavista Bay, and had many friends as well as relatives among the *Newfoundland* sealers. Gaulton asked Abe Kean if he thought the crew of the *Newfoundland* had gotten aboard their ship all right.

"Yes, most decided!" Kean growled in a dismissive tone.

Gaulton walked away. While leaving the bridge, he heard the captain say to someone near him, "Keep the whistle sounding in case the *Newfoundland*'s crew are travelling towards us."

Outside the fortress of steel, the polar winds had tired of toying with the warm gusts daring into its realm. Now the north wind pushed it aside altogether and ripped around the *Stephano*, screaming through its rigging and yawing over the ship's superstructure. Finding no entry, it bore away, seeking easier prey. Cavorting over the frozen plain, the wind spiralled and swirled and rejoiced when it found what it was looking for. Triumphant, it moved down to intercept the defenceless ice hunters who were stripped of all shelter.

*　*　*　*　*

A BITTER COLD CAME WITH the changing wind baffling out of the north. The fleeting spring-like warmth was over, and those who had not heeded the warnings, those who had discarded articles of warm clothing were paying a terrible price. The men's necks, exposed with no coat collars to protect them, were burning with the frost. They turned up their shirt collars and drew their heads down between their shoulders, hoping to find some relief.

Around the shuffling feet of those men who were able to walk lay the forms of others who were too weak from hypothermia and exhaustion to walk, too filled with despair. The falling snow was slowly burying them. One of the sealers stopped and lashed out with his foot, unceremoniously kicking first one and then another of the downed men.

"Get on yer feet, fer God's sake!" Jesse Collins roared at the top of his lungs. "What are yous l'id down fer? Nappy time fer 'e, is it? Nish as a bloody fish merchant, the lot of 'e!"

The men he had kicked were slowly getting up. Collins bent down and grabbed at them, hauling them to their feet.

"Come on, b'ys, 'aul 'em up. Get 'em on der gams! We're all

ice hunters, by God. We stands our ground! We don't lie down on it like mucked dogs!" Jesse continued shouting while others helped them to their feet. "Tramp now, b'ys! Tramp 'round the harbour wit' us dis fine snowy night! Tramp yer feet and flise yer arms as we go! Rally on, b'ys, rally on!"

Slowly, Collins revived the sealers' spirits and got them going. Off they went, chasing Collins, flising and tramping "'round the harbour."

Flising was the tried-and-true method used by everyone from loggers to fishermen all around outport Newfoundland for keeping warm. A simple action, it involved flinging both arms as wide as they could go, then wrapping them in a quick, violent motion around the upper body as hard as possible. The harder the arms were slapped against the rib cage, the more heat they generated. Now the sealers looked like a troupe of mummers seeking Christmas merriment. They shouted and yelled and flised as they walked around the perimeter of the huge ice pan.

But behind them, one of the forms lying prone on the ice had not risen to the call. Thomas Jordon from Pouch Cove was so cold he was shaking uncontrollably. He had never been so cold in his life. Jordon was among the sealers who had removed his coat and left it behind earlier that morning. He had fallen through shortly after leaving the *Newfoundland* and had gotten soaked to his waist, as had many others. Jordon figured he would get a chance to dry up when he boarded the *Stephano* and maybe even spend the night aboard the modern ship. He was one of the first men to board her and had even gotten a cup of hot tea. He had only started to remove his wet clothing when he was ordered back up and over the side before he even got a chance to finish his tea.

He was wearing hand-knitted underwear. Sodden as it was, at first it chafed his inner thighs. Then the temperature dropped, the wool froze solid, and with every step he took it burned his skin. When the second hand called a halt for the night and ordered the sealers to group in their various watches to avoid overcrowding the pans, Jordon had stayed with his own group. He didn't know if it was his watch, nor did he give a damn. He just wanted to stop and rest. Then he started shivering and his teeth began to chatter beyond his control. The shivers always started in his upper mid-spine and sent spasms all over his body. He slapped his hands together until the tips of his fingers stung with the pain of it, and when it pained so hard he couldn't take it anymore, he stopped.

Jordon wished he hadn't left his coat behind. He had flung aside his heavy flagpole after the first two hours of walking and kept the flag. It was now wrapped around his neck like a rough scarf. The rough fabric was frozen solid, but it kept some of the biting wind and snow from his throat. His knees began twitching and shaking with the cold. He pressed his upper arms against his chest and bent his head between them, forcing his breath inside his shirt collar. It felt warm and comforting for a moment, and he decided he would lie down and curl up in the snow. His fingers were numb inside his wet cuffs. Both his hands were clenched into fists, his thumbs pulled out of the knitted thumb holes and held tightly between his fingers. Surprisingly, his uncovered ears didn't feel cold. There was no feeling in them at all.

A sudden urge to urinate came over him. He squeezed his thighs together, fighting the need, trying to hold his water back. Shaking all over, Jordon got up and turned his back to the wind as he removed his right cuff. He bent forward and fumbled with the buttons of his fly, his fingers burning with the sudden bite of the wind. Again and again he tried to force his fingers to grip the smooth buttons, but they would not answer. Jordon was shocked that his fingers were too scrammed with the cold to work. His need to pass water was becoming painful. He squirmed and twisted his legs. Finally, he pulled his left hand free of the other cuff to aid with the buttons. Bent double and shaking like a man with palsy, and with the merciless snow pelting his exposed neck, Jordon felt the first dribble of urine against his left thigh. It felt warm and soothing. Frantic, he tried to release the buttons, but it was too late. He urinated and couldn't stop. The water ran down his leg, radiating heat wherever it went. Jordon gave up trying to stem the flow and let his bladder void itself. Tears filled his eyes. He could not remember wetting his pants in his lifetime and he was embarrassed. What was happening to him?

The bouts of shivering came again, worse than before. He was so tired and so cold, he had to lie down and rest. Staggering forward, he fell to his knees. His right foot had no feeling at all and would not support his weight, nor would it move when he willed it to. It didn't even feel like a part of his body anymore. He stared all around, dumbfounded. It took a while to realize his foot was frozen. Another bout of shivering enveloped his body so violently his stomach convulsed and he vomited in great heaves. When it passed, he felt a little better. Letting himself fall gently down on the bitter snow, Thomas Jordon curled into the fetal position from which his life had begun and, thus comforted, his life blissfully ended.

Richard McCarthy of Carbonear found Jordon's body among the drifting snow at 10:00 p.m. Richard stared at the form in disbelief. Bending down, he touched Jordon to see if he was still alive. Jordon's face was icy cold and had partly drifted over with snow and there was no movement from the man at all. Snow was drifting inside the man's mouth. McCarthy wondered why he wasn't crying. Why, when he felt such a God-awful loss deep in his gut, did no tears come to his eyes? Richard knew Thomas Jordon had a brother, Stephen, who had left the *Newfoundland* with the others. McCarthy had not seen him since. He wondered if he had died, too.

McCarthy tried to close Jordon's mouth, but it was frozen solid. He hauled Jordon's cap down until it covered the man's face. McCarthy walked to a nearby pan where George Tuff was with a group of thirty or so men. Tuff was walking and stamping his feet. With every step he took he was slapping his hands together and McCarthy heard him say, "'Tis ol' man Kean's fault. 'Tis ol' man Kean's fault." With very word Tuff uttered, he slapped his hands harder. Tuff yelled to the sealers who were lying down to get on their feet, to keep moving at all cost. It was the only way they were going to survive.

Some of them did as he ordered and staggered on. Some tried and were too frozen to move. Some did not move at all. And the long night had only begun.

19

*S*TEPHEN JORDON SAT ABOARD THE *Newfoundland* drinking a cup of tea. He had gone on the ice just as eagerly as the others early that morning. He was one of the men who had seen the two sun hounds, one on either side of the rising sun. To Stephen they looked like miniature suns with a hazy yellow cast. He knew they meant bad weather was not far off, probably from the southeast. Stephen was walking with his chum, William Evans, and by 10:00 a.m. he figured they had covered five or more miles toward the *Stephano*. To Stephen the ship still looked far away. Looking back at the *Newfoundland*, he was surprised he could barely see her through the falling snow.

Maybe we should all turn back, he thought.

As if reading his mind his friend, William said, "Let's go back to our own ship, eh, Steve?"

Before Stephen could answer, he heard Tobias Cooper from Bonavista say he was going back to the *Newfoundland*. The men standing around argued about it for a few minutes. In the end, most of them went on toward the *Stephano*, but Stephen and his friend Evans turned back and headed for their own ship with Tobe Cooper in the lead. Stephen heard the men behind them calling them sissies, and one even called them cowards, but they paid no heed and walked on toward the *Newfoundland*. It took four hours to follow their own trail back to the ship. Somewhere on that long walk back, Stephen Jordon found a coat by the path. He was sure it belonged to his brother, Tom. He wondered if he should take it with him or leave it behind. If his brother returned with the others that evening, they would have to follow this same path, so Stephen left the coat on the ice and walked on.

He endured the dressing-down from Wes Kean as they approached their ship and replied, "I could see nutting ahead of us but death, sir." By now visibility was less than a few hundred feet and Cooper pointed out this fact to their irate captain, but Kean raged on. Stephen walked aboard and entered the after hold, where he stayed until that evening. He went on deck to have a look at the weather before dark. The sky was filled with biting snow and he couldn't see the bow of the *Newfoundland* when the flaws came. The blizzard the two sun hounds had promised was here.

While he stood there buffeted with wind and clutching his shirt collar around him, Stephen realized he wasn't wearing his coat. He shivered and thought about his brother's coat out there in that driving snow. While he stood there peering into the wind, the ship's whistle blew twice and then stopped. Stephen had a strong feeling that his brother needed his coat. They had two nephews who had gone toward the *Stephano* with the others, and now their faces filled his head, too. It disturbed him. Unable to bear the storm any longer, he went below and sought his bunk, where he tried to sleep but could not.

*   *   *   *   *

IT TOOK REUBEN CREWE TWO full hours to find his son. Albert was bounding ahead with the younger sealers he had made friends with while aboard the *Newfoundland*, seemingly oblivious to the danger they were all in. But as was the way of boys and men, when dark was upon them and no ship was near, they all gathered around. Their leaders talked gravely of their plight. Reuben found his son among the group. He would not let him out of his sight again. The men beat their hands and flised their arms and stamped their feet to keep warm. The snow kept coming and it started to drift with the drop in temperature. The wind stung their eyes and the snow spun around them when they hunkered down behind clumps or pinnacles. A keening sound came over the Great White Plain as the winter gale pressed down.

"Was it like this when the *Harlaw* went down, Pop?"

Albert's question was sincere and innocent. Reuben could have told his son the truth but decided against it.

"Naw, my son. The *Harlaw* was swallowed up be the ice, as ye know. Our ship is jest beyond the driftin' snow and lookin' fer us, fer sure. We'll be found before long. An' if we 'ave to make a night of it, we'll be a' right till the marnin'. A fine story we'll 'ave to tell yer mother, eh, Albert John? The two of us dis time. She'll never let us come swilin' again, I 'lows."

"Too far fer us to walk ashore, is it, Pop?"

"Walk ashore? Where to, my darlin' b'y?"

"I 'eard 'em say we was offa Bonavist' Cape. Maybe we could walk right 'ome instead of walking around in circles."

Albert stopped walking. The snow swirled around father and son while dark shapes of silent men stood all around them.

"Oh, Albert John, my b'y, we're miles from the Cape. Could be forty or more miles. Keep walkin', my son, 'twill warm yer blood."

"My feet are stingin', Pop. I went in to me knees dis marnin' an' now me feet are freezin' and stings wit' every step I take."

"The stinging is yer warm blood pumpin' against the cold, my b'y. 'Tis the numbness ye must fear. Marl on, my son."

Taking Albert's hand in his for the first time since his son was a small child, Reuben Crewe led on in a vain attempt to keep warm.

Albert didn't tell his father that his feet weren't all that were freezing. His upper body was getting colder as well. He walked beside his father for a few steps until they approached several other men who were huddled together. Feeling embarrassed with his hand in his father's, he pulled away and walked in the lun of his father's broad back. He was shivering and his hands were cold inside the mitts his mother had knitted. Then he thought about the scarf his mother had also knitted, which he had left behind in his bunk aboard the *Newfoundland*. Albert wished he had never left the warmth of his mother's kitchen.

He remembered the night before he and his father were to leave for St. John's. Both their bags were packed and would be loaded on his father's little sled in the morning. Albert John had been surprised to see his father coming from the shed with the little slide tucked under his arm. Reuben had kept it hidden, even though he had never planned to use it again. It looked like it needed a new rope—mice had chewed the old one—and now it leaned against the outside door jamb waiting for the morning journey. Albert couldn't wait to begin. He would be pulling a real ice hunter's sled!

His mother stuffed spare socks and mitts and a shift of clothing for both men into their duffle bags. His father's was a real genuine seaman's bag. In Reuben's bag she packed a small Bible and admonished him to read it when among "them heathen ice hunters." Mary began folding something else into Albert's bag when he stopped her. It was a thick red scarf that she had made especially for her son. Albert told her he wouldn't carry it with him. Wearing it would make him look like a sissy, he said. After all, everyone knew ministers and schoolteachers were the only ones who wore scarves. His father had laughed. "If you had yer way, Mary maid, Albert John would have a string running around his neck and down his sleeves fastened to his cuffs like a chil'!" Clearly disappointed, his mother had taken the scarf away.

Days later, on board the *Newfoundland*, Albert had found the scarf folded neat and tidy in the bottom of his bag. He smiled when he found it and was more pleased than ever that he had a gift to take back to his mother. He showed the scarf to no one and wore it in secret, on cold nights when the wind seemed to penetrate into the very seams of the *Newfoundland*'s thick planking.

Albert found it cold even with all of his clothes on. He hated the ship's blankets. They were tattered and lumpy and smelled of bilge and the general rank smell of the old ship. They looked as though they had never been washed. Under the pale light of the lamp, the snoring sealers' breath appeared above them. In the shadows he sneaked his mother's woollen scarf out of his bag and wrapped it around his neck. It still carried his mother's smell and brought back many comforting memories: of bread baking and a stove pinging, of a curtain softly drawn against the winter night, of a soft voice humming, and knitting needles clicking, a feeling of home. Every night after that, Albert John had drawn the scarf out of his bag and draped it around his neck.

He wished to God he was wearing it now. The top button of his coat collar was missing and snow flawed inside his neck. His right hand, which kept a tight hold on the collar, was numb and without feeling. He kept walking on behind his father.

When that ashy night had passed and the dismal day came, still swooning with snow, its first light revealed the snow-covered mounds of crumpled men. All of them were crude, nondescript figures and didn't look like men whose work was done and who should have lain straight and true in death. Among the men still walking between the mounds were Reuben Crewe and his son, Albert John. Now they were walking side by side, the one leaning on the other. In the snow that blew around them, it was difficult to tell who was leaning hardest, the father or the son.

*   *   *   *   *

CECIL MOULAND WAS SO TIRED he started looking for a place to lie down. He couldn't remember the last time he had rested. His legs ached with weariness and he was getting cold and sleepy. Snow was piling up. Even with his head turned from the biting wind, his face burned with the cold. Walking was difficult, even with the line of men breaking trail ahead of him. Someone at the head of the line had been shouting encouragement all night. It was long after midnight, he figured; Cecil didn't own a watch. They were passing a high ice formation over which the howling wind sent skeins of fine flakes. Cecil stepped out of line and lowered his body down at the base of the ice formation. He felt instant relief from most of the bitter wind. The other sealers walked past him, herded together like sheep returning to the fold. Bending into the misery of the storm, they soon disappeared in the scudding snow.

Mouland curled into a ball beneath one of the larger knolls that stood several feet above him. He was amazed to feel the ice move under him like a cradle. It was like a living thing, and though it was cold and unfeeling, its motion brought him some comfort.

The realization that thousands of feet of icy water lay beneath his moving bed startled him for a moment, but he dismissed his worries and closed his eyes. A pleasing shiver ran up his spine. It made him tremble all over, so he tucked his body tighter against the cold. He heard muffled voices from what seemed a great distance. Like a lullaby, the voices soon led him to sleep.

He was awakened by a hard blow to his ribs accompanied by an angry voice.

"What in the 'ell're ye doin' lyin' down on the job? Get to yer feet, b'y!"

Jesse Collins had kicked him without mercy. Mouland just stared up at him. Several more sealers stood around in a cluster, watching. He recognized Jacob Dalton with his stowaway friend, Offie Chalk, standing next to him. Peter Lamb was not with them.

"I'm tired, sir, an' sleepy, too," Mouland whimpered.

"Tired? Sleepy? A young man like you, after only a few miles of tramping?"

Collins kicked him again, softer this time, but his foot connected with the same tender spot. Angry now, Cecil Mouland got to his feet.

"Why are you kickin' me? I can lie down if I wants to! You are not my master watch. I don't 'ave to take orders from you!"

Collins pushed his face up close to Cecil's and leered at him.

"Mouland, is it? From Doting Cove?"

"Yes, sir, I am."

"You the one I 'eared about who is buyin' a ring fer 'is girl?"

"You've near broke me ribs!" Cecil said angrily. He was shivering badly.

"Look at you! Shiverin' like a dog shakin' a rat's neck, you are! Yer girl! What's 'er name?" Collins persisted.

"Jessie, sir. Jessie Collins!" The very sound of his sweetheart's name quieted him some.

"Jessie! Jessie, did ye say? Do you know my name, b'y?"

"Yes I do, sir! Collins, you are, from Newport."

"Aye, Collins 'tis, my boy! Don't know me first name, do 'e?"

"No I don't!"

"'Tis Jesse, my son! Jesse Collins. The same as yer girl. Ha ha!"

Collins laughed at the look on Cecil's face. Then, in a serious tone, he pointed toward two rounded mounds fifty feet away from them. They looked like spent sled dogs that had let themselves drift in.

"Look over dere, Mouland. Dem fellers laid down, too. Sleepy and tired like you, they was. I can't rouse 'em. Too far gone, dey were, when we found 'em. They will never get up again, my b'y. They're dead." Collins's voice sounded defeated.

"I t'ought 'twas banks of snow, sir! Why are they dead? 'Ow can they be dead in such a short time?" Mouland was devastated to learn that these weather-hardened ice hunters could die so easily.

Jesse Collins put his arm around Cecil's neck and said in his strong, penetrating voice, "Deat' comes easy when a man gives up the fight, Mouland. Out 'ere on a night like dis, 'tis every man fer 'imself. Master watches er no."

He looked around for emphasis. "A man down is a dead man! You eats an' drinks on yer feet! You sleeps on yer feet, and if ye falls over I'll wake ye up to start all over again."

Then in a softer voice, yet one filled with warning, he said for Cecil's ears alone, "Dotin' on a girl from Dotin' Cove, eh? And she be the name o' Jessie Collins. Ha ha! A promise I'll make to 'e." He leaned closer. "If you gives up and dies out 'ere, I'll 'ave yer woman!"

"You'll what? No man will have my Jessie but me, sir! Pledged fer marriage, we are! I'll die on me feet first!"

An indignant Cecil pulled away from Collins, who only smiled and walked away again, shouting to the others to follow.

"Two Jesses and two of 'em Collins on the one mattress, by God! One of 'em pretty as a picture an' t'other an ugly bugger!"

Collins laughed and sang a ditty.

> *"I wish me jammies was close to yer nightie,*
> *Not in the bed but on the line,*
> *No one's dere but yours an' mine."*

His voice faded away, laughing as he marched in the gusting snow. The others followed him, but none of them as briskly as the young suitor from Doting Cove. Cecil Mouland would not lie down again.

20

THE PERSON ABOUT WHOM SUCH talk brought the young Cecil Mouland to his feet, and his senses, was unaware of these happenings. The young woman, Jessie Collins, was sleeping comfortably in her own clean and warm bed in Doting Cove.

She awakened suddenly without any apparent reason and sat up in her bed. On the dresser beside her sat a lamp she had placed there herself. She had turned its wick down hours ago after reading her Bible. The oil lamp guttered with its need for fuel and gave off a dull, yellowish light in the small room. Her dashing new beau, Cecil Mouland, was on her mind, and images of him angrily chasing after hundreds of laughing men came to her. It was these images that had awakened her. The thought made her a bit uneasy. Unable to sleep, she threw back the heavy quilts, turned up the lamp until its light flooded the room, and stepped to the lone window overlooking a frightful storm.

The wind whistled around the eaves of the house just a few feet above her window. Pulling back the lace curtain, she peered out but could see nothing save for veils of snow rushing past. The gale had worsened since she went to bed, and she wondered if her young ice hunter was safe. There was no heat anywhere in the house. She had let out the lone kitchen stove and dampened it with water before bedtime. Now she settled back under the blankets and picked up her Bible. She read from the book every night before she slept. She seldom selected any particular passage, and now her eyes fell to these words:

> Yea, though I walk through the valley of the shadow of death, I will fear no evil: for Thou art with me; Thy rod and Thy staff comfort me.

Jessie Collins had read these same lines of scripture many times before, but never had it given her such peace of mind. It would forever be her favourite Bible verse. She turned the lamp down again, settled under the warm blankets, and went back to sleep. The lamp, starving for oil, gave a few fast sputtering sounds and died. By now the first pallid light of day had come. Magnified as it passed through the frosted windowpane, it fell gently upon the face of the peacefully sleeping young woman.

*　*　*　*　*

THE NEW DAY BROUGHT ANOTHER round of misery to the Great White Plain. The temperature had dropped severely and the wind blew harder than ever out of the northwest. It roared and moaned and burned exposed flesh. Its icy breath freeze-dried the snow and dashed around the frozen sealers. Blowing snow was everywhere, bearing steadily on them in a never-ending assault. It clung around their legs and bit into their faces and their eyes, robbing them of sight. It came at them from all directions as the ice underfoot rose and fell in great rolling waves.

Beards and moustaches were now frozen, crystallized white; tiny ice candles hung from their eyelids. The sealers beat at the ice on their skin with fingers too numb to grip, and sometimes their mates broke away the ice for them. They were hungry and bone weary. These were the lucky ones, for scattered all around them were the bodies of the dead.

Of the sealers who had left the *Stephano* less than sixteen hours before, twenty of them were already dead. Dozens more were down on the ice and, though still alive, were so filled with despair at the thought of being left to die they would not get up. Others were so far gone they could not get up even if they wanted. Hypothermia would soon kill them. As morning wore on toward brilliant day, the wind increased, the temperature dropped even further, patches of blue sky appeared above the blowing snow, and the deaths of good men continued. The reason they were on the ice in the first place was forgotten in the struggle for life.

Someone spotted two adult seals and one whitecoat nearby. With a yell, a couple of men who still had their gaffs went after them. Their usual zeal for the hunt was replaced with the primordial need to hunt for survival. They were tired, but they killed all three seals in quick order and knifed open their warm flesh. One of the seals had died with its cleft tongue hanging out of its oval mouth. The man who had killed it said he loved seal tongue fried in pork fat.

The sealers took turns dipping their frozen hands into the animals' hot blood. They wrapped their hands around the steaming carcasses and held them there for a while, letting the blood sting their fingertips when the feeling returned. They opened up the bellies of the dead animals and pushed their hands inside to hold their entrails and viscera. When they hauled their mitts over their bloodstained hands, the liquid stuck to the wool like glue.

They removed the hearts and livers from the seals along with strips of black meat and the tenderloins that ran along the animals' spines. Laying them on the ice, they allowed the meat to drip and stiffen before cutting off pieces and eating them raw. One sealer was chewing into the half-frozen meat and had started to swallow it when his taste buds rebelled against the gluey, fishy taste, forcing him to vomit.

Another of the sealers who was bending over one of the seals lowered his head to drink some of its warm blood. He staggered to his feet with blood dripping from his jaws like a dog that had just torn open a lamb. His stomach heaved and urged as if he would throw up, but he kept the blood down and walked away.

The low drift coming over the plain soon robbed the dead seals of their warmth. The snow melted on contact with the blood, which quickly coagulated into gelatin, and the sealers struggled away. They now walked without direction or purpose, like drunken men returning from a late party. They walked to keep warm, to stay alive. The day passed, slow and hard. A ship's whistle, no matter how far off, would have lifted their spirits. The crack of a gunshot or a single shout from their fellow swilers would buoy them and could mean the difference between life and death, but there was nothing, only the terrible moan of the wind.

With their heads together, they talked in low tones about removing the clothing from the dead to save the living. Most of them agreed; it was the practical thing to do. They walked toward a pan where the dead bodies of several of their companions were laid.

"After all," said one, as if justifying what they were about to do, "if he was alive, he would give me his coat."

He worked at the fastenings of his dead friend's coat. One fellow approached another of the downed sealers who was nunnied into a ball and drifted in with snow. He placed his hand on the man's shoulder and was about to unbutton his coat collar when the sealer moaned. The startled robber jumped back in surprise.

Then, through the curtain of snow, a ship's topmasts and rigging, stark against the late evening sky, beckoned them to safety. It was two miles away, but the ship was headed toward them. The strong shouted words of encouragement to the weak. From scattered pans, the different watches started for the ship. Their ordeal was over. They were saved!

* * * * *

ON BOARD THE SS *BELLAVENTURE*, the second hand, Abraham Parsons, was busy guiding the ship through the ice, picking up seal pelts and men as they went. The wind was bitter cold from the northwest with heavy ground drifting. Parsons was from Bay Roberts and had spent twenty-seven years at the seal hunt, a few of them on the *Newfoundland*. Through hard work and dedication he had worked his way up through the ranks from sealer to second hand. He loved his job, especially when he was on the bridge and directing the work of loading seal pelts. Looking out the bridge window at the work in progress, Parsons heard the clinking sound of the forward winch hauling a large tow of pelts up over the starboard side of the *Bellaventure*. He could see over the drift from his vantage point; sometimes the heavy wind flaws obscured his men completely. Other times the snowdrift cut them off at the waist until their upper bodies seemed to float on a swirling white cloud. Parsons watched the sealers jump around flising their arms and holding their hands over their ears to ward off the biting cold wind.

The pelts swung on the rope strap hanging from the heavy steel cable. The winch stopped as it cleared the gunnels, the strap was let go, and fifty or more sealskins slid onto the greasy deck, the smaller whitecoats as bloodied as the larger adults. The men on the ice clambered up over the side sticks and Parsons ordered the big ship slow ahead, toward the next pan with seals marked with the *Bellaventure*'s flag.

Away in the distance, directly over his bow, he thought he saw a few men. They were moving slowly, as if they were killing seals. Probably men from the *Newfoundland*, Parsons thought, which he could see beyond them. The *Bellaventure* came to the next bunch of her own sealers and Parsons ordered the ship stopped. They loaded the pelts, three strings of them this time, and the sealers climbed aboard. Parsons ordered hard a-starboard and the ship lumbered away.

Framed in the eastern sky of the after window on her bridge, where no one was watching, a dead man's coat was raised on a pole.

*   *   *   *   *

SIDNEY JONES WATCHED AS ARTHUR and Elias Mouland left to walk toward the *Bellaventure*. Jones heard Arthur yell to his men to stay where they were on the pan and he would send help back as soon as he reached the ship. Jones, master watch from Newtown, had stood on a pan earlier in the day and had watched helplessly as three of his friends dropped. He had never seen men die like that before. They had wandered from one quarter to the other, shivering and moaning with the burning pain of frostbite as they went. One of them stumbled after the others and fell into the water, encasing his boots with ice. The laces were swollen to three times their size and frozen stiff.

Warning the three men did nothing to sway them wandering dangerously close to open swatches of water. They were dead on their feet. One after the other, the trio fell and no amount of yelling or poking could rouse them. Jones had stood over them, incredulous. Tears filled the man's eyes as he spoke their names over and over. Unable to stay where they had fallen, Jones walked away to another pan and others joined him, leaving the three corpses of their downed comrades as they had died—together.

Now as the day was ending, Jones was on a different ice pan with another man who was dying. Henry Dowding was from Templeman and the two were good friends. They had both eagerly shipped aboard the *Newfoundland* and had stayed together throughout the ordeal. Jones called Henry "Harry," and Harry called Sidney "Sid." Sid knew Harry was going to die. The man was shivering so violently he couldn't speak. He flised his arms feebly, going through the motions of it with little effect.

"Cheer up, Harry b'y. The b'ys are 'eaded fer the *Bell*. 'Twon't be long now an' you'll be aboard o' 'er wit' a cuppa 'ot tea in yer 'ands."

Harry brightened as Jones delivered the good news. Supported by Sid, he walked in the direction of the *Bellaventure*.

"Oh praise the Lard, Sid b'y, I'm all but done. I 'lowed I wudn't goin' to make it," Harry said weakly. His teeth were chattering so badly, Jones could barely understand him.

Suddenly, Jones stopped. He watched in disbelief as the *Bellaventure* turned her stern to them and sailed away, leaving her dirty spoor smeared across the evening sky. He watched as tiny groups of men who were headed toward her stopped walking. He saw a raised gaff, with a garment of clothing at its point, fall down. Even from a distance, Jones could feel the despair of the men who had tried so hard. Then he saw the figures turn and walk in the opposite direction, carrying the gaff with them.

Jones turned his gaze in the direction they were headed. They were walking toward their own ship, the *Newfoundland*! She was much farther away than the *Bellaventure*, but she appeared to be coming their way.

Then, to his horror, the *Newfoundland* turned her bow and sailed away from them.

Jones told Harry they had failed to reach either of the two ships. Harry folded into a crump on the ice, in utter despair, and Jones was sorry he had told him. No amount of coaxing could get him on his feet again. Jones cradled his friend in his arms. He cursed at him to get up. He pleaded with him. He cried over him. But five minutes after the second ship had abandoned them, Henry Dowding died. Sidney Jones, who had just seen his best friend die, walked away sobbing.

*   *   *   *   *

GEORGE TUFF HAD ORDERED JONES to stay with the dying men and left for the *Bellaventure* with Jesse Collins, who Tuff considered to be the smartest man on their pan.

"Cheer up, men," he said. "We'll soon be aboard the *Bonaventure*." Tuff had mistaken the distant *Bellaventure* for the *Bonaventure*. "They've seen us fer sure! We're goin' to be all right!"

He assured Jones he would send help back to the dying men as soon as possible. Collins was carrying the gaff tied with a jacket taken from a dead sealer. Tuff and Collins crossed another pan where every man on it, twelve or more, was dead. Their fellow sealers had dragged them together, and the snowdrift had entombed them in a mass grave.

Approaching another group, still alive but suffering badly, Tuff and Collins told them to hang on and asked them to hoist the crude flag. Shortly, five of them stood on the highest rafter of ice they could find and held the flag high, waving it back and forth. From their vantage point it looked as though Cecil Mouland and the four men with him were almost aboard the *Bellaventure*. They yelled with excitement beneath the makeshift flag. Then, to their dismay, they saw Mouland and his men turn as the *Bellaventure* sailed away from them.

Tuff spotted the *Stephano* and thought Abe Kean was searching for them. She was miles away and seemed to be looking for open water that would bring the ship to them. The sealers' spirits lifted again, until the *Stephano* too turned and steamed away.

Then their own ship, the *Newfoundland*, was spotted a little more than two miles away. She appeared to be coming for them despite the fact she was jammed in the ice. Determined, George Tuff and a few others headed her way. They figured that even though the ship was stuck in the ice, they could get close enough to make themselves heard before the deep night came. They stopped walking. In stunned amazement, they watched as the *Newfoundland* turned away to the northwest, hull down among the tumbled ice.

Defeated, the sealers dropped the flag on the ice. They would never be found. No one was looking. No one gave a damn. They were all going to die within sight of their would-be rescuers, the men who had put them here. Even the indomitable George Tuff's spirit was broken.

"Well b'ys, 'twould seem it only remains fer us to fix away a place to die and wait fer our end."

He leaned his tired back against the rough ice and slid down. The snow curled around his feet and legs as he buried his face in his trembling hands.

Their second night without shelter was upon them. The wind had lessened but it still cut like a knife. The sealers with Tuff cut bavins of wood from their gaffs and tried to get a fire going, but their fingers were shaking so badly they lost their last wet match without making one spark.

Between the scudding flaws, the lights of ships on the horizon taunted them. The clouds were scattered and the full moon stood out like a pearl in the starry, wintry sky. The glittering firmament peered down in silence, and now the stalk of death on the Great White Plain had changed. For two days and a night it had preyed on the weak, but now it turned toward the strong, intent on weakening and harrying them and taking every last man.

21

*T*HE SECOND NIGHT, WEDNESDAY, APRIL 1, was even more unforgiving than the first. The sealers' resources were dwindling. Many of those sealers who had fought so valiantly would lose the battle, but they would not die easily.

With the night came a low snowdrift, which at times the men could see over when they had the strength to stand. The wintry clouds scudded away, taking into the heavens what little heat remained, and the cold deepened. All of the ice hunters were hungry, exhausted, and freezing. Many of them couldn't bring themselves to believe there was any hope of survival. Combined with hypothermia, the loss of will to live created a state of body and mind that could only end in death.

Hypothermia occurs when the body's core temperature drops below the temperature needed to sustain normal metabolism. Shivering begins as the nervous system becomes agitated, warning of danger. Mental confusion sets in. Muscles won't do as they are asked. The surface blood vessels contract as the brain directs blood to the vital organs deep in the chest cavity. Extremities such as the fingers, toes, ears, and nose turn pale with the sudden removal of blood. When the warm blood leaves, the cold rushes in, and they turn blue and puffy. Speaking is a challenge. Walking becomes a wandering, irrational, stumbling exercise in futility. The organs fail. The bladder muscles will not hold water. The mind is sluggish, incoherent, and sees things that aren't really there. In a mindless paradox, the victim may remove his clothes, thus hastening his death. Burrowing into the puniest of shelters, they sometimes seek warmth but find colder temperatures.

Twenty or more sealers had gathered on one pan. Some cowered for shelter on the ice while others walked. Jacob Dalton was one of the latter, and stumbling weakly next to him was Theophilus Chalk. Around them, between the pans, were a few swatches of water, some big enough for a man to fall through. Others were hundreds of feet across, black and dangerous, promising a quick end. Starshine glittered on the surfaces of these, what the people of the Arctic regions called polynyas. They are mysterious bodies of water that never freeze despite their frigid environs.

Talking became confused stammering, brought on by hypothermia. Those standing around looked like black-robed priests sequestered in a nave, praying for penance. Those bent over looked like parents weeping over an empty cradle.

A loud voice came across the pan from Chalk and the others. Jesse Collins was still trying to rally them. Collins had more of a mothering instinct than he had for leadership. The sealers heeded him. He was answered with shouts from those who would not give up. They appeared like tired soldiers marching home after a lost battle.

Jacob Dalton managed to ward off cold more easily than most men. He always seemed to be warm and seldom wore mitts on his big hands. He had a quick stride, unusual for a fisherman who spent a lot of time on a rolling deck, and he was seldom idle when on his feet. But Jacob was cold now. He had stayed on his feet since they left the *Stephano*. Despite that first night, and the next day fraught with disappointment, he had kept moving. His arms were idle only when he was forced to cover his ears with his hands. He alternated from ear to ear in a constant effort to keep them warm. Now several of his fingers wouldn't function as they should. His wet coat sleeves had shrunk with the frost and his right wrist was blue and swollen. Two toes and the heel on one foot were numb. His eyes were watering and he feared he was becoming snow-blind.

Theophilus Chalk was in a bad way. He was staggering around without any knowledge of where he was, and without Jacob's help he would wander away from the group. He was talking through chattering teeth and kept staring at the ships' lights in the distance with a strange expression on his face, which had taken on an alarming blue cast.

"'Ow come we don't go in outta the cold, Jake?" he stammered.

"What do you mean, Offie? Go in where?" Jake asked, flinging his arms around his body.

Offie stared off toward the twinkling lights again. "Why, dere in the 'ouses, Jake b'y! I can see the lamplight from the upstairs windows. Don't s'pose dey're all gone to bed an' left us, do ya? I needs to dry me mitts, Jake b'y. Me 'ands are perishin' cold."

With that, Offie started to remove his wool mitts. Before Jacob could answer his confused friend, a shout rang out.

"Help, b'ys, help! Someone's gone in the swatch! Come on, fer God's sake, I can't hold 'im much longer!"

Jake ran off toward the noise, leaving Offie to stare eerily at the mirage of house lights. It took Jake a few minutes to find the caller in the dark and the blowing snow. Others had arrived by the time he got there. One of the sealers was holding onto one hand of a man who was in the water at the edge of a pan. The sealer in the water was groaning pitifully and shaking so badly he could not offer any assistance with his own rescue. Jacob Dalton knelt down and grabbed the man's other hand. Men pitched in and clutched the man's clothing, and with everyone hauling, he emerged from the water and onto the ice like a large seal.

His clothing quickly froze solid. He had lost his hat in the water and now his head was bare. The man became encased in ice from head to toe. His face was covered with slush and he couldn't get his eyes open. There was nothing the sealers could do. They had no fire, no heat of any kind. There was no warm clothing to replace his wet outfit and no warm food or drink to ease the man's final moments. One man knelt beside him and started to brush the ice from his face. In total misery but seemingly without effort, the doomed man began crawling like a child toward a cavity at the base of a knob of ice. Someone tried to stop him, but another laid a hand on his arm and said, "Leave him bide. 'Tis fer the best." He squeezed himself head first into the icy valley until he was visible only from the waist down. He tried to draw his legs up to his chest, when suddenly he grew still. Snow drifted all around him, covering what could be seen of him below the frozen white headstone.

"I seen 'im comin' across the pan," the man who had called for help explained to Dalton and the others. "He was 'eaded fer the swatch an' I bawled fer 'im to stop. 'Twas no use. He was like a crazy man! I couldn't go near 'im. He 'ad his sculping knife in his 'and, skearin' it around as if he were stabbin' at somet'in', and yellin' he was. 'I'll stab the bugger, I will,' he was sayin'. 'Twas the damnedest t'ing I ever seen, b'ys! I knowed him all me life. A real gentleman, he was. Wouldn't kick a crackie bitin' at his feet, he wouldn't." The sealer shook his head as if he couldn't believe what he had seen. "Walked right out into the black swatch as if 'twas not even there, he did, still lungin' with that knife. I ran to the edge after 'im. He went right under and came back up real quick, like. The knife was gone from his hand. I grabbed him and sung out fer you fellers. Why would he do sech a t'ing? And who do ya t'ink he wanted to stab?"

"Ol' man Kean, I'd say," one man said without hesitation.

"Yes, by God," said another.

Jacob remembered the strange way Offie was acting when he left him. He ran back the way he had come and fumbled in the dark, wondering why his step was so slow. Despite the need for haste, he couldn't get his muscles to work faster. It took him a while to reach the pan where he had left his friend, but Offie wasn't there.

Jacob thought he had taken a wrong turn somewhere and he was on the wrong pan. But then, staring up at him from the snow was a pair of woollen mitts. They looked as if they had been laid down with care. Beside them was a woollen hat. They were both Offie's. Jake shouted, "Offieee! Offieee!" again and again. He ran, calling as he went, heading toward the lights of the ships. He stumbled across a pan where more men were grouped together trying to keep alive. He inquired about his friend. No one had seen anything. Jacob was sure Offie had left to walk home. He wondered if he would make it.

* * * * *

JACOB DALTON HAD NO WAY of knowing it, but the lights of Little Catalina, which Theophilus Chalk had imagined in his hypothermic state, bore west-northwest of them by just forty nautical miles. The gale of northwest wind from yesterday had pushed the ice steadily south. The men from the Bonavista Cape area were dying abeam of their homes.

A few miles north of Little Catalina, in the community of Elliston, moonlight glinted on the frost-covered window upstairs in one such home. The frosty window was partially draped with a pretty white curtain Mary Crewe had made herself. A beam of light fell diagonally across the clean wooden floor, the bed, and the woman's face. She was awakened not by the pleasant light on her face but by the feeling of someone touching her gently through the blanket's fold. The touch didn't frighten Mary, as she later said. She knew what she would see when she sat up. Strangely, she had somehow expected it.

Kneeling at the foot of her bed were her husband and her son. Reuben was in shadow to the left of the boy and had his arm around his boy. Albert John was leaning across his father's chest and was staring longingly at his mother with the moonlight full on his face. Though she didn't hear anything, Mary knew her husband was praying. Her boy's hands, covered with the new cuffs she had knitted, were clasped together under his chin, as if he too were praying. Her husband's rugged face looked drawn and haggard and filled with regret. Her son's face was a steely white, his cheeks looked puffy, and he was shivering all over. Mary Crewe neither swooned nor cried out, though she knew she was looking at the dying moments of her lifelong mate and her young son. The vision was so clear that Mary recognized her own unique double stitching in the clothes they were wearing. Instinctively, Mary reached toward her son.

Her fingers were within a few inches of the boy when he and his father faded away on the moonbeam coming through the window. With a pitiful cry, Mary hurried to the window, threw the curtains aside, and stared out. The distraught woman fell to her knees and leaned her arms on the sill. Pressing both hands against the frosted pane, she wept. At first she saw nothing out the window, just the scudding clouds shadowing the bright moon. But as her hands melted the frost, she saw the harbour below filled with Arctic ice. Across it, the moon path led her gaze seaward. The ice glittered and sparkled in places like diamonds, but in others Mary saw scattered black forms. They could have been moon shadows or the forms of men. She felt the cold seeping through, but she held her hands there until she couldn't bear it any longer. Drawing them away, she clasped them together for warmth and to begin the age-old supplication of women who pray to the Almighty for their men upon the sea.

Mary stayed there on the cold floor as the frost stole across the pane again, clouding her view. She stayed there in the same position, sobbing and shivering and welcoming the cold, until her joints weakened and she slumped to the floor. She remained there, beneath the window, until the night turned to day.

* * * * *

FORTY-TWO NAUTICAL MILES TO THE southeast from Elliston and from the window where Mary Crewe was kneeling, her husband, Reuben Crewe, and their son, Albert John, were also on their knees. The same moonlit night revealed a scene identical to that which showed itself to Mary in her tiny bedroom. Albert John Crewe was dying, cradled in his father's arms. Reuben was strong enough to carry on alone, but he would not. He would rather die with his son.

Reuben Crewe could not believe what was happening. He knew when the *Stephano* had turned away from them that they were in serious trouble. The reason why he had returned to the seal hunt was to look after the boy, and he had secretly thought it would not be necessary. His ordeal when the *Harlaw* had gone under the ice paled in comparison to the challenge that lay ahead of him. Reuben doubted if he was up to it, but with the life of his young son hanging in the balance, he would not die without a fight.

Albert John had shrugged away his father's concerns for several hours, but when the first night deepened and the blizzard rose to a terrific gale, the boy stayed near his father's side. All through that terrible night he walked by his father's side, sometimes behind him, and Reuben shielded him from the worst. Sometime during that night they had seen a man fall down and not rise again. It was the first time Albert had seen anyone die. In the full light of the next day, he saw many more die. Now it was night again, and still no one came to rescue them.

Albert ate the cakes of hard bread he carried in his pocket and several more from his father, who told the boy he wasn't hungry. He washed the bread down with snow, which he found took longer and longer to melt in his mouth. As the second night wore on, Albert wished he had worn the scarf his mother had hidden inside his bag. He would not feel embarrassed to wear it now.

The night lost some of its clouds, and when the moon shone

down on the field of death, Albert Crewe's frostbitten feet gave out under him. He stumbled and fell face down on the ice. His father went to his side.

"Get up, Albert John! You must get up, my son! You cannot lie down! 'Twill be the end of ye!"

"I—I can't get up, Pop! Me feet ent got no feelin' in 'em! They doubled up under me. I'm awful cold, too, Pop. An' sleepy. I'll rest me eyes fer a bit." The boy's voice was low and incoherent. His father had to bend close to him to understand what his son was saying.

"You cannot! You must not sleep, Albert John." The moonlight showed how badly his son's condition had deteriorated. His face was blue and puffy with frostbite. He was shaking like a lone autumn leaf in a gale of wind and his teeth were chattering.

"Oh my God! No! Not my boy, Lord! Take me, Lord, an' keep my boy safe!" the anguished father cried.

He went to his knees and pulled his dying son hard against his chest. Albert mumbled something Reuben could not understand, but he managed to get the boy on his knees beside him. He wrapped one arm around his son's shoulders and pulled Albert's head under the shelter of his coat. Albert tucked his folded hands under his chin. Reuben removed one of his mitts and placed his hand on the boy's face. It was icy cold. Shivers came over the boy in spasms, and when they did they were so severe they shook both father and son. Albert's chin quivered and he burst into tears. Reuben Crewe was crying, too, as he rocked his son back and forth.

A group of men discovered them. Among them was Jacob Dalton, who began flising his arms back and forth.

"Why are ye lying down, Uncle Reub? Yer always tellin' us to keep movin'."

"'Tis Albert John, Jake b'y. He can't walk, you see. An' his face is awful cold." Reuben looked up at the men standing around him. "I'll warm 'im, though, b'ys, and then we'll come along wit' you fellers again."

"No, Uncle Reub, you can't stay dere in the cold. You'll freeze solid," one of the sealers said. He reached down to help pull the old man to his feet, but Reuben pulled away from him.

"'Ow can I stand to me feet wit'out my boy?" he asked. "I'll keep 'im warm wit' his head tucked under me arm. He'll be all right. I promised his mother I would look out fer him, you see. 'Tis why I come back. An' by God, I will. 'Ow can I walk into my Mary's warm kitchen wit'out Albert John? What will I say to her when she asks me where the boy is? No, b'ys, I'll bide yere and keep me promise to my Mary."

Tears came to the sealers' eyes. They knew they could offer no help to the Crewes.

"By God, wouldn't I like to have ol' man Kean in reach of my 'ands right now," said Dalton, angrily clenching his big hands into fists.

The ice hunters walked away from father and son. One of them looked back and noticed that the breath from only one of the figures was rising into the sky.

Reuben Crewe watched his fellow sealers walk away. Jacob Dalton was singing again, but none of the others had joined him. Reuben's knees were cramped and freezing cold from kneeling on the ice. He wanted to remove his hand from his son's frozen face long enough to put his mitt back on, but the boy looked so peaceful he kept it there. He suddenly noticed that Albert John wasn't shivering anymore.

"Sleep well, my son," he said quietly, "while I keeps watch."

* * * * *

PHILLIP HOLLOWAY, THE TRAPPER, WAS faring well. So far he had come through the ordeal without serious incident. He had helped Jesse Collins keep the others going and had walked to keep warm without stopping. He was used to walking. His trapline was a long one over rough terrain. He was hungry now and dropping for sleep, but he marched along with the others, nodding and dozing on his feet as he went. He would have liked to have another orange. His brother, Josh, had taken two of them from the *Stephano* and had given him one last night. The two brothers had eaten them quickly before they could freeze solid in their pockets. Oranges were a rare treat, and Phil discovered he loved them. He slowed down and stopped walking. He had to get some sleep. Just a few minutes would do him.

"Not t'inkin' of lying down, are ye, Phil?" bawled his friend Jesse Collins, who had come up behind him. Joshua and a few others from the Bonavista North area were with him.

"Naw, Jess b'y, just feeling a bit groggy is all."

"Fred Collins has died, Phil b'y," Josh said sadly.

"We're still on our feet, though, by God," said Collins, not allowing the death of their friend to sink in. "Come on, b'ys, we've a boat to haul up on the other side of the 'arbour an' the tide is leaving."

He pointed to a big swatch of moonlit water nearby, and with that the unstoppable Jesse Collins got the men swinging their arms and running around the imaginary harbour. Phil was revived by Jesse's enthusiasm. Brushing aside the need for rest, he followed behind them. It took them nearly twenty minutes to navigate around the pan and return to the swatch of water.

Phil was jogging along behind for the second time and was swinging his arms wildly when he felt the first taste of hot liquid in his throat. He knew immediately what it was: blood. He tried to ignore it and swallow it, pretending it was saliva. But it was no use. He stopped in the trail as hot blood bubbled out of his nose and erupted from his throat in a burst of red that covered the snow at his feet. It was the worst nosebleed he had ever experienced. It kept coming and he was afraid. He tried to call out to the men who had gone ahead of him, but his voice came out in a guttural, liquid sound that went nowhere. The tough trapper who had survived the cold was bleeding to death. He staggered on his feet near the dangerous black water. His balance was leaving him, but he had to stay on his feet. To lie down meant death. He used his hand to try and stop the blood from his nose, but there was just as much blood coming up out of his throat. His clothes were soaked with it and it blackened the snow around him. He staggered backwards and was surprised when he heard a splash of water.

When the sealers made their round again, they saw a string of blood leading from the path to the water and couldn't make sense of it. They called and called for their friend without success. But Joshua Holloway kept staring at the bloodied snow and knew what it meant.

22

CECIL MOULAND WAS HUNGRY. HE fished inside his jacket pocket for another cake of the hard bread he had taken from the *Stephano*. The sea biscuits were like granite and he was tired of chewing them. They required teeth of iron to crack—he often broke the cakes open on his knee—but he had none left. His pocket was empty of bread, but his hand brought up a bag of chewing tobacco. He had completely forgotten about it. Holding the cloth bag tied with a string, the memory of the man who had given it to him filled his eyes with tears.

His grandfather had gone to the ice for years and had endured many a time of bitter cold. He had told him he must keep his jaws moving above all else. Cecil's grandfather was convinced that if he did this simple thing, his brain would never freeze. There was only one way to keep your jaws moving, he maintained, and that was to chew tobacco. Cecil had never chewed tobacco in his life. He had tried smoking it once or twice but had gotten into such a fit of coughing he had given up on it. There was another reason why he was against tobacco. His girlfriend, Jessie Collins, was a member of the Salvation Army and he had become a convert, also. The Army considered the use of tobacco to be sinful. When he became a "soldier" of that army, he had taken a sworn oath not to use it. Cecil had asked his grandfather if food would serve just as well to keep his jaws moving.

"Ah, me darlin' b'y," he had said. "What 'appens to yer grub after you chews it fer a spell?"

"Why, you swallows it!" said Cecil.

"Swallies it indeed, my b'y! Nah, my son. Baccy's the answer! Baccy and flisin'. 'Tis the proper t'ing to keep a man's head straight and his bosom warm."

Now Cecil's grandfather's advice resounded in his ears and he loosed the string on his "baccy bag." He placed the plug of tobacco in the corner of his jaw and gnawed off a piece. At first it didn't taste too bad—a bit strong with a faintly sweet and spicy taste. Then, as his saliva warmed it and his teeth ground it to a pulp, it burned his tongue like hell! He wanted to spit the revolting substance out of his mouth, but he suddenly realized his jaws were warm for the first time in two days. He kept on chewing.

He was on a pan with many other sealers, most of them still on their feet. Cecil fell in step with them again. Rolling his first wad of tobacco to the side of his jaw, he began singing a church hymn. He reasoned that as the tobacco was sinful, the singing of hymns might make it less so. He was surprised when many of the others joined in. Jacob Dalton's voice was loudest of all. From other pans came the sound of men singing, too. The songs rose and faded as they stumbled on, their voices buoying their steps as they went.

> "Let the lower lights be burning, send a gleam
> across the wave / Some poor fainting struggling
> seaman, You may rescue You may save."

Many of them stared at the lights they had no hope of reaching and wept openly. They sang "For Those in Peril on the Sea" and "Throw Out the Lifeline." All the hymns they sang represented the sea in a figurative sense, but some of them who raised their voices in song would not live to see another day on the cold Atlantic Ocean.

*   *   *   *   *

HEDLEY PAYNE OF GREENSPOND WAS seventeen years old and at the seal hunt for the first time. He followed his master watch, Arthur Mouland, without question or complaint. He started with six cakes of hard bread in his pockets and chewed them slowly, making them last. He didn't think about dying at all until his best friend dropped. Job Easton was walking beside Payne when he just fell over, curled up on the ice, and died. The sealers had to drag young Hedley Payne away from Job's corpse.

Joseph Randell was from Bonavista. He was thirty-five years old and had been to the ice for two years previous. Randell ate nine cakes of hard bread and sucked pieces of ice only when he had to get the pulpy bread down his throat. He held his urine until his bladder caused him pain and then forced himself to dribble it like a dog, holding his precious body heat inside as long as he could. He wore heavy, store-bought underwear lined with fleece. The sleeves of his rough canvas jacket chafed his wrists and left them frostbitten. He was on a pan where ten men had died, and when the eleventh fell down at his feet, Joseph could take it no more and walked away to join the living.

John J. Howlett from Goulds was one of the men with William Pear when he died on the first night out. John couldn't believe a man could die so easily, and it frightened him. Dog tired and cold, he wouldn't allow his body to stop for rest. The fear of death kept him alive.

Thomas Ryan was from Turks Cove, Trinity Bay. Though he was thirty-two years old and unmarried, this was his first year at the ice. He shipped aboard the *Newfoundland* as bo'sun's mate and was considered one of the ship's officers. Before leaving the *Newfoundland* early Tuesday morning, Thomas dined on a nourishing hash of meat, potatoes, and turnip served with bread, hot butter, and tea. Aboard the *Stephano* he was given more bread and butter and tea. He was in prime physical condition. He saw the first man in his company die just before dawn on Wednesday morning. The long night came again, and when it was over, in the full light of day, Ryan counted twenty-six dead men scattered around the pan. Many of them were friends and it sickened him so much he vomited in grief.

This was nineteen-year-old Cecil Tiller's third year at the hunt. He was from Newtown and knew George Tuff well. Tiller was a tough but easygoing fellow who took orders without question and feared nothing. He was sure they would be spending the night aboard the modern *Stephano*. He was looking forward to it. When Abe Kean ordered them back on the ice and the big ship disappeared in the mist of snow, Cecil was more disappointed than anything else. He stared in disbelief as hard men died. It wasn't until he heard Jesse Collins say in his usual offhand, casual way, "The *Greenland* disaster won't 'ave a peck on dis one," that Tiller thought he could actually perish. Even with several frostbitten toes, he refused to give up.

Wesley Collins was also from Newtown. He was nineteen years old, not married, and had no intention of ever getting married. He was a sombre, deep-thinking sort, and though he appeared distant, he was very friendly. He had an angular face which he always kept clean-shaven. Now it sported a grizzly beard and he didn't like it, but a two-day beard was the least of Collins's worries. He had fallen between the pans twice. His left leg was freezing and two of his toes were burning like fire. His right leg had no feeling at all. He kept walking with the others for as long as he could before the frost moved up his foot into his leg. It gave out and he went down, but he didn't stop moving. For twenty-four hours he kept flising his arms and twisting his body as vigorously as he would have if he were standing. He would never give up.

Theophilus Chalk and Jacob Dalton were not the only

sealers who hailed from Little Catalina. The little fishing village on the north side of Trinity Bay had a long history of sealing. George Carpenter, age thirty-five, had shipped aboard the SS *Newfoundland*, as had Abel Tippett, fifty-six years, William J. Tippett, thirty-one, Norman Tippett, twenty-seven, and Edward Tippett (no relation to the other Tippetts), who was twenty-four years old.

Late Wednesday night, the sealers from Little Catalina were gathered on the same ice pan with fifteen others. All of them were suffering from severe fatigue, frostbite, and hunger. Some were also suffering from despair and were heard to say many times, "We're lef' to die, b'ys! Dere's no more'n that to it." On this coldest of nights, after having gone so long without rescue, many more walked under the same cloud of despair.

* * * * *

IT MATTERED LITTLE NOW WHOSE watch they were under, for though the master watches struggled to save their charges, in reality every man was under his own watch. Anyone who could stand was on his feet and moving. They had carved shelters out of the larger ice formations that gave them some relief from the bitter wind, but they didn't stay there for long. They kept stamping their feet and slapping their hands and arms, anything to keep the cold out of their blood. To lie down on the ice for more than a few minutes meant death.

Jacob Dalton told the men about Offie's strange behaviour and the boy's disappearance. By now they had all witnessed death close at hand, but the death of one so young and from their small community troubled them greatly. Theophilus Chalk was the first sealer among the group from Little Catalina to die. He would not be the last.

Of the four Tippetts, the youngest, Edward, was in the best shape. George Carpenter and William Tippett were good friends and stuck together. For the most part the fleet-footed ice hunters had been hobbled, reduced to a shuffling walk. Low murmurs of talk came from the men. During the pauses between the walk-arounds they stared at the lights of the ships burned down against the winter night.

They talked about the skippers who had put them on the ice—they cursed them; they damned them—and of home and wives and especially their children. Then Norman Tippett fell to his knees as though he had been shot. It was so unexpected he dragged Abel down with him, who had been helping him stay on his feet. Abel was Norman's uncle and considered the young man more as a son than a nephew. Norman was one of the sealers who had wrapped a *Newfoundland* ice flag around his neck in an effort to keep out the cold. The flag was made of rough, coarse cloth that had chafed his neck until it was sore, and the frost worked its way into the wound. Norman's fingers and feet were also frostbitten, and now he was past hope. When Abel spoke to him, Norman tried to reply but was unable to utter more than a soft moan. Abel wasn't much better off than his nephew. At fifty-six, kneeling defeated on the ice, he suddenly looked much older. Edward Tippett walked up behind and knelt down between them. Through chattering teeth Abel told Edward that Norman was dying. The old man cried and cried.

"Where's William to, Ed? 'Ave you seen me other nephew?"

"He's keepin' company with Carpenter an' the others," Edward replied. "He's still on his feet, Abel b'y."

"My God! My God, Ed! What's 'appenin' to us, my son? I can't feel me fingers. They've gone all scram on me, an' I can do no more than keep Norman in me lun.'"

"I'll bide wit' you for a while, Abel b'y. We'll nunny together, the t'ree of us, an' share our heat and our lot as is our way, eh, Abel?" said Edward in a calm, reassuring voice. He put one long arm around Abel's shaking shoulders and tucked Norman into the shelter of his body.

"Oh, Edward, my b'y, 'tis wonderful good o' you to keep us

warm. I feels better already, an' Norman is not shiverin' as he was."

Edward did not answer. He hadn't told Abel that he was freezing cold himself. He bent his head down and they rocked back and forth. Now the three men looked like children in a huddle, like they were sharing a secret and would soon burst away to continue with their game.

But they stopped moving after a while, and when the other sealers came upon them and touched them, there was no response. The living walked away, as they must, and behind them, kneeling, sculpted together with the cold, remained the epitome of the human bond: two were bonded by blood, but all three were joined by the greatest bond of all—love.

* * * * *

CHARLIE MARTIN FROM ELLISTON WAS coughing. He was weak and faint but still on his feet. Just before dark on this second night of misery, he had taken a gaff from a dead man's hands and left his hometown friends with the intention of following George Tuff in search of their ship. Everyone now considered Tuff as their ice master. Trying to cross between two loose pans of ice and using the gaff for leverage, his stiffening limbs had betrayed him and he fell into the water. Pulling himself out, he was soon coated with frost. He tried to dry his clothing, but the cold beat him to it. His wet clothes froze solid and he was now in serious trouble. Eight of his friends from Elliston lay dying near him.

He had passed the frozen bodies of Reuben Crewe and his son, Albert John, several times during the night. Now the grey dawn was coming and the two men, frozen as one, were on display before him. It touched his heart until he couldn't bear the sight of it any more. Charlie staggered past them and looked for a place to get warm, a sheltering place, a place to escape from it all.

He found his refuge: frigid mounds of ice banked with the white moss of snow. He half fell, half stooped and began crawling toward them. Through eyes glazed with weariness and a mind confused with hypothermia, he burrowed his way among the mounds. After a bout of coughing, he fainted away. The living had found a haven among the dead, for they were not mounds of ice at all, but the frozen bodies of dead sealers.

23

*T*HURSDAY MORNING, APRIL 2, 1914, would change the lives of hundreds of Newfoundlanders, most of whom didn't know it yet. The sun rose up over the rim of the frozen sea without mountains or hills to challenge its arrival. It burst over the Great White Plain, revealing the carnage below.

The SS *Newfoundland* had drifted farther south and east during the night. Greenspond now bore seventy-nine nautical miles to the northwest. Elliston was forty-six miles away, also bearing northwest, and Little Catalina bore west-northwest at forty-two nautical miles. The steamer was paralyzed in the ice and Captain Westbury Kean was in the barrel.

The rising sun was to his back, and with the glasses held before his eyes he could see a great distance. He panned the horizon as the maw of the white wilderness glistened with the new day. Something was moving. He pulled the glasses down quickly, not wanting to see. Just as quickly, he raised them again. He refocused the lenses and saw a scattered line of men making its way toward his ship. There were so few. The glasses dropped from his hands and hung by their leather thongs around his neck. His legs went weak, his face turned deathly white, and he felt a sickening bile rise in his throat. If not for the sturdy barrel around him, he would have fallen to his death.

He was trembling so badly he doubted he could scale back down the rigging. Stepping back, he hauled up the trap door by its rope loop and began his descent. Staring again at the men out on the ice, he saw one of them go down. He staggered against the ratlines, lost his grip, and nearly fell before he made his way back down to the deck.

"Oh my God! Oh my God, my God!" Kean cried. "Green! Some o' my men are comin'. 'Tis only a few, nine I believe, an' they appear to be in grave distress. Oh my God, my God! Somet'ing terrible has happened. Sweet lovin' Lard! The starm! The starm! What in the name o' God 'as the ol' man done?"

Kean was like a panicked child now, confused and disoriented. "Get a signal aloft," he managed to blurt out, hysterically walking to and fro, not wanting to accept what he knew was coming. Charles Green took temporary command of the *Newfoundland* and ordered a flag run up the signal halyards with a bucket beneath them. Normally there would be a ball hanging under the flag, but the *Newfoundland* didn't carry one. A ball on the signal halyards was the signal of distress.

* * * * *

ROBERT RANDELL WENT UP ON the bridge of the SS *Bellaventure* before daylight. They were doing well with the seals, and judging by the pleasant eastern sky, they would top up their catch and sail home. The ice was tight when he ordered his vessel southwest for a quarter-mile or so. Then he veered to the southeast after a more promising lead as the sun rose full and bright over the butting bows of the *Bellaventure*.

"Some men on the ice, sir!" the barrelman in the foremast shouted below. "Two miles or so on the nart' side of the sun. Two of 'em 'eadin' our way, looks like." Then he shouted again, this time in a voice filled with concern, "One of the two is down, sir! Up again, sir! He's staggerin', by God! Like a man crippled, 'e is!"

"Full ahead," roared Randell. "Ram the bugger towards

those men! They've been out all night, by God!" He turned to a few men on deck. "Over the side and tend to them!"

They raced down the side sticks, jumped from the ship, and ran ahead of her bows. The man who was in front fell again, and when he saw his rescuers running toward him, he stayed down. The man behind him staggered on. It was Jesse Collins, barely on his feet.

The men from the *Bellaventure* grabbed the first man and helped him along. The courageous sealer delivered the terrible news: the men of the SS *Newfoundland* had been on the ice since the beginning of the storm on Tuesday.

Randell wired the fleet.

* * * * *

ABOARD THE *NEWFOUNDLAND*, WES KEAN was stricken with grief. He sent men to help the sealers walking toward them like drunkards. They stumbled and fell but kept on coming. Then he spotted two more men who were walking quickly, with obvious strength, and Kean's spirits lifted. But as they came within shouting distance, he learned they were two of the *Stephano*'s men. Their ship was jammed in ice and their captain had sent them to inquire about the flag flying from the *Newfoundland*. Kean told them that it was a distress signal and then asked a question.

"Are my men aboard o' the *Stephano*, b'ys?"

"No dey are not, sir! Dey was put on the ice along o' twelve o'clock on Tuesday, sir!"

Kean was devastated. He ordered Charles Green to hoist the international signal for distress at sea to alert the *Stephano*.

At 8:00 a.m., the first of the survivors were near enough to identify. George Tuff, his trusted second hand, was in the lead, but he looked much different now than he had when he left the *Newfoundland* on Tuesday morning. He was haggard and appeared to be on the verge of collapse, but he was still leading.

With him were Stanley Andrews from Pound Cove, Sidney Jones and Jacob Bungay from Newtown, Arthur Mouland and his friend Elias Mouland from Bonavista, John Hiscock of Carbonear, Henry Squires from Topsail, and Samuel Russell from Bonavista. The news they had for Wes Kean was devastating. Tuff told his young captain he feared more than half of his men were dead. Kean ordered hot tea laced with rum for the survivors and turned away, dejected.

Staring out the bridge windows, Wes Kean watched as smoke billowed up from the *Stephano* and then the *Bellaventure*, six miles away. The modern technology he was denied was being put to good use. The other ships had learned the plight of his crew and were doing their best to get through the ice to assist.

Stephen Jordon had seen the men come aboard and had waited until they reported to their distraught captain. To Jordon, Wes Kean seemed to have aged since daylight. Many of the men were dead, but he heard no names mentioned. He walked toward Arthur Mouland, who saw him coming.

"Your brother died the first night of the starm, Jordon b'y. I could not save him! No one could."

Stephen felt the pain of loss and frustration well up in his eyes. "What about me two nephews?" he asked, feeling sure they were safe.

But Mouland lowered his head. "I'm wonderful sorry to tell 'e, Steve b'y, but the two of 'em died along o' two o'clock er so yesterday."

Stephen turned away, shocked and lost for words. He kept thinking of the ice where his brother had left his coat.

* * * * *

THE TWO *STEPHANO* MEN CLIMBED aboard gasping for breath. Abram Kean, dressed in his long greatcoat, had been watching from the barrel. By the time they got on board, he was standing on deck, waiting impatiently.

"Well?" he barked.

"The men of the *Newfoundland*, sir," one man blurted out. "Dey've all been on the ice since you ordered—I mean since dey left dis one on Tuesday, sir!"

Kean's thick eyebrows rose and his steely blue eyes pierced the speaker. But it was a fleeting thing. Old man Kean rarely showed his emotions to anyone.

"Away to the rescue! Take grub an' matches an' flasks of spirits wit' 'e!" he bellowed. "Get back to the *Newfoundland* and ask Westbury where his crew is. You there, aloft! Scan the ice fer men!"

Kean roared into action like a raging bull, flinging directions at his crew. He stormed back on the bridge and ordered a message to the *Bellaventure*, but there was no need. Captain Isaac Robert Randell had already mustered his own troops.

* * * * *

THE MEN FROM THE *BELLAVENTURE* walked away from their ship after getting directions from the survivors. The ship was still battling her way through heavy ice when Randell ordered them to carry rum and blankets, stretchers, firewood, and coal oil to get a fire started. Food and kettles of hot tea were hurried to aid the living.

Alfred Maidment, from the little hamlet of Shamblers Cove just across the tickle from Greenspond, was barely alive when the men from the *Bellaventure* reached him. While one of the rescuers fished in his pack for a flask of brandy, another cradled Alfred in his arms and bent down to put his mouth close to the man's badly swollen ear. He asked his name. "Maidment," the suffering man told him through swollen, cracked, blue lips. The brandy was placed to his mouth and a dollop poured down his throat. The old ice hunter raised his head a little, coughed a few times, and died in the arms of a stranger.

Another crewman was too far gone to chew the food he was given. It fell out of his mouth minutes before he succumbed to the elements.

One sealer, still alive, was lifted away from a pan with twenty dead men on it. But when they rolled him onto a stretcher, his head drooped lifelessly over the side of the canvas deathbed.

Men walked in silence, in awe of the catastrophe wrought by the storm. They approached white mounds they suspected were humans and touched them with their hands. They walked around quietly, searching among the dead. Some of them would be haunted by what they saw until the day they died: dead men with their eyes sealed in icicles; faces burned and blistered with Arctic cold. Some of the dead looked as though they had been tortured: bodies contorted, and fingers forever pointing somewhere, to someone.

One sealer dropped to his knees without warning and clasped his hands in prayer. When his rescuers placed their hands on him to take him to safety, he toppled over. He died thanking Almighty God for his rescue.

The *Bellaventure* finally made her way through the ice and loomed over the carnage. The brilliant sun shone down and a warm wind came from the south. Those who could walk aboard did so on their own while many more needed help.

*　*　*　*　*

JACOB DALTON WAS ON HIS feet though he had fallen many times as he approached the *Bellaventure*. He fell once again but, determined, stayed down and started to crawl. However, he had twisted and was crawling away from the ship that could save him. Jacob was blinded, and around him were swatches of blue water.

He had found the pain of snow blindness seeping into his eyes before dark yesterday and had suffered through it all night. The brilliance of this morning's sun stung his eyes like burning sand while tears froze solid to his whiskered face. He tried to stand when he heard his name.

Aboard the *Bellaventure*, his uncle had seen him coming, and when he saw him go down he cried out in anguish. He ran down the ladders and yelled to Jake not to move. He reached his nephew just in time: Jacob was only a few feet away from a water hole. He was one of the last men to be rescued, the only sealer of the seven from Little Catalina to survive.

* * * * *

NOW THAT THE LIVING WERE aboard, the floating hearse began the morbid task of collecting the dead. During the day the *Bellaventure*'s men helped the living—nursing them, feeding and warming them, giving them tea and spirits, carrying them aboard on stretchers.

The *Stephano*, the *Florizel*, and the *Bonaventure* had aided in the rescue, every ship responding as they were able. With the exception of the *Stephano*, they were miles away and the heavy ice hindered them all. Men from the *Stephano* carried Simon Trask of Elliston, who was near death, for two miles over the rough ice, and the ship's doctor nursed him back to health. They picked up two dead men. One of them was Eli Kean, Abram Kean's cousin. Patrick Hearn of St. John's was able to walk aboard the *Stephano*. The *Florizel*'s men collected nine dead sealers.

The *Bellaventure* was nearest and saw the worst of it. When her crew had brought aboard all the sealers who had survived, they began to search for those who had not. They gathered the dead on separate pans of ice; the loading of the corpses began at 3:00 p.m. and was finished by four o'clock. The ice pans on which the dead had been laid were flagged with the *Bellaventure*'s own colours. The wheelsman followed the shouts of the scunner aloft in her barrel and the ship forced her way through. The flags that were once used to mark the carcasses of seals now led them to carcasses of hunters and Randell ordered his men to search as far as they felt was necessary. The body of young Peter Lamb, the would-be troubador, was found alone, a short distance away from a pan filled with dead bodies.

One of the *Bellaventure*'s crew was walking around the far western perimeter of the disaster area when he spotted a mound that didn't look like ice. He approached it warily. It was the lone body of another dead sealer. Theophilus "Offie" Chalk had perished walking toward the lights of his home.

On one of the pans, the bodies of the three Tippetts were frozen together. Not far away, Reuben and Albert John Crewe were both found dead, on their knees and huddled together.

The rescuers talked in murmurs. They discussed how to load the dead sealers. They decided that the bodies of the men who had died together would not be separated. One man suggested they use the *Bellaventure*'s winch and the others stared at him. They would not have any part of slinging their fellow hunters aboard like a strap of seal pelts.

When the gangway was lowered, they carried the dead aboard, individual corpses first. The *Bellaventure*'s men had discovered the bodies of twenty men on one pan. Some had their arms folded on their chests as if they knew they were dying. Some were curled into fetal positions. Others were found lying straight. They were all frozen solid.

Grasping the arm of one of the sealers who was nearly buried among the dead, the rescuer jumped back in alarm. The arm was soft and pliant in his hand—and it moved! Recovering from shock, he approached the still figure and gingerly touched it again. The arm twitched in response and the near-dead man opened his eyes and groaned. A shout brought help, and the survivor was hurried across the ice and up over the waiting gangway. He recovered within the warmth of the ship. It was Charlie Martin. Sheltered among his dead comrades, he had survived.

None of the dead had the pallor of men who had been laid out for days. Those who had not suffered from frostbite had wind-browned faces and looked as if they would soon awaken.

The bodies of the two Crewes and the three Tippetts posed a temporary problem for the men, but they soon came up with a simple solution. They brought out a piece of ship's canvas around which they gathered the Tippetts, then the Crewes. The dead bodies were lifted up and carried aboard the *Bellaventure*.

Some of the sealers who were watching had to turn away while others did not. One man, who was a churchgoer, voiced aloud the sentiments of many.

"Whit'er Thou goest I will go." And then, "Greater love hath no man than dis, who lays down his life for a friend."

* * * * *

WES KEAN WENT THROUGH THE motions that day like a man who had just lost all of his best friends. The *Newfoundland* was stuck and could not help. He watched in frustration as the other ships rescued his men. He stared through his binoculars until his eyes were red and swollen.

No ship was able to get near the *Newfoundland* all day. Runners were required to bring news and updates to her. The day finally ended, and Charles Green's log read, in part:

> 1:pm—distress signals were hoisted and S/S *Stephano* and *Bellaventure* began searching the ice for men. 4:pm—*Bellaventure* reports having picked up sixty of our crew at noon and *Stephano* one. Ice close and heavy. Ship not making any headway. 8:pm—Light breeze from SE. Clear weather and overcast sky. Lat -48.32N. Long -52.1W.

The three ships burned down for the night, the *Newfoundland* cloaked in her usual shadowy darkness. The *Stephano* was aglow with bright lights. The softer lights of the *Bellaventure*, which men watched from the deck of the *Newfoundland*, made her look like a funeral pyre.

* * * * *

LATER THAT NIGHT, THE WIND shifted from southeast to north-northeast. The ice slackened, and at 8:00 a.m. both the *Bellaventure* and the *Stephano* steamed up alongside the *Newfoundland*. Abram Kean crossed the ice and came aboard, as did Captain Randell. The two *Newfoundland* men he had on board walked across with him and the two dead were carried aboard the *Bellaventure*. Those sealers of the *Newfoundland* who were ill and crippled with frostbite were carried aboard the *Bellaventure* for the trip home with the dead. On the bridge of the *Newfoundland* the ship's roll was called, and when a man didn't answer to his name, Abram Kean ticked it off the ship's articles. With the *Newfoundland*'s dead now aboard the *Bellaventure*, Randell walked back to his ship. She powered up with a smear of smoke across the sky, veered away, and headed south for St. John's. Wes Kean signalled to the *Florizel* that he was leaving and swung the old *Newfoundland*—empty of seals and filled with grief—into the *Bellaventure*'s wake. Old man Kean turned the *Stephano*'s broad stern to it all and went back hunting seals.

The body of trapper Phil Holloway, who had a wife and six children waiting in Newport, was never found. Likewise the bodies of Henry Dowding and James Howell of Templeman. And somewhere beneath that Great White Plain were Henry Jordon of Pouch Cove, David Locke of St. John's, Michael Murray of Carbonear, and Art Mouland (not Arthur) of Bonavista harbour. The body of the old ice hunter Uncle Ezra Melindy, the quiet man from Cat Harbour, Notre Dame Bay, who had survived the *Greenland* disaster, had disappeared. In life he was loved by all. He had refused to talk of his first sealing disaster, and now he would never get the chance to talk of his second.

The skipper of the *Bellaventure* had wired Harvey and Company of the tragedy and to let them know that he was sailing home with the victims at full speed. His ship made good time, and at 5:00 p.m. on Saturday, April 4, he slipped through The Notch with the red ensign at half-staff. And the city was waiting.

It was customary for the city of St. John's to greet the first ship returning from the seal hunt with great fanfare. Ships in port would repeatedly blow their whistles. People lining the docks celebrated with shouts and cheers. Church bells rang over it all. The *Beothic*, captained by Billy Winsor, steamed through The Narrows with all her flags aloft and her whistle blowing. The citizens crowding the docks and the shoreline had been waiting for the *Bellaventure* to enter, but the *Beothic* was the first ship back. Although he knew about the *Newfoundland* disaster, Winsor expected a hero's welcome on account of the full load of pelts he carried on board his ship. He was mistaken. Instead, he was met with total silence and disdain for entering the harbour so gaily in a time of such loss and grieving.

Shortly after, the flag on Signal Hill was raised again in preparation for the entry of another ship, the long-awaited *Bellaventure*. When she steamed slowly up the harbour to Harvey's Wharf, a large crowd of people came and watched her approach. No one cheered and not one church bell rang out to greet her. The people of St. John's were in mourning, the city black and silent.

The *Bellaventure* closed the north side of the harbour and nudged up against the pier, where her bowsers forward and aft were fastened to the bollards. Thus secured, the ice hunters, cold and dead on her deck, awaited the next indignity.

*   *   *   *   *

WHILE THE *BELLAVENTURE* TIED UP to the land, the *Newfoundland* was stuck in ice again many miles abeam of Baccalieu Island. The old ship wasn't the only vessel having a hard time getting through. Hull up on the ice behind her were the SS *Eagle*, the SS *Diana*, and the *Adventure*. The *Newfoundland* would be tormented by the ice for three more days and as many nights while the other ships passed her. Many bunks in her hold were empty. The remaining sealers were quiet. No yarns were spun of disasters at sea; they were living through one of their own. The ship finally slipped away from the ice edge into open water on Tuesday.

Charles Green's log:

> 3:pm, left the ice. Weather fine and clear. 5:pm, Cape Spear bore NW by W. Distance 14 miles. 8:pm, entered the narrows and proceeded to quarantine station.

The *Newfoundland* edged into the old harbour without the city's knowledge. The sealers stood mutely at her gunnels, and above them, framed in her bridge windows, her young captain was silent, too. She slunk to her moorings under the shadows of evening. The last of the ice hunters had come home.

The city of St. John's went out of its way to take care of the surviving sealers. Doctors and nurses scurried about. Men were bandaged, given medicines, and consoled. Hospitals and clinics worked steady to aid the sick. Local citizens opened their homes and their hearts to the returning sealers awaiting passage back to the outports. Busiest by far were the city's morgues. The morticians ran out of caskets and more had to be built. Pine coffins were hauled to the harbourfront on horse-drawn drays and sleds and the off-loading of the dead began. People turned their faces in horror or watched in mute fascination at the sight of so many bodies. Many of the corpses had limbs so constricted in death they would not fit into the coffins. These were carried off on draped stretchers, with legs and arms sticking out. Men, women, and the children standing at their side wept. As coffins draped in black were carried down the *Bellaventure*'s gangway, the clutter and whine of the *Beothic*'s winch off-loading her cargo went on. The crowd paying homage to the dead glared at the ship, but the work continued.

The dead were taken into the basement of the Seamen's Institute, where medical personnel began the grisly work of thawing them out, of thawing them apart. Eventually the bodies were identified and transportation arranged to take them home. John Keels of Bonavista was given the best of medical help in hospital, but he could not recover from his trial by cold. He died on April 18. His death brought the death toll to seventy-eight.

In death, many of the sealers returned home aboard the trains they could not afford to ride in life.

The work of preparing the *Newfoundland* for her future life at sea went on after a time. Hundreds of pounds of leftover provisions were taken off and Harvey's employees removed the crude bunks of lumber. On one of the bunks, under the filthy curvies, someone found a red scarf. Rolled neatly inside the scarf, wrapped in brown paper and tied with a seaman's knot of twine, was a set of hair combs inlaid with pearl.

Under another bunk, looking as if it had been forgotten, was a dented harmonica. The worker blew through it once. It sounded cowed. Neither of the items was ever claimed.

* * * * *

IN ST. JOHN'S, NORTH BY the coast to the barren bill of Cape Freels, and beyond to Elliston by the sea, men wept and women cried a thousand tears. They cried in sorrow for the loss. They cried in fear for their children.

Some of the survivors told their stories and some never would. The dead have been covered and now lie beneath the sod.

Our tale of adventure, heroism, agony, pain, misery, and defeat has just about ended, but for those who wonder about such things, we must return to the sea again, so that our tale will end where it began: on the ice.

Nights are shorter now. Days are longer and warmer. The bright spring sun shines its sweet benediction as if to atone for the agonies of winter. The sea is warming and the ice is melting. Dissolving, shrivelling, weakening, foundering, and wasting away, the Great White Plain is dying.

The seals now swim in the widening blue lakes of open water. Then, on a warm night without a moon, they leave, almost without a sound. The new day reveals nothing but a watery plain, its surface bereft of all life. And the seals are wending their way north, toward that long polar night where the Arctic sages are already spinning a new tale.

Epilogue

STORIES ABOUND OF ALL THE sealing captains. The sealers who sailed with them gave them glory or vilified them as was befitting, but the tales told of Abram Kean surpass them all. Few were endeared to this most famous of all the sealing skippers. Berths aboard Abram Kean's ship were still the most coveted, yet he was the most hated of all the skippers. Sealers fought for berths aboard any ship on which he was captain, yet few liked him. He earned the respect of the sealers for one reason only: Abram Kean had an instinct for finding seals. Few men could face the icy blue stare of his eyes or the lash of his tongue, but there were other ways to vent frustrations, as this story handed down through the years relates.

John Hounsell was a hardened fisherman from Paul's Island, on the north side of Bonavista Bay. Hounsell, like so many others, continued sealing for many springs. A good hunt meant the only sure cash money in his pocket for the entire year. One of the captains John Hounsell sailed with was Abram Kean. The old man was eager to have Hounsell with him; although Hounsell was short, he was powerfully built, quick on his feet, and a fearless hunter besides. Although Hounsell was just as eager to sail with Kean each spring, he hated the man's arrogant, domineering attitude toward his men.

John Hounsell was also well-known as a trickster, a real sleeveen.

Late one evening, the sealers from Abe Kean's ship returned from a hard day's hunt. They were wet, dead tired, and very hungry. They had complained all day about the food handed out to them each morning. It was always cakes of hard bread with jars of water and little else. They were tired of crushing hardtack between their teeth. They also complained about the salt fish—most of which was smatchy—served them every day for supper. They all knew about the cases of sweet jams and other delicacies that had been brought aboard the ship. Some of them had helped with the loading of it. All of it was stowed forward and never seen again. The sealers chose John Hounsell to speak to someone about their concerns.

Hounsell told the master watch that he and the others had heard the officers were eating fresh beef smeared with sweet sauces between thick slices of bread. They heard it was called "san'wiches." The master watch said he would pass their concerns along to the second hand. He also added that he had no idea what a san'wich was.

The next morning the sealers were served their usual cakes of hard bread. When they returned that evening, weary and hungry, Abe Kean was waiting for them on deck. The sun was going down and the brilliant winter twilight above the ice illuminated the sealers as they climbed up the side sticks to gather before their skipper. They were a hard-looking bunch of men. Few of them had shaved or washed for days. Their faces and hands were smeared with dried blood, and around their feet were hundreds of bloody pelts reeking of heavy fat. Abe Kean looked down at them like a stern schoolmaster.

Dressed in rich fur from head to boots and carrying a tall gaff in his right hand, he dressed them down without preamble. He called them buggers and a bunch of complainers. They'd be lookin' fer a bert' in another ship next spring, by Christ. Chewin' 'ard bread was the very thing that kept a man's brain from freezin'—every sealer knew that! And as fer salt fish, "'twas what most of ye was reared on." Kean finished his tirade without interruption. His clear eyes glistened like frost in the dying light as he stormed towards the forepeak. He yanked open the scuttle door and proceeded to descend the stairs.

When leaving deck to go below, most seamen will turn and descend the stairs backwards, their hands sliding along the polished handrails, but Abe Kean did not turn around this evening. He began climbing down the companionway facing forward, further dismissing his men with the broad of his back.

John Hounsell saw his chance and sprang into action. Around Fair Islands, of which Paul's Island was one, John Hounsell was known as a champion rock-slinger, acquiring the skill as a boy. Hounsell would take rocks aboard his punt while hunting bull birds and, instead of wasting expensive lead shot, he would kill them with rocks. Granted, the birds had to be quiet and the seas steady, but Hounsell always managed to kill a good meal of seabirds this way.

John's pockets were filled with rock-hard cakes of bread, just right for throwing. He dug his hand into his coat and pulled one out. Gripping one end with his index finger and forefinger, he threw the cake with all his might toward the scuttle opening.

It flew straight, turning over and over, its brown and white colours flashing in the evening light. It made contact with the back of Kean's head and shattered on impact. There was a sound like a wooden mallet hammering home a short thole-pin, just before Kean disappeared from view. Then the sound of Kean clattering head over heels down the companionway arose from the dark stairway. Not one sealer spoke or moved to their skipper's aid as he unleashed a storm of curses. John Hounsell rushed forward and clambered down the stairs. Kean lay sprawled on the floor at the bottom of the stairs.

"What's wrong wit' 'e, Skipper?" Hounsell yelled innocently. "I 'eard ye bawlin' out. Tripped an' fell down the stairs, did 'e?"

"Tripped? Tripped? And that I did not, John Hounsell! I was

poleaxed, sir! Poleaxed, I tell 'e! By one of me own men! Did ya see the bugger who done it to me, John? I'll reeve me gaff t'rough his gizzard, by God!"

Abe Kean reached for his gaff on the floor and struggled to stand. John helped his captain to his feet.

"I t'ink you was felled be a cake of 'ard bread, Skipper," he ventured.

"'Ard bread? Why, you must be daft, man! 'Twas a blow from a maul, fer sure, John. Brought the blood from me pate, it did!"

Sure enough, Kean's hand came away from the sore spot at the back of his head with blood on it. There were pieces of bread scattered over the floor beneath the steps. John noticed that a few of them were flecked with blood. He was about to bring this fact to Kean's attention but decided not to tempt fate.

Kean was not over his fury. He glared at Hounsell without blinking, his eyes narrowed to slits that bored into John's very soul. Hounsell looked away.

"Find 'im fer me, John. Surely someone seen the bugger who did it. Find the bastard who felled me and you'll never have to look fer a bert' on any ship of mine ever again, sir!" With that, the captain walked to a chair and sat down.

Hounsell stepped quickly to the companionway. With his face as straight as he could manage, he said as he ascended the steps strewn with bread crumbs, "An' dat I will, sir. An' what will I tell the men, sir? Struck wit' a cake of 'ard bread or no. Jest to be sure of finding the bugger, sir!"

"A maul, sir! A sledgehammer blow, it was! Wielded be a coward! Tell 'em that, sir!" yelled an indignant Kean.

Hounsell stepped lightly out on deck, slammed the scuttle door behind him, and burst into laughter. When he went below deck to the sealers' quarters, they were all waiting for him. Several of them had cakes of hard bread in their hands and were laughing.

The only time anyone ever knew Abe Kean had been knocked down was the spring when John Hounsell of Paul's Island let fly with a well-aimed cake of hard bread.

Author's Note

I HAVE COME TO THE end of yet another tale, this one about Newfoundland's most valiant of men—her sealers. I have written the story as much for myself as for my readers. Of all the myriad stories told about our past, this is the one that resonates most in our communities. Because of this, I feel I owe you, the reader, a further explanation as to how the events in my story came to be.

Given that 100 years have passed since the SS *Newfoundland* disaster took place and there is no one left alive who could give a first-hand account, I had to do some extensive research. I was aided in this endeavour by my faithful friend and wife, Rose. We scoured cloudy, scratchy microfilms in the different museums and archives in our province. We read faded, 100-year-old newspapers and collected thousands of pages of information I would need to tell the story. My heart pines when I think of the many questions I could have asked Cecil Mouland on that long-ago day aboard my old truck. I will forever cherish what I did learn from the old man, who eagerly shared his incredible tale of surviving against man's greatest obstacle—despair. I am pleased his tale is now bound here forever. I thank Cecil Mouland posthumously.

One of my favourite means of obtaining information before

writing a story is interviewing people directly involved, or talking to those who have had the story told to them. I am not one of those who dismisses out of hand the oral, anecdotal history passed to us by generations of storytellers. Terse documented recordings often miss the human compassion relayed by the spoken word. No matter how many times the story is retold, the basic truth remains. One has only to listen.

The story of one of the surviving sealers was told to me by his son. Jake Dalton of Catalina is the son of Jacob Dalton, whose story has been mentioned in our tale. Rose and I sat in Jake's kitchen for hours and listened while he told us the story passed down to him from his father. Jake was very honest, direct, and sometimes emotional. From him I learned his father was easygoing and slow to anger, a powerful man with big hands. He was seldom cold and, when abroad on a winter's day, kept flising. I learned his father was not a religious man, but he sang hymns during those bitter nights on the ice. He told his family that if he could have found young Offie he would have saved him. Jacob did marry young Theophilus Chalk's pretty sister, Delilah. He went back to the ice for twelve more years, and until his last days he blamed "old man Kean" for the disaster. Thanks so much, Jake.

I read forty-eight sworn statements recorded at the magisterial inquiry that was held after the disaster. They were all the fourteen-inch page lengths of the day. Some of them were as short as two pages and many were as long as twenty-five. I found many typos as well as different spellings of names (e.g. Dowding spelled as Downing, Joshua spelled as Josiah). Some of the sealers from the communities around Newtown were listed as being from Newtown and many from Little Catalina were recorded as being from Catalina. A few compass bearings were wrong. I spent many hours trying to get it all right. It wasn't easy to do. If there are errors—and there are bound to be—I take full responsibility.

Geography is very important to me. I always have to know my bearings, my position on the map. When I read a book there will usually be a dictionary hard by me, and always an atlas. I have taken the exact coordinates of the ship from a copy of Charles W. Green's logbook, which I have in my possession. I wanted the reader to know exactly where this disaster took place in relation to our coast. During the months of writing the first draft of the manuscript, I asked dozens of people where they thought the event happened. Most people thought it was in Labrador. Others thought it was somewhere around the Grey Islands or off the northern tip of the Great Northern Peninsula. While I am able to follow basic compass bearings and can get my bearings from the heavens day or night, finding my direction by latitude and longitude is beyond my talents. I was aided in this venture by my nephew Tom Collins.

Tom is not only a navigational officer who has sailed the world over but is currently chief officer on an ocean-going ship. He came to my home with a huge chart in hand. I quickly learned it is sacrilegious for seamen to call maps of the sea "maps." They are charts! Maps are for landlubbers. With compass, dividers, slide rule, and protractor in hand, Tom made quick work of the coordinates that I had given him. It was like magic to me. Now I knew exactly where the tragic events took place. The ordeal for the swilers began on the north end of Bonavista Bay and ended outside of Baccalieu Island, on the north side of Conception Bay. I found it amazing that seventy-five per cent of the sealers died abeam of their own snug homes by the water. Those who waited at home had no idea their loved ones were dying not far across the mysterious sea. When Tom had finished his detailed work with carefully plotted lines and notes, my son, Clint, photographed it. Thanks to both of them for putting my story on the chart.

Reading the sworn statements of the sealers and officers at the inquiry was fascinating. Abram Kean's was the longest, stern and at times condescending:

> So far as risk is concerned there is no man
> that goes to the seal fishery can possibly avoid

taking risks. It is a risky voyage from start to finish, and if any man makes up his mind that he is not going to take any risks, his only way is to stay at home.

So states Abram Kean regarding the hunting of seals on the ice floes. When his judgment was questioned, he had this to say:

I don't think that because this bad accident has happened under very peculiar circumstances that we should allow our sympathy to get the better of our judgment and talk of things which at other times we would never think of. I do not think I did err in my judgment in not going to the *Newfoundland* and making certain that the crew was aboard on Tuesday night or afterwards.

He also said about the crew of the *Newfoundland*:

Now that I have looked back upon the past, and that everything is over I have concluded that there is only one action of mine would have saved them from that terrible catastrophe, and that is an action of total indifference towards the crew.

Meaning that if he had not picked them up, they would have probably made it back to their own ship. Abram Kean was not afraid of stating his opinion publicly. He also gave credit where it was due:

One man in particular, Collins from New Harbour, displayed some considerable courage in trying to preserve the lives of his fellow men: One man reported, that in his opinion twenty men would have died the first night if it had

not been for Collins. One man said, "I am alive,
Captain but I do not thank myself, I should
have been dead long ago if it was not for Jesse
Collins." Tuff the second hand also in my opinion
deserves great credit. I sincerely hope that a
report should be made on this matter by the
survivors and that we make in some substantial
way, a recognition of the services rendered.

During the many days of the inquiries, hundreds of people
lined the streets of St. John's where Abe Kean would have to walk
in and out of the courts. They shouted taunts and accusations at
Kean, but when the "ol' man" stepped unafraid into the street,
his back hunched against the verbal blows to come from the
gauntlet he must walk, they often fell to muted rumblings. The
few accusations shouted at him were silenced when the great
man stopped and turned his icy stare upon the speaker. Abram
Kean was under a lot of scrutiny from newspapers, sealers, and
the public. The map he had drawn, which he provided to the
inquiry to show the positions of the ships involved, as well as the
crew of the *Newfoundland* on the ice, was deemed to have been
contrived to vindicate himself. For the most part the sealers
blamed him for the disaster.

To quote Samuel Russell of Bonavista in his sworn statement:

I blame Captain Abram Kean for the whole
business of this transaction.

In the eyes of the public, at least, Abe Kean's broad shoulders
carried the burden well. Some of the sealers blamed George Tuff.
Thomas Dawson of Bay Roberts:

In my opinion George Tuff was the responsible
man for our crew, to look out for them. He was
given charge of them. He should have informed

> Captain Kean that we had been five hours travelling to his ship and made arrangements with the captain to come pick us up after we had killed the seals; or not to have left the ship (*Stephano*) until the following morning.

Lemuel Squires of Topsail:

> When I got overboard the *Stephano*, I was thunderstruck because I understood we were going to stay there the night. It was spitting snow about a half hour before we got to the *Stephano*. It was George Tuff's duty to have seen that we stay aboard the *Stephano* for the night.

George Tuff's sworn statement:

> I never for one minute protested to Captain Abram Kean about my men leaving the *Stephano*. Not one of my master watches for one minute objected to me their leaving the *Stephano*; none of my master watches reported to me that any of our men did object to leaving the *Stephano*.

The transcripts vary on the distance the men walked from the *Newfoundland* to the *Stephano*, but clearly Wes Kean had underestimated the distance between the two vessels; the sealers testified the *Stephano* was anywhere from five to seven miles away. However, the distance is probably less important than the time: no matter how far, they had walked for four and a half to five gruelling hours over some of the most formidable terrain on earth. When they reached the *Stephano* they were exhausted, thirsty, and hungry. The time they spent aboard her also bears noting. The testimonies vary from as short as ten minutes to no longer than twenty minutes.

The "dinner" Abe Kean had reportedly ordered for them was bread and tea, hot or cold depending on where you stood in the lineup. It is doubtful that even today's modern fast-food venues could serve 132 hungry men in less than twenty-five minutes. The sealers were asked at the inquiry if food was available for the taking when they were ordered to leave the *Stephano*, and their answers were the same: yes. This did not mean they could avail of the ship's stores. It simply meant they could fill their pockets with cakes of hard bread. On a diet of starch, and lacking protein and suitable hydration and without rest or even dry clothes, the sealers were ordered back on the ice ill-prepared for the ordeal that awaited them.

The manner in which the sealers of the *Newfoundland* disembarked from the *Stephano* after their short respite aboard that modern ship is also noteworthy. Far from the jubilation with which they had sprung over the sides of their own ship, now they were laggard and morose. The spirit was gone out of them. They had not felt welcome aboard the *Stephano*.

Westbury Kean's sworn statement:

> There is no special regulation or order that I know of requiring them to take food with them. They are expected to look out for themselves. I have heard a good many of the men who were lost did not have food enough to last them until they died. Many of them also carry a little can in which they put molasses and a liniment: The tins are for sale and careful men carry them. It would be extremely difficult to force the men to properly provide for themselves. They are often very careless.

Wes Kean showed genuine remorse for the loss of so many of his men. Few of his sealers or the public at large placed any blame on him.

Jesse Collins was also asked about their diet while aboard the SS *Newfoundland*. His sworn statement:

> We had extra bread served out to us once a week. I could not safely say if it was once but I think that was all it was. I can't remember if we had any fresh meat of any kind. I can't remember that we had any potatoes. I can't remember if we had any fish and brewis for breakfast at any time. I don't remember any fish and brewis. I don't remember having any onions, potatoes, or turnips. I can't remember any soup served to us.

Jesse Collins never returned to the ice, though he was proud to tell his stories. They have been handed down through his extended family for 100 years. One of his granddaughters is my next-door neighbor. She is also my aunt, Pearl Collins. Aunt Pearl remembers one story in particular that her grandfather told her when she was a young girl. He had not been burned by the frost, he said, though he had a bladder on his knee, but that was "only a chill and not to be paid any mind. I wore warm wool drawers knit be your grandmother's own nimble hands, and a thick flannel shirt—store-bought, it was. Warm, though."

He had his pockets stuffed with cakes of hard bread, he told Pearl. Collins also had a strong set of teeth, but many of the other sealers, especially the older ones, did not. The cakes of hard bread had to be broken into pieces against their knees, or, as was more often the case, against the ice, before it could be chewed. When some of the sealers' hands became too "scrammed" with the cold to hold the bread with their fingers, Jesse broke it for them. And he did more than that. Collins chewed on the bread for them, crunching it between his own teeth before spitting it into the palm of his hand and handing it to them. And they took it willingly, he said. Pearl found this hard to believe and told her grandfather so.

"Ah, 'twas a wunnerful bad time, my pretty dear," he replied.

Wesley Collins barely survived the ordeal. He had fallen into the icy water twice and both legs and some of his fingers became severely frostbitten. Unable to walk and suffering from hypothermia, he was carried aboard the *Bellaventure*. He hung between life and death in a St. John's hospital for days, where doctors tried to save his limbs. To save his life, his right leg was amputated below the knee; surgeons also removed two fingers from his left hand. Eventually his leg was fitted with a cork prosthetic and, amazingly, Wes went back to sea. He was told the cork for his leg came from the hills of sunny Spain. Collins always boasted that his Spanish leg never, ever got cold.

Many of the swilers carried physical scars of frostbite to their graves. Many more carried scars hidden more deeply which were seen by no one.

All six sealers from Little Catalina who died were buried in a common grave in the Methodist Church Cemetery in that town. With rasping saw, ringing hammer, and willing hands, the people of Little Catalina had just finished building a church of their own. In the spring of 1914, the very first service held in the new church was the burial ceremony for the six sealers. The church was lacking its complement of pews and there was not enough seating room, so many of the mourners stood against the walls. There was no church bell, so a flag was raised in farewell. An organ was graciously provided for the event by a woman of the town and the funeral dirge was played. That summer, a white marble gravestone was erected over the ground where the bodies were laid. The single stone was a monument for them all. As in life, so in death: together. And it stands there still.

The stories the sealers told while aboard the SS *Newfoundland* are true. The SS *Harlaw* is well-documented in Newfoundland history. The tale told about the trappers and the poison is one that was handed down orally. It was told to me by my friend John Lush of Gander. Thanks, John.

The magisterial inquiry which dealt with the tragedy

concluded by accusing Abram Kean, Westbury Kean, and George Tuff with negligence. No one was charged. It was said that George Tuff never had a nightmare after.

During the research for this book, I soon discovered that the statements the sealers gave at the inquiry were different from the ones they quoted for years after. From the documents it is evident that few of them were asked directly if they blamed anyone. With the exception of those mentioned, most of them would not have blamed the ship captains publicly. My research revealed that most of the sealers feared persons of authority, especially skippers who could easily affect the sale of their fish if they so wanted. The hushed halls of justice were intimidating to men who were mostly illiterate. These men, who could face the dangers of a rolling sea of water or vast reaches of ice unafraid, were cowered by the authority all around them recording their every word. They were intimidated by the formality, the influence, and the power of it.

But away from the lorded halls and while safe at home, they blamed the Keans for not doing something as simple as blowing the ships' whistles. It would have saved them all, they reasoned. The first night on the ice, the assurance of the dawn bringing sure rescue kept them going. But when all three ships turned their sterns to them the next day, many of them just gave up. The most formidable foe for any man to conquer is despair. Some men have great depths of courage to draw from. Some do not. It is the way of things. We are all different.

Maybe no one was to blame. The fact remains, though, 132 sealers were left on the ice, with a storm in the offing, and seventy-eight of them died.

* * * * *

CECIL MOULAND NEVER WENT TO the ice again. He and his wife left Newfoundland to work in the United States and stayed there for years. They were lifelong professing Christians, and while in the states Cecil was an active supporter of evangelist

Billy Graham. He worked at setting up the great tents used for the preacher's venues before attending the meetings himself. Both he and his wife, Jessie, returned to Newfoundland to enjoy their retirement and to end their days where they had begun.

After his wife died, Cecil spent his remaining years in a seniors' home in St. John's. There he would live quietly and cause trouble to no one until death found him in his bed on September 4, 1978, in his eighty-fourth year. As per the old gentleman's request, his body was laid beside his one true love, Jessie Collins, in a plot of ground overlooking the sea in Hare Bay.

Though Cecil Mouland has long been recognized as the last living survivor of the SS *Newfoundland* disaster by many, including the news media, in actual fact he was not. There was another survivor who outlived Cecil by four years.

Hugh Mouland was born in Bonavista on February 7, 1892. He was one of the sealers who survived that terrible ordeal on the ice floes in 1914. Hugh was a tough, work-hardened man of twenty-two years. He had fallen into the water late Wednesday evening after sighting the SS *Bellaventure*. He was suffering badly with nearly frozen feet, but on Thursday morning Hugh was one of the few sealers who walked aboard the *Bellaventure* without aid. Hugh even assisted with the loading of other, less fortunate sealers. He attributed his survival firstly to the "cossack" he was wearing—which his grandson Cyril Abbott still owns. Secondly, Hugh told his family, "I would see them [his fellow sealers] all under my feet before I lay down to die."

Hugh shipped back to sea again in the early summer of 1914 on a sailing schooner and fished the north coast of Labrador that season. The schooner he sailed on was wrecked and Hugh barely escaped with life for the second time in just a few months. He continued to sail the sea, and three times more the ocean tried to shorten his life but failed.

Hugh Mouland died in Gander on February 6, 1982, just one day before his ninetieth birthday. He was the true last living survivor of the SS *Newfoundland* disaster.

Acknowledgements

I would like to thank the following people for their assistance while I wrote this book: Bronson Collins; Elizabeth Collins; Jesse "Jed" Collins III; Christopher Collins, Sr.; Marie (Pardy) White; Carl Howell; Keith Greening; John Lush; Clementine (Gill) Smith; Jacob Dalton; Wilbert R. Goodyear; Fred Keats; Katrina Pickett; and Steve Hounsell.

I would also like to acknowledge The Rooms Provincial Archives and the Centre for Newfoundland Studies (CNS) and Maritime History Archives divisions of Memorial University of Newfoundland.

Special thanks to my nephew, First Mate Tom Collins, for the navigational details.

Also, special thanks to my son, Clint Collins, for illustrating this and all my other books.

I wish to sincerely thank Flanker Press for entrusting this story to me.

Bibliography

Brown, Cassie. *Death on the Ice: The Great Newfoundland Sealing Disaster Of 1914*. Doubleday Canada, 1972.

Bruneau, Stephen and Kevin Redmond. *Iceberg Alley: A Journal of Nature's Most Awesome Migration*. Flanker Press, 2010.

Burroughs, Polly. *The Great Ice Ship Bear: Eighty-Nine Years in Polar Seas*. Van Nostrand Reinhold Company, 1970.

Butler, Paul and Maura Hanrahan. *Rogues and Heroes*. Flanker Press, 2005.

Chaulk Murray, Hilda. *More Than 50%: Woman's Life in a Newfoundland Outport, 1900-1950*. Flanker Press, 2010.

Chaulk Murray, Hilda. *Of Boats on the Collar: How It Was In One Newfoundland Fishing Community*. Flanker Press, 2007.

England, George Allan. *The Greatest Hunt in the World*. Tundra Books, 1969.

Fiennes, Ranulph. *Captain Scott*. Hodder & Stoughton, 2003.

Galgay, Frank and Michael McCarthy. *A Sea of Mothers' Tears: Sea Stories from Atlantic Canada*. Flanker Press, 2003.

Horwood, Andrew. *Newfoundland Ships and Men: Schooner Square Rigger Captains and Crews*. The Marine Researchers, 1971.

Kean, Abram. *Old and Young Ahead*. Flanker Press, 1999.

Kirwin, W. J., G. M. Story and J. D. A. Widdowson, eds. *Dictionary of Newfoundland English*. Second Edition. University of Toronto Press, 1990.

Lincoln Library of Essential Information, The. Twenty-ninth Edition. Buffalo, New York: The Frontier Press Company, 1966. Catalogue card number 24-14708.

Noseworthy, Daphne. *Blue Ice: The Sealing Adventures of Artist George Noseworthy*. Creative Book Publishing, 2010.

O'Flaherty, Patrick. *The Rock Observed: Studies in the Literature of Newfoundland*. University of Toronto Press, 1979.

Ryan, Shannon. *Haulin' Rope and Gaff: Songs and Poetry in the History of the Newfoundland Seal Fishery*. Breakwater Books Ltd., 1978.

Ryan, Shannon and Martha Drake. *Seals and Sealers: A Pictorial History of the Newfoundland Seal Fishery*. Breakwater Books Ltd., 1987.

Shackleton, Ernest. *Shackleton: The Polar Journeys*. Birlinn Publishers, 2002.

Smallwood, Joseph R. *Encyclopedia of Newfoundland and Labrador, Vols. 1 and 2*. Newfoundland Books Publishers, 1967.

Thoms, James R. and Scott Stirling. *Our First Thousand Years: Including the Vikings' 1000th Anniversary and the Newfoundland and Labrador Who's Who Millennium Edition 2000*. Stirling Communications International, 2000.

Wright, Guy David. *Sons and Seals: A Voyage to the Ice*. Institute of Social and Economic Research, Memorial University of Newfoundland, 1984.

GARY COLLINS was born in a small, two-storey house by the sea in the town of Hare Bay, Bonavista North. He finished school at Brown Memorial High in the same town. He spent forty years in the logging and sawmilling business with his father, Theophilus, and son Clint. Gary was once Newfoundland's youngest fisheries guardian. He managed log drives down spring rivers for years, spent seven seasons driving tractor-trailers over ice roads on the Beaufort Sea of Canada's Western Arctic, and has been involved in the crab, lobster, and cod commercial fisheries.

Gary's writing career began when he was asked to write eulogies for deceased friends and family. Now a critically acclaimed author, he has written nine books, including the children's illustrated book *What Colour is the Ocean?*, which he co-wrote with his granddaughter, Maggie Rose Parsons. That book won an Atlantic Book Award: The Lillian Shepherd Memorial Award for Excellence in Illustration. His book *Mattie Mitchell: Newfoundland's Greatest Frontiersman* has been adapted for film.

Gary Collins is Newfoundland and Labrador's favourite storyteller, and today he is known all over the province as "the Story Man." His favourite pastimes are reading, writing, and playing guitar at his log cabin. He lives in Hare Bay, Newfoundland, with his wife, the former Rose Gill. They have three children and three grandchildren.

Gary's email address is nicholasc68@live.ca.

Index

Adventure 308
Africa 181
Akpatok Island 41
Amundsen, Roald Engelbregt
  Gravning 242
Anderson, John 85
Andrews, Stanley 300
Anguille Mountains 241
Antarctic 242
Antle, John 89, 90, 95-98, 105,
  106, 120-123, 127, 140, 189,
  200, 201, 227
Appalachian Mountains 71
Arctic 21, 40, 41, 45, 55, 57,
  68-71, 93, 94, 101, 107,
  112, 136, 251, 279, 283,
  302, 310
Arctic 93
Arendal, Norway 241
Atlantic engine 28
Atlantic Ocean 26, 36, 42, 44,
  46, 49, 64, 66, 70-72, 78,

85, 87, 128, 137, 179, 180,
  291
Aurora 116, 192

Baccalieu Island 190, 194,
  307, 317
Baffin Bay 41
Baffin Current 42
Baffin Island 93, 94
Baine Johnston and Company
  191, 229
Baldwin, Peter 85
Banks Island 93
Barbour, George 117, 191-194
Barbour, Sam 118
Barbour's Tickle 56
Barents Sea 87
Basque 72
Battle Harbour 70, 71
Bay de Verde 194
Bay of Fundy 202
Bay of God's Mercy 93

Bay Roberts 120, 231, 273, 319
Beaufort, Francis 105
Beaufort scale 105
Beaufort Sea 93
Bellaventure 273-276, 298-308, 323
Belle Isle 71, 72
Beothic 93, 178, 307, 309
Beothuk 135, 136
Best, Abram 254
Bird Island Cove 43
Black River 129
Bonaventure 197, 232, 276, 303
Bonavista 101, 120, 189, 190, 200, 239, 261, 291, 300, 306, 309, 319
Bonavista Bay 23, 43, 52, 62, 75, 78, 108, 113, 116, 139, 205, 228-230, 235, 255, 311, 317
Bonavista North 106, 287
Bonavista Peninsula 43, 116
Borchgrevink, C. E. 242
Bowring Brothers 103, 188
Branchy Rock 113
Brigus 242
Britannia 90, 129
British Admiralty 90
British Empire 90
Brookfield 163, 228, 255
Brooklyn 13
Brown, Cassie 18, 19
Brown, Robert 109

Bungay, Jacob 120, 236, 245, 300
Butchers Cove 75
Button Island 70

Cabot Island 117, 118
Canada 13, 41, 85, 93, 202
Cape Bauld 43, 70
Cape Bonavista 43, 113, 126, 178, 189, 194, 233, 263, 282
Cape Breton 43, 202
Cape Farewell 42
Cape Freels 51, 108, 111, 121, 130, 135, 309
Cape Hatteras 42
Cape Kakkiviak 41
Cape Norman 70
Cape North 42, 49, 202
Cape Onion 70
Cape Pine 43, 243
Cape Ray 241, 242
Cape Sable 202
Cape St. Francis 195
Cape Verde Islands 181
Carbonear 253, 259, 300, 306
Carpenter, George 293, 294
Cartier, Jacques 136
Catalina 78, 121, 122, 316
Cat Harbour 306
Charleston 85
Chaulk, Delilah 122, 316
Chaulk, Theophilus "Theo" "Offie" 121, 122, 140, 201, 206, 234, 266, 279-282, 292, 293, 304, 316

Chesapeake Bay 201
Christianity 12, 22, 41, 324
Christmas 53, 56-60, 62, 64, 257
Church of England 23
Clarenville 11, 78, 101
Clarke, George 242, 243
Collins, Alice 17
Collins, Fred 109, 110, 231, 287
Collins, Jesse 16, 17, 23, 24, 26-28, 30-35, 37, 38, 59, 109, 110, 150, 163, 185, 187, 190, 205, 206, 231, 233, 237, 256, 257, 266-268, 276, 279, 286, 287, 292, 299, 319, 322
Collins, Pearl 322
Collins, Rose (Gill) 11, 15, 16, 315, 316
Conception Bay 242, 317
Connors, Thomas J. 243
Conway, Ambrose 252, 253
Cook's Harbour 70
Cooper, Tobias "Tobe" 205, 206, 226, 261, 262
Cornwall 129
Cranford, Garry 18
Cranford, Jerry 18
Cranford, Margo 18
Crewe, Albert John 45-48, 60, 61, 101-103, 106, 126, 127, 141, 161, 162, 167, 171, 189, 206, 234, 237, 262-265, 282, 284-286, 295, 304
Crewe, Benjamin "Ben" 46, 47

Crewe, Mary 45, 47, 48, 60, 61, 161, 171, 190, 264, 282-284, 286
Crewe, Reuben 45-48, 60, 61, 101, 161, 166-169, 171, 172, 190, 205, 206, 234, 237, 262-265, 282, 284-286, 295, 304
Crystal Crown stove 126
Cuba 85
Cuff, Daniel 124

Dalton, Jacob "Jake" 122, 123, 150, 201, 206, 234, 239, 266, 279-282, 285, 286, 290, 292, 293, 302, 316
Dawson, Thomas 120, 219, 231, 235-240, 244, 319
Death on the Ice 18, 19
Defoe, Daniel 105
Diana 137, 308
Doting Cove 13, 51, 52, 61, 108, 124, 126, 127, 267-269
Dover 75
Dowding, Henry "Harry" 54, 274, 275, 306, 316
Dundee Shipbuilding Company 118

Eagle 109, 115-117, 119, 308
Easton, Job 35, 237, 291
Eclipse Sound 94
Ellesmere Island 41
Elliston 43, 44, 47, 49, 59, 78, 101, 122, 126, 234, 241, 282,

284, 295, 297, 303, 309
Ellis, William 43
England 88, 129
Escape Point 135
Europe 36, 41, 43, 64, 72, 87,
    88, 136, 180, 229
Evans, William "Bill" 261
Exploits River 51

Fair Island 109, 110, 313
Farquhar, James Augustus 85
Flanker Press 18
Florizel 103, 121, 128, 177-
    179, 183, 188, 197, 232, 252,
    254, 303, 306
Flowers Island 118, 119, 141,
    229
Fogo 119, 120, 122
Fogo Island 119-121, 194
Foxe Basin 41
France 72, 243
Funk Island 130, 135-137,
    139, 166, 178, 183, 189

Gambo 75, 77, 78
Gaulton, Garland 255, 256
Golden Glow flour 84
Gooseberry Islands 113
Goulds 291
Graham, Billy 149, 325
Grand Banks 42
Green Bay 139
Green, Charles W. 90-94, 105,
    112, 113, 116, 118, 120, 121,
    142, 174, 182-184, 186, 226,

227, 248, 249, 298, 299, 305,
    308, 317
Greenland 41, 42, 87, 93, 180
Greenland 56, 116, 117, 166,
    172, 191-195, 237, 239, 292,
    306
Greenspond 28, 30, 33-36, 78,
    82, 83, 114, 117, 237, 291,
    297, 301
Greenspond Island 33
Greenspond Tickle 110
Gulf of Mexico 42, 180
Gulf of St. Lawrence 42, 46,
    49, 70-72, 89, 167, 241, 242

Hannie and Bennie 229
"Hard Times" 172
Hare Bay 12, 16-18, 52, 62,
    75-77, 325
Harlaw 101, 167-170, 263,
    284, 323
Harry's Ground 113
Harvey, Alick J. 129
Harvey and Company 37, 86,
    91, 104, 129, 130, 218, 243,
    307, 309
Hatton Headland 70
Hearn, Patrick 303
Hebron 70
Hiscock, John 300
Hispaniola 181
Holloway, Joshua 28, 30, 31,
    34, 109, 110, 206, 231, 233,
    234, 287, 288, 316
Holloway, Maryann 58, 59

Holloway, Phillip "Phil" 23-25, 28-32, 34-38, 58, 59, 109, 110, 163-165, 206, 231, 286, 287, 306
Horwood, Samuel 253-255
Hounsell, John 311-314
Howell, James 54, 56, 306
Howell, Mark 56
Howlett, John J. 291
Hudson's Bay 41
Hudson Strait 41

Îles de la Madeleine (Magdeline Islands) 42, 49, 167, 202
Indian Gulch 135
Inuit 87
Ireland 44, 191

Janes, Robert 93, 94
Jellyfish Cove 72
Jensen, Bernard 242
Jones, Sidney "Sid" 120, 245, 274-276, 300
Jordon, Henry 306
Jordon, Stephen 259, 261, 262, 300
Jordon, Thomas "Tom" 257, 259

Kane Basin 41
Kean, Abram "Abe" 35, 37, 54, 55, 90, 92, 103, 116, 119, 127, 151, 162, 174, 176-179, 183, 187-189, 192, 194, 195, 200, 206, 228, 229, 231, 234, 237, 239, 240, 252, 254, 255, 259, 260, 276, 281, 286, 292, 298, 300, 301, 303, 306, 311-314, 316-321, 324
Kean, Eli 303
Kean, Joseph "Joe" 103, 121, 128, 155, 178, 179
Kean, Samuel 255
Kean's Island 119
Kean, Westbury "Wes" 37-39, 54, 55, 59, 83, 90-92, 95, 98, 103, 104, 107, 110, 112-114, 116, 118-122, 128, 130, 133, 139, 152, 155, 173, 174, 176-179, 183, 184, 186, 189, 190, 197, 200, 201, 206, 225-228, 230, 231, 240, 246, 248, 249, 262, 297, 300, 301, 306, 320, 321, 324
Keels, John 309
Kikkertavak Island 41
King George V 90
Kite 93

Labrador 70, 71, 80, 191, 317
Labrador Current 42, 71, 72, 180
Labrador Sea 41, 42, 70, 71
Lamb, Peter 88, 89, 94, 95, 127, 141, 172, 189, 266, 304
Lancaster 200, 239
Lancaster Sound 41
Landing Rock 135
L'Anse aux Meadows 72

Little Cabot Island 117, 118
Little Catalina 121, 122, 150, 234, 282, 293, 297, 303, 316, 323
Locke, David 306
Lundrigan, John 89, 95, 127

Marconi, Guglielmo 129
Martin, Charlie 295, 304
Martin, William J. "Bill" 251, 252
McCarthy, Richard 259
McClure Sound 93
Melindy, Ezra 306
Melville Island 93
Methodism 43, 323
Morgan, James 252-254
Morris, Edward 90
Mouland, Art 306
Mouland, Arthur 120, 200, 239, 274, 291, 300, 306
Mouland, Cecil 11-17, 19, 51, 52, 61-63, 108, 124-126, 128, 141, 148, 149, 161, 166, 172, 177, 189, 200, 220, 266-269, 276, 289, 290, 315, 324, 325
Mouland, Elias 274, 300
Mouland, Jessie (Collins) 12, 13, 16, 52, 61-63, 127, 149, 189, 267-270, 289, 325
Mouland, Ralph 108, 124, 220
Muddy Point 51
Murray, Michael 306

Nachvak Fjord 41
Neptune 93, 94
Newfoundland Sealing Company Ltd. 85
New Harbour 35, 39, 318
Newnes, George 242
Newport 16, 17, 23, 24, 26-28, 33, 35-39, 57, 109, 110, 233, 234, 267, 306
Newtown 53, 54, 56, 107, 117, 120, 236, 274, 292, 300, 316
New York 13, 201
New York, Newfoundland and Halifax Steamship Company 167
Nobel Prize 129
North America 40, 72, 201
North Carolina 42, 85, 201
Northern Hemisphere 136, 142, 180
Northwest Territories 93
Notch, The (The Narrows) 64-66, 68, 90, 104, 105, 179, 307, 308
Notre Dame Bay 51, 75, 78, 108, 139, 306
Nova Scotia 43, 49, 85, 202

Old Harry 113

Parsons, Abraham 273, 274
Paul's Island 311, 313, 314
Payne, Hedley 237, 291
Pear, William 238, 244-246, 250, 251, 291

Philadelphia 201
Pickett, Jonas 109
Pistolet Bay 70
Placentia Bay 89, 127, 129
Pollux 241
Pond Inlet 93
Pond Tickle 33
Pool's Island 110
Port au Port Peninsula 241
Portia 243
Pouch Cove 257, 306
Pound Cove 107, 300

Quebec 85
Quirpon 70

Randell, Isaac Robert 155, 298, 299, 301, 303, 306
Randell, Joseph 291
Random Island 129
Ranger 137
Rangoon Beans 84
Red Bay 72
Red Island 89, 127
Robinson Crusoe 105
Royal Household flour 84
Russell, Samuel 300, 319
Ryan's Bay 70
Ryan, Thomas 291, 292

Sable Island 43, 49
Saglek Bay 41
Sagona 114, 118, 119
Sahara Desert 181
St. Andrew 121, 184

St. Anthony 174
St. Bride's 252
St. George's Bay 241
St. John's 12, 13, 16, 31, 34, 36, 37, 39, 45, 47, 64, 66, 75-78, 80, 81, 86, 89, 95, 101, 102, 104, 109, 113, 118, 122, 123, 127, 139, 161, 162, 167, 178, 190, 191, 194, 195, 200, 214, 215, 224, 229, 242, 245, 251, 254, 264, 303, 306-309, 319, 323, 325
St. Lawrence River 85, 202
St. Mary's Bay 86, 243
St. Paul Island 42, 167, 169, 170, 202
Saint-Pierre and Miquelon 243
Salt Water Pond 24, 25, 28
Salvation Army 51, 52, 289
Savage Cove 70
Sawyer, Tom 52
Scotland 118, 167
Scott, Robert Falcon 242
Seamen's Institute 309
Seldom 119
Shackleton, Ernest Henry 242
Shamblers Cove 110, 301
Shanawdithit 136
Sheppard, Mark 254
Signal Hill 129, 307
Silver Fox Island 109
South America 181
South Carolina 201
Southern Cross 89, 241-243

Spain 72, 323
Spanish-American War 85
Squires, Henry 300
Squires, Lemuel 236-238
Stephano 103, 121, 128, 151, 162, 174, 175, 177, 179, 183, 184, 187-190, 197-199, 202, 203, 205, 206, 227, 228, 230-240, 244, 249, 251-257, 261, 262, 271, 276, 279, 284, 287, 289, 292, 299, 300, 303, 305, 306, 320, 321
Strait of Belle Isle 42, 70-72
Sturge's Island 119

Templeman 53, 56, 107, 274, 306
Tiller, Cecil 292
Tippett, Abel 293-295
Tippett, Edward 155, 293-295
Tippett, Norman 153, 154, 293-295
Tippett, William J. 153, 154, 293, 294
Tizzard, John 226, 248
Topsail 236, 300, 320
Trans-Canada Highway 11
Trask, Simon 303
Trinity 75, 168
Trinity Bay 43, 78, 121, 291, 293
Tuff, George 53-56, 107, 119-123, 130, 133, 137, 138, 150, 166, 172, 183, 187, 188, 190, 191, 194, 195, 197-199, 203,

204, 207, 227, 228, 230-239, 244-246, 250, 251, 259, 260, 276, 277, 292, 295, 299, 300, 319, 320, 324
Tunungayualok Island 41
Turks Cove 291
Twillingate 174, 175

Ungava Bay 41
United States 13, 71, 324

Vidi, Lucien 182
Vikings 75, 102

Wesleyville 75, 98, 105-107, 109-111, 114, 115, 117, 118, 124
Whitbourne 89
White Sea 87
Wild Bight 70
Winsor, Billy 178, 307
Winter Harbour 93
Woolwich 105

Yetman, Fred 228, 232
Young Harry 113

SS Newfoundland Disaster 1914: Those Who Died

David Abbott, Doting Cove, 18

Raymond Bastow, St. John's, 17
James Bradbury, Shearstown
John Brazil, St. John's, 43
Robert Brown, Fair Island, B.B., 21
John Butler, Pouch Cove
Valentine Butler, Pouch Cove, 26

George Carpenter, Little Catalina, 35
Fred Carroll, Bonavista, 44
Benjamin Chaulk, Elliston, 35
Theophelus Chaulk, Catalina, 17
Charles Cole, Elliston, 24
Fred Collins, Newport, 21
Patrick Corbett, Clark's Beach, C.B., 23
Albert J. Crewe, Elliston, 17
Reuben Crewe, Elliston, 47
Daniel Cuff, Doting Cove, 32
Simeon Cuff, Bonavista, 26

Charles Davis, St. John's, 28
Stephen Donovan, Goulds, 21
Alphaeus Dowding, Newtown, 22
Harry Dowding, Templeman, 22
Daniel Downey, St. John's, 22

Job Easton, Greenspond, 17

William Fleming, Bonavista, 19
Charles Foley, St. Bride's, P.B., 21

Alexander Goodland, Elliston, 22
Patrick Gosse, Torbay, 23

Fred Hatcher, Cat Harbour, 21
Thomas Hicks, Bonavista, 48
Joseph Hiscock, Carbonear, 23
Philip Holloway, Newport
Adolphus Howell, Newtown, 19
Edgar Howell, Newtown, 19
James Howell, Templeman, 23
Mark Howell, Newtown, 22

Bernard Jordan, Pouch Cove, 18
Henry T Jordan, Pouch Cove, 22
Thomas Jordan, Pouch Cove, 50
Michael Joy, Harbour Main, 23
Eli Kean, Pound Cove, B.B., 21

Percy Kean, Valleyfield, 28
John Keel, Bonavista, 25
Arthur Kelloway, Perry's Cove, 25

Peter Lamb, Red Island
William Lawlor, Horse Cove, 20
David Locke, St. John's, 21

Albert Maidment, Shambler's Cove, 52
Robert Maidment, Shambler's Cove, 30
Benjamin Marsh, Deer Harbour, T.B.
Samuel Martin, Elliston, 52
Robert Matthews, New Perlican, 26
Ezra Melindy, Cat Harbour
John Mercer, Bay Roberts, 34
Nicholas Morey, St. John's, 25
Arthur Mouland, Doting Cove
Ambrose Mullowney, Bay Bulls, 32
Mike Murray, Carbonear, 22

William Oldford, Elliston, 22
Charles Olsen, St. John's, 20

William J. Pear, St. John's, 27
Fred Pearcey, Winterton. T.B., 24
Joseph Pickett, Fair Island, 21
James Porter, Long Pond, Manuels, 33

James M.J. Ryan, Fermeuse, 19
John A. Ryan, Goulds, 18

Hezekiah Seaward, New Perlican, 40
Peter Seward, New Perlican, 47

Ernest John Taylor, Long Pond, 25
Abel Tippett, Little Catalina, 56
Edward Tippett, Little Catalina, 24
Norman Tippett, Little Catalina, 27
William J. Tippett, Little Catalina, 31
Noah Tucker, Elliston, 22

Allan Warren, Hant's Harbour, 31
Charles Warren, New Perlican, 31
George Lee Whiting, Hr. Grace, 26
Joseph Williams, Ferryland, 21

SS Newfoundland Disaster 1914: Those Who Survived

Arthur Abbott, Bonavista, 15
Philip Abbott, Doting Cove, 41
George Adams, Harbour Grace, 18
Stanley Andrews, Pound Cove
John Antle, Turks Cove, 42
John Antle (Stowaway), St. John's, 15
E. Barrett, St. John's
James Barrett, Old Perlican, 27
Patrick Bennett, St. John's
James Brace, St. John's, 38
Jacob Bungay, Newtown, 21
Thomas Chard, Bonavista, 44
Jesse Collins, New Harbour, 30
Wesley Collins, Newtown
Henry Constantine, Pouch Cove
Jerry Conway, Turks Cove, 38
John Conway, Turks Cove, 39
William Conway, Turks Cove, 45
John Cooper, Bonavista
Richard Cooper, Bonavista, 23
Tobias Cooper, Bonavista, 33
Ronald Critch, Trinity Bay, 38
Tom Cuff, Doting Cove, 54
William Cuff, Doting Cove, 17
Jacob Dalton, Little Catalina
Thomas Dawson, Bay Roberts, 46
James Donovan, Goulds, 30
Thomas Doyle, Harbour Grace
William Eagleton, St. John's
Charles Evans, Hant's Harbour, 31
James Evans, Pouch Cove, 29
William Evans, St. John's
John Fisher, Bonavista, 48
Joseph Francis, Hant's Harbour, 18
Noah Greeley, Kelligrews, 37
Ariel Green, Hant's Harbour, 19
Charles W. Green, St. John's
Thomas Groves, Bonavista, 46
Josua Halloway, Greenspond, 30

Levi Handcock, Newtown
John Alpheus Harris, New Chelsea
Alfred Hayward, Bonavista
John Hayward, Bonavista, 23
Patrick Hearn, St. John's
William Hickey, St. John's
Robert Hicks, Doting Cove, 39
John E. Hiscock, Carbonear, 15
John Howlett, Goulds, 23
Fred Hunt, Wesleyville, 33
Sydney Jones, Templeman, 31
Stephen Jordan, Pouch Cove, 43
J.B. Kean, Wesleyville
Westbury Kean, Flowers Island, 28
Henry C. Kelloway, Perry's Cove, 25
Benjamin Leary, Carbonear, 38
William Leary, St. John's
George Lenthorn, Bonavista
William Lundrigan, Peter's River, 17
John Maher, St. John's
Fred Marsh, Bonavista
Charles Martin, Elliston, 20
Eric Martin, Pouch Cove
Richard McCarthy, Carbonear, 19
Azariah Mills, New Perlican, 50
Terrence Moore, Turks Cove, 41
Hubert Moores, Turks Cove
Arthur Mouland, Doting Cove
Cecil Mouland, Doting Cove, 21
Elias Mouland, Bonavista, 71
Hugh Mouland, Bonavista
Hugh Mouland, Bonavista
John Mouland, Bonavista, 56
Ralph Mouland, Doting Cove, 20
Samuel Mouland, Bonavista
Thomas Mouland, Bonavista, 27
Headley Payne, Greenspond, 18

Ed. Peddle, New Perlican, 27
Benjamin Piercey, New Perlican, 32
George Pitts, New Perlican
James Porter, Elliston, 46
William Porter, Elliston, 24
John Power, St. John's
Joseph Randell, Bonavista, 52
Thomas Ring, St. John's
Joseph Rogers, St. John's
Richard Rogers, St. John's
Samuel Russell, Bonavista
Frank Ryan, Turks Cove
Thomas Ryan, Turks Cove
Frank Seward, Heart's Ease, 29
Mike Sheehan, St. John's, 19
Edward Short, Hant's Harbour, 24
John Skinner, St. John's
Lemuel Squires, Topsail, 23
George Stagg, Bonavista, 23
Sam Street, Bonavista, 20
Philip Templeman, Newtown, 54
Thomas Templeman, Newtown, 24
Cecil Tiller, Newtown, 21
John Tizzard, St. John's
Mike Tobin, Fermeuse, 27
Simon Trask, Elliston, 20
George Tremblett, Bonavista, 35
George Tuff, Templeman, B.B., 33
Edward Whalen, St. John's
Luke White, Somerville
William J. White, New Perlican, 44
Thomas Williams, St. John's
Robert Winter, Poole's Island
William Woodfine, Northern Bay
William Woods, St. John's

Above names taken from the website www.homefromthesea.ca, March 31, 2014
Also found during research the following names: John Dooley, St. John's; William Pitts, New Perlican
Source Sealers Agreement: The Rooms Provincial Archives
Note: New Harbour, Bonavista Bay, was changed to Newport